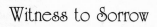

Witness to Sorrow

William John Grayson, about 1830(?); attributed to Samuel F. B. Morse.
Collection of Henrietta Barnes Parker.

Witness to Sorrow

The Antebellum Autobiography of William J. Grayson

"I witness the Death of the Great Republic with sorrow."

Edited by Richard J. Calhoun

University of South Carolina Press

To the memory of

HUGH HOLMAN

He initiated my interest in the antebellum South many years ago as director of my dissertation on literary criticism in Southern antebellum magazines. It was while working on this dissertation that I first discovered William J. Grayson. Grayson's contemporaries, Simms, Hayne, and Perry, praised his character as gentleman. Those of us who worked with Hugh Holman have nothing but praise for his character as teacher.

Copyright © University of South Carolina 1990

Published in Columbia, South Carolina, by the University of South Carolina Press

Manufactured in the United States of America

Library of Congress Cataloging-in-Publication Data

Grayson, William J. (William John), 1778-1863.
  Witness to sorrow : the antebellum autobiography of William J. Grayson / edited by Richard J. Calhoun.
      p.   cm.
  First published, in part, in scattered issues of the South Carolina historical and genealogical magazine of 1947-50 — Cf. Introduction.
  Includes bibliographical references.
  ISBN 0-87249-690-2
  1. Grayson, William J. (William John), 1778-1863 — Political and social views. 2. South Carolina — Biography.   3. Poets, American — 19th century — Biography. 4. Secession. 5. Nullification. 6. South Carolina — Politics and government — 1775-1865. I. Calhoun, Richard James. II. Title.
  F273.G66   1990
  975.7'03'092 — dc20   90-33491
                                                         CIP

Contents

Illustrations

Foreword

Long before the War the world, or at least New York and New England—the part of the world that counts—was being told what has since become Yankee gospel: The men of the Old South had no minds, only temperaments. That prejudiced reading continues to plague American letters. The Old South had no intellectual life worthy of note, at least according to a great majority of our intellectual historians, who do not so much condemn as ignore it. In recent years, thanks largely to a small band of determined warriors led by Michael O'Brien, that allegedly nonexistent intellectual life has miraculously been intruding itself into academic circles. Better late, even well over a century late, than never, and the publication of William J. Grayson's autobiography comes as a powerful salvo in what promises to be a protracted war. That the salvo comes buttressed by Mr. Calhoun's illuminating Introduction, temperate style, and judicious editing makes it all the more encouraging.

The kernel of truth in the old charge may be found in the backwardness of southern fiction relative to northern. As is well known, Simms was no Hawthorne. For poetry the record is less clear, except for those who transform Poe into an honorary Yankee and choose to forget Henry Timrod, Richard Henry Wilde, and Thomas Holley Chivers. I do not wish to argue. With due respect for Timrod, Wilde, and Chivers, whose best work remains impressive, the Old South did not produce an Emily Dickinson. But then, apart from Miss Dickinson herself, neither did the North. Still, it is a strange bias that makes the novel, even if poetry is added, the sole measure of intellectual accomplishment.

Grayson's warmest admirers would not, I suspect, consider him more than an interesting minor poet, but even his detractors ought to be able to appreciate his general intellectual quality and to recognize, if only from reading this book, that he was participating in a transatlantic community with a rich intellectual life. Suffice it to note that, whatever the extent of and reasons for the Old South's

backwardness in the output of literature, narrowly defined, it produced intellectuals whose work ranked with the best the North had
to offer and in some cases overmatched it: George Tucker and Jacob
N. Cardozo in political economy; John Randolph of Roanoke, John C.
Calhoun, and Albert T. Bledsoe in political theory; James Henley
Thornwell, Robert Breckenridge, and Robert L. Dabney in theology
and ecclesiology; Thomas Roderick Dew and William H. Trescot in
the interpretation of history; George Frederick Holmes and Hugh
S. Legaré in social and cultural criticism. To the list we might well
add William Harper, James H. Hammond, N. Beverley Tucker, T. R.
R. Cobb, George Fitzhugh, Henry Hughes, Henry A. Washington,
Edmund Ruffin, Joseph LeConte, and others.

With the exception of Randolph and George Tucker they all
defended slavery, and even Randolph and Tucker joined the others
in a spirited defense of traditional southern values. Their work, for
the most part, went onto the garbage heap of history on "the night
they drove Old Dixie down." Yet they did a good deal more than
defend slavery, and much of their thought has passed into some of
twentieth-century America's most penetrating social and literary
criticism at the hands of southerners who, alas, are largely ignored
in Academia: Allen Tate, John Crowe Ransom, Donald Davidson,
John Gould Fletcher, Richard Weaver, and, more recently, M. E.
Bradford, Thomas Fleming, and John Shelton Reed. Influence aside,
the best of the work written in the Old South would repay careful
reading today. Let me settle for two personal favorites: Thomas
Roderick Dew's astonishing study of the history of Western civilization, *A Digest of the Laws, Manners, Customs, and Institutions
of the Ancient and Modern Nations,* and Thornwell's four volumes
of sermons and discourses on theology, ecclesiology, and society and
politics.

The place of poetry in the Old South has yet to be studied
thoroughly. The few books of poetry published in the South or by
Southerners do not appear to have sold well—a circumstance that
underscores the modest success of Grayson's *The Hireling and the
Slave*—and too often historians, literary and other, have erroneously
concluded that the southern people, the planters in particular, had
little interest in poetry of any kind. Yet Shakespeare's work may
well have been, after the Bible, the most widely read and discussed
in planter circles, where it was readily quoted with ease. The religious
and agricultural journals regularly published the work of known,

fledgling, and perfectly dreadful poets. Slaveholders, male and female, wrote poetry, or what they hoped would be received as poetry, all the time. Southern college students read major poets and filled notebooks with their own poetry. Young gentlemen sent the young ladies they were courting love poems, mostly their own creations, as a matter of course. Battle-hardened politicians like S. S. Prentiss of Mississippi and Zebulon Vance of North Carolina wrote poetry that won the admiration of some contemporaries. Planters and their ladies filled diaries, correspondence, journals, and even plantation account books with their favorite printed poems and, more often, their own efforts. In short, Mr. Jefferson found little support for his opinion that poetry should be eschewed almost as readily as novels.

What it all means remains debatable, but the widespread passion for poetry may help account for the respect accorded well-known poets, at least in elite circles, when they spoke up on social and political questions. And a number of poets turned in yeoman service for the proslavery cause. Wilde defended southern rights as a member of Congress. Chivers entered the lists with newspaper articles that blistered the free-labor system of the North, where he spent much of his time. Timrod, the poet laureate of the Confederacy, celebrated the slaveholding South as the beacon for a new world order. Father Abram Joseph Ryan, the politically militant Catholic priest, became the Poet of the Lost Cause. But no single effort had the circulation and impact of Grayson's *The Hireling and the Slave*.

Mr. Calhoun, in his searching and wide-ranging Introduction, suggestively points to a correlation between literary and political styles, most notably with respect to the quarrels between the politically conservative and poetically neo-classical Grayson and the politically visionary and poetically romantic Timrod. He would, I am sure, agree that such correlations should be pushed only so far and that it would be an injustice to both men and a sin against the canons of literary criticism to reduce their poetical styles to political bedrock. Yet, as Mr. Calhoun notes, Grayson's cultural and political conservatism does provide an intriguing contrast with the romantic Timrod's politically radical flights of fancy.

Mr. Calhoun draws our attention to Grayson's brave defense of the Union, which has largely been forgotten, much as his defense of slavery has not been forgiven. Mr. Calhoun recognizes what some historians sadly do not—that proslavery and unionism coexisted comfortably in the minds of such unionists as South Carolina's Ben-

jamin F. Perry and James L. Petigru. Grayson's thinking brought
him close to the position taken by a wavering James H. Hammond
in the 1850s and much closer than is usually recognized to the world
view of Timrod and the extreme proslavery theorists. Mr. Calhoun
suggests that, unlike Timrod, Grayson did not recommend the social
system of the South as a model for a new world order—that, in
effect, he did not take the high ground of Timrod's *Ethnogenesis*
which, in some respects, reads like a poetical version of Fitzhugh's
Sociology for the South.

Mr. Calhoun is certainly right so far as Grayson's explicit ideological stance is concerned. But we would do well to pay careful
attention to Mr. Calhoun's *caveat*: Grayson did not reflect much on
the logic of his own position. Had he done so—had he sought the
ideological consistency expected of a social theorist rather than a
poet—he would have ended with Fitzhugh, much as Timrod did, in
seeing some form of slavery as the only solution to the "social
question" (the struggle between labor and capital) that was wracking
Europe, troubling the North, and threatening to destroy Western
civilization. To appreciate the course of Grayson's thought we must
take full account of the extent to which the defense of "slavery in
the abstract" (slavery as the natural and proper condition of labor
regardless of race) was sweeping the educated circles of South Carolina in the 1840s and 1850s.

The proponents of "slavery in the abstract" included fire-eaters
as well as unionists, but here we are concerned with the unionists
with whom Grayson identified and whose particular version of the
ideologically exterme proslavery view paradoxically led to political
moderation. Indeed, Fitzhugh himself opposed secession until the
final hour. In South Carolina the great and influential Presbyterian
divine, James Henley Thornwell ("the Calhoun of the Church"), also
held out against secession as long as he could and also proclaimed
that the capitalist countries were inexorably being driven to restore
some form of slavery. Thornwell did not have to read Fitzhugh to
arrive at that conclusion, which in fact had been drawn by a good
many southern theorists before Fitzhugh came on the scene. (Fitzhugh did make original contributions to the discussion, but they
need not concern us here.) Thornwell deduced his conclusions from
a study of the reigning laws of Ricardian and Malthusian political
economy, which like other well educated Southerners he knew well
but reinterpreted in the light of Christian ethics. As for Grayson,

it was enough that he followed the practical workings of those so-called laws in the parliamentary reports on the ghastly conditions of British working-class life.

But if we grant that Grayson deplored the fate of the working classes under the wages system and that he held up slavery as a humane alternative, does it follow that he, like Fitzhugh loudly or Thornwell gingerly, advocated the enslavement of all labor? Grayson himself denied it. He wrote, in his notes to *The Hireling and the Slave*, that he sought only to defend black slavery and that he believed the racially superior whites of Europe might find their own solution to the social question. Yet he admitted that he saw no solution in sight and that conditions were growing worse. More to the point: the poem itself is not merely a defense of black slavery; it is a damning attack on free labor as a system. Even in the notes, where he recited the slaveholders' familiar litany of capitalist crimes—no work, no food, no home, no human fellowship, no social responsibility for the working classes—he added, with emphasis: "*This is seen among hirelings only.*" The schemes of reformers he dismissed as "vain," for the misery was inherent in the system. In *The Letters of Curtius* he was blunter: "Slave labor is the only organized labor ever known. It is the only condition of society in which labor and capital are associated on a large scale in which their interests are combined and not in conflict. Every plantation is an organized community, a phalanstry, as Fourier would call it—where all work, where each member gets subsistence and a home and the more industrious larger pay and profits to their own superior industry." Did Fitzhugh or Henry Hughes ever write more forcefully?

The unionists who took that extreme ideological ground denounced secession as madness. They agreed with James H. Hammond, whose heart but not head lay with secession, that the South lacked the requisite human and material resources to win a war of national independence and that slavery could only be secured within the Union. They took the measure, as most secessionists did not, of the moral and political isolation of the South and pleaded with their southern adversaries not to play *va banque* with the very existence of the South and its social system. After all, if they were right in arguing that "free society" was sailing into a catastrophe, that its social system was doomed, and that some form of slavery was the wave of the future, then their politics made sense. As Francis W. Pickens wrote Benjamin F. Perry from Europe during the 1850s, all the South had to do was to restrain its hotheads and wait for European society to unravel. The hostility of the bourgeoisie to slavery would abate as it found itself pushed by the threat of revolution to abandon its system of class relations. Grayson spoke in such accents, no doubt with less dialectical rigor than some but with considerably more rhetorical power than most.

In other respects, too, Grayson should be read in the context of the debates within an intellectually vigorous slaveholding class in South Carolina and, more broadly, the South. I do not wish to be understood as suggesting that he should be viewed primarily as a social critic, much less as an ideologue. Respect for the man and his life's work require that we begin and end with his own primary concern — poetry — as Mr. Calhoun has done. But, however we assess the relation of his poetry to his social and political thought, Grayson clearly acknowledged that relation and took it seriously. In so doing, he contributed more than he knew to the struggle for a slaveholders' world view and, despite his overt political stance, to the struggle for a southern nationality. That he so clearly foresaw the terrible outcome measures the extent to which the tragic history of his beloved South and his social class was also his own.

Eugene D. Genovese,
Atlanta, Ga.

Acknowledgments

I wish to acknowledge generous assistance provided by the following. First of all, I remember the staff of the Charleston Library Society many years ago when I first did research on Charleston periodicals. At that time they invited visiting scholars to their coffee breaks. My greatest debt is to Allen Stokes, the Librarian, to Eleanor Richardson and other reference librarians, to Herbert Hartsook and the efficient Manuscript Room librarians at the South Caroliniana Library of the University of South Carolina. I am grateful to the Institute for Southern Studies for providing me with an office and housing on a Summer Fellowship, making possible my transcription of the manuscripts of William J. Grayson. I owe a special debt of gratitude to the reference librarians at Clemson University, especially to Marian Withington and Myra Armistead, and to the Special Collections staff.

One always owes something to the administration of his university. I am obligated to Dean Robert Waller and to Provost David Maxwell for making possible a Provost Award, which helped fund much of my research.

For response to requests for information I wish to acknowledge the reference staff at the South Carolina Historical Society in Charleston and at the Georgia Historical Society in Savannah. I would also remember John Broderick and his reference staff at the Library of Congress; Robert Bass and the late Samuel G. Stoney for their work on the manuscript of the autobiography; Louis Rubin, Eugene Genovese, Elizabeth Fox-Genovese, Theodore Rosengarten for their past research and for their present suggestions.

Finally, I thank the South Caroliniana Library for the most important thing of all—permission to publish the manuscript of the autobiography, the war diary, and photographs in their collection. Above all, I am grateful to the prose style of William J. Grayson, which deserves today some of the respect that he received for it from his contemporaries.

Witness to Sorrow

─────────── Introduction ───────────

William J. Grayson:
Autobiographer

William J. Grayson is now remembered solely as a minor figure in the history of Southern literature who wrote a pro-slavery pastoral poem, *The Hireling and the Slave*. When he died in Newberry, South Carolina, on October 4, 1863, in the midst of a war he had opposed, he left behind two manuscripts on which he must have believed that his reputation would rest, the biography of his closest friend and staunch fellow antisecessionist, James Louis Petigru, and his autobiography. Both texts recount the lives of men who had fought for the survival of the Union and who died believing that it had been shattered forever. Only the lesser work, the biography, was published, posthumously in 1866 by Harper in New York, because his friend Petigru was esteemed there as an antisecessionist. Its publication was sponsored by both the New-York Historical Society and the Massachusetts Historical Society. The superior work, Grayson's autobiography, was not published until 1947-50, even then only in part, scattered through several issues of the *South Carolina Historical and Genealogical Magazine*. The chapter affirming his literary judgments, which to Grayson were as important as his political opinions on slavery and secession, was left out as of little interest.

Grayson has always been viewed too narrowly, most often as a defender of slavery, rarely as a significant South Carolina antisecessionist. There has been more attention paid Grayson by literary historians as a minor man of letters than given him by historians as a proslavery apologist or as an antisecessionist. This attention has been mostly brief accounts of his contributions to literary magazines, as part of a study either of literary criticism or of Southern magazines. J. B. Hubbell in the older standard history of Southern literature, *The South in American Literature*, covers *The Hireling and the Slave*, makes use of brief passages from the autobiography and his biography of Petigru to show that Grayson bitterly opposed secession, but fails to see the autobiography itself as of any literary importance. *The Hireling and the Slave* is remembered in the now authoritative *History of Southern Literature*, but the autobiography fails to earn even mention. Fred Hobson in *Tell About the South* makes the unkindest cut of all, classifying Grayson as just another proslavery polemicist.[1]

My own interest in Grayson began nearly thirty years ago as part of a study of literary criticism in antebellum Southern periodicals. I was interested then exclusively in his conservative opposition to Romantic poetry and criticism, as testimony that neoclassical tenets and judicial criticism had a longer tenure in criticism in Southern literary magazines than in Northern. Later, when I wrote on *Russell's Magazine*, I focused attention on Grayson's defense of neoclassical standards in his essay, "What Is Poetry?," answered by a youthful Henry Timrod, eager to champion the new Romantic ideas.[2] I tried to show that Timrod was absolutely correct in identifying Grayson's critical positions with those in Kames' *Elements of Criticism* (1762), needing only to add Blair's "Rhetoric," the law student's guide to persuasive writing. I acknowledged Grayson as one of a conservative older generation of Charleston professional and literary men, trained in Scottish common sense philosophy and rhetoric, who still subscribed to the tenets of neoclassical literary theory and Age of Reason rationality. He was interesting to me as a type of Southerner sometimes overlooked in the histories of the antebellum South—the professional man (doctor, lawyer, professor, government official), conservative on most matters, at times including secession, who fancied for himself a gentleman's avocation as a man of letters, even if this meant writing only occasional reviews for a literary magazine. His younger friends, Henry Timrod and Paul Hamilton Hayne, might have been receptive to the more fashionable Romantic ideas; but Grayson was more concerned with sustaining the traditions and standards of the past, in literature and in government.

My acquaintance with Grayson's autobiography has disclosed larger considerations than my knowledge of his periodical writings and my slight familiarity with his poetry acknowledged. Grayson's posture is that of the true conservative, supportive of *all* things in literature, in politics, in society that further stability and order and against all things that threaten to produce chaos. He was capable of criticizing what was going on in the South as well as in the North. By the 1850s, the taste for Romanticism in literature in Charleston and the passion for secession in politics in South Carolina had become almost as threatening to Grayson's sense of the proper order of things as abolitionism in politics and abolitionist propaganda in literature were from the North.

In his long poem *The Hireling and the Slave*, Grayson had defended the South and its agrarian way of life built on slavery by portraying in verse a simple pastoral way of life that contrasted with the strife and conflict between managers and hirelings already evident in the industrial system of England and certain to come in the North. His autobiography takes a larger perspective. He turns his attention beyond defense of region to a much more objective account of what had lost the battle to save the Union. After reading the Stoney version of Grayson's autobiography, Theodore Rosengarten observed: "This engrossing memoir has been mysteriously ignored by historians, perhaps because they think they know what Grayson had to say. But readers familiar with the picture of happy Negroes and kind masters pulling at the same end of the rope in *The Hireling and the Slave* will find a more sober, less ideological, and profoundly self-critical vision in Grayson's later work written but six years after the polemical poem."[3]

Grayson intended his autobiography to be read by his contemporaries principally as an account of a political battle lost by one who had fought that battle, but also, not incidentally, as a case for neoclassicism as preferable to romanticism. He anticipated interest in what he wrote, as one who had both defended and criticized his region and the Union. He did not foresee that he would be so nearly forgotten that he would have to wait more than a century to be heard.

I

Who was William J. Grayson? Grayson's autobiography presents his own character more intimately than a brief biographical introduction can sketch it. But then the stress in autobiography is more on the discovered meaning of a life than on the actualities of that life. Grayson was a man of the eighteenth century, born on November 12, 1788, in the Beaufort District of South Carolina. Beaufort was at that time a pleasant village of about 200 inhabitants.[4] Though it was not far from the cultural center of Charleston, areas of the region could be as remote from culture as the faraway hill country of the upper Piedmont. But, with the introduction of Sea Island cotton, Beaufort was fast becoming one of the wealthiest communities in

South Carolina. The planters, even then, thought of themselves as self-sufficiently cultured and refined, and Beaufort was soon to value itself as "the Newport of the South." It was the home of intellectuals, chief among them the Elliotts — Stephen Elliott, Sr., the chief botanist of South Carolina and the first editor of the *Southern Review*; William Elliott, agriculturist and author of *Carolina Sports*. The Beaufort Library Society, reinforced by the bequest of the library of Hugh Swinton Legaré, came to think of itself as one of the best libraries in the Southeast. The cultural seeds were there in Grayson's youth, but the full flowering was to come later.

Through a blunder, some biographical entries, beginning with that in the *Library of Southern Literature* and including the official biographical directory of the United States Congress, curiously list him as the son of a United States Senator who was a member of George Washington's staff, the distinguished Virginian, William J. Grayson. Very little of record exists about Grayson's actual father, William John Grayson of Beaufort, except that he was born in 1760, died in 1797 at the age of 37, and served as a first lieutenant in Roberts' Artillery at Charleston until May 12, 1780, when on the fall of Charleston he was taken prisoner by the British. He apparently read law and served as sheriff of the Beaufort District. He married Susannah Greene on October 9, 1787, and he died, almost exactly ten years later, on October 10, 1797, in debt to his father's estate. Grayson's father is only briefly mentioned in his son's autobiography.

On September 11, 1798, Susannah Grayson married advantageously William Joyner, English native and wealthy planter from Beaufort. Her son spent much of his youth with his grandmother on nearby Parris Island, fishing, swimming, and enjoying the life of a prosperous country youth. His new stepfather had money, but it was through his own family that he could claim family connections with the aristocracy of the Sea Islands — the Wiggs and the Hazzards. At the local grammar school he studied the classics and read *Don Quixote* before he was twelve. The stepfather recognized his stepson's intellectual capabilities and determined to prepare him for higher education where the best Beaufort families sent their intellectual sons, at Harvard or Yale. In 1801 he was shipped North and enrolled in a school at New Utrecht, Long Island, taught by an old Scotch dominie named Todd. The quaint Dutch village life there remained one of his pleasurable images of idyllic life at the turn of the century. On Todd's unexpected death he was sent to another school, Newark Academy, at Newark, New Jersey, which proved inadequate for a student with Grayson's interest in reading.

His early education pretty much a failure, Grayson returned home in 1803 to Beaufort Grammar School, at that time one of the best schools at its level in South Carolina, studying there until he was sixteen, when he began college preparation at a private school taught by Milton Maxcy. Maxcy recognized the brilliance of his pupil and packed him off to his brother, Jonathan Maxcy, the first president of the new South Carolina College and a distinguished educator, previously the president of Brown University and of Union College in New York. After a personal interview with Maxcy and an examination requiring the explication of a text from the classics, on February 7, 1807, Grayson was admitted to South Carolina College with sophomore standing, and he was graduated on December 4, 1809. An illness prevented him from taking his final examinations and apparently cost him first place in his class. Out in the real world, he soon saw the vocational limitations of his classical education in the practical world of the nineteenth century, leaving only two pursuits open to him, that of author or schoolmaster. The former was not practical since "The South, fifty years ago," he observes, "offered no field for authorship." For four years Grayson enjoyed a life of reading and leisure on the Sea Islands. Images from this time of drum fishing, boat trips through the channels, and journeys to Charleston remained with him and appear later in his autobiography as remembrances of a simpler and better life. His pastoral excursion ended when the state representative from St. Helena's Parish, James H. Cuthbert, died, and through efforts of his friends, Grayson was elected in November, 1813, as his replacement in the South Carolina legislature. A long life of public service was begun.

In 1814 Grayson married Sarah Matilda Somarsall, the daughter of a wealthy Charleston merchant and planter. Through her grandfather, Colonel Daniel Stevens, hero of the Revolution and former mayor of Charleston, she had ancestral ties to Cotton Mather and to other distinguished New England divines. Grayson soon found employment as an assistant principal at Beaufort College. On August 17, 1815, he resigned to become principal in the Savannah Academy at Savannah, Georgia. An outbreak of malaria in Savannah sent him back to Beaufort, after only one year away, to be endangered by a more dread disease there.

When the yellow fever epidemic in 1817 threatened Beaufort and closed the school, he abandoned teaching for the study of law. The actualities of practice soon conflicted with the virtues of the classical humanist ideals he had learned from reading Cicero. He found what was always of paramount concern to him — "Right, justice, truth" — to be secondary considerations in the practice of law. He departed law and returned to politics, winning election as state representative from Beaufort, serving from 1822 to 1826, then advancing to the state Senate in 1826, where he became a spokesman for higher education in South Carolina.

Grayson also found financial success in business investments. For twenty-one years he served as a director of the South-Western Railroad, and he acquired property in both the Beaufort and Charleston districts, with town lots in Charleston and two plantations on the Wando River, one small (523 acres) and one large (4462 acres). He owned 170 slaves in St. Helena Parish by 1850. In 1831 he was elected commissioner in equity for Beaufort District, and he was chosen the next year as a States Right representative to the Twenty-third United States Congress from the Beaufort-Colleton District. His election came about partly from his campaign support for nullification, but mostly from his work editing the *Beaufort Gazette*, a newspaper that spoke for this movement. In his autobiography the older staunch unionist and antisecessionist says little in defense of his earlier activities for nullification except that he joined in the mood of the moment. Succumbing to a mood was an uncharacteristic act for Grayson. When he undertook in the 1850s his attack on the secessionists, he contended that being a supporter of nullification in the 1830s did not logically dictate being a secessionist in the 1850s.

In Congress during the time of Jackson and Calhoun, Grayson was more an observer of squabbles of the great and not so great men of the time than a political activist himself. He was constantly active in the move to establish a naval base at Charleston. After two terms (1833-35, 1835-37) he was defeated when he decided to run after all, too long after first informing his constituents that he would not seek reelection.

Grayson returned to Charleston to rethink his political commitments. He devoted time to contemplation and to private study, finally deciding to become active in the Whig party and to sever all his nullification connections. In 1840, when the Whigs regained control of the Presidency, he was appointed collector of customs at Charleston, serving in that office from July 9, 1841, to March 17, 1853, under both Whig and Democratic administrations. He was perceptibly an effective public servant and a leading citizen of Charleston, serving as a trustee for South Carolina College (1821-1829), as commissioner to establish a bank in Columbia (1831) and commissioner to value land (1837), as a member of both the New England Society and the Society of the Cincinnati, as vestryman for St. Michael Parish, and as president of the Charleston Port Society (1846).

In the 1850s South Carolina passions were not soothed by compromise, and a radical movement led by Robert Barnwell Rhett was afoot to push secession, with the cooperation of other Southern states if possible, but alone, if necessary. Momentarily, there seemed no strong voice to counter this radicalism. Joel R. Poinsett in Greenville, a leader of the fight against nullification, was now too old and feeble to be effective; even Grayson's friend Petigru thought that the Compromise of 1850 meant peace in his time. Grayson believed otherwise, sensing that South Carolina was now the most radical state in the South; and, with his pen, he soon took over leadership of the Unionist movement in Charleston. He published a *Letter to His Excellency Whitemarsh B. Seabrook Governor of the State of South-Carolina on the Dissolution of the Union* (1850), an argument, *The Union, Past and Future. How It Works and How to Save It* (1850), and an anonymous, witty, Swiftian satire on secession, *The Letters of Curtius* (1851). His satire was spiced with ironic commentary on the South's unpreparedness for war, describing how Charlestonians might have to freeze over Charleston harbor and skate across to attack Fort Sumter, or bombard Washington with secessionist propaganda, after acquiring the flying island of Laputa.

Charlestonians could listen to political argument but not tolerate satire that insinuated military insufficiency on the part of a region that prided itself on its military traditions. When his identity as the author of *The Letters of Curtius* became known, Grayson was soon under siege in Charleston for engaging in political matters while holding federal office. He turned from use of Swiftian satire to use of a Rabelaisean story of Master Janotus de Bragmardo, who was to receive six baskets of sausage for returning bells stolen by Gargantua. He compared several of the secessionist leaders to Master Janotus with their six baskets of sausages interpreted as the "offices of influences" they sought from their constituents. Under hostile fire for political activity while holding office, Grayson did not hesitate to defend himself publicly, replying that holding a public office did not disfranchise him as a citizen of the state from speaking out on a matter of great national concern.

Secessionist talk temporarily abated when the Nashville Convention of 1850 produced no support from any other Southern state to join South Carolina in anything other than resolutions of protest. A middle group between secessionists and antisecessionists, the cooperativists, who did not want to act without the cooperation of other Southern states, prevailed for the moment. A South Carolina state convention, assembled on April 26, 1852, produced only protests. Grayson may not have had direct influence, but he had been read and he had stirred up hostility against himself. After the election of Franklin Pierce in 1852, Charleston pressure on Washington finally forced him out of office, ironically for defending the Union. His antisecessionist writing was done, but his autobiography registers his persisting doubts about the South's capabilities to wage war against the North and articulates his personal distaste for anything that smacks of rebellion and disorder against established government or organized society.

In the later 1850s Grayson's writing took on a more literary bent. There were other threats to order and to reason. If secessionists in South Carolina were using demagoguery to attack the Union, those other extremists, the abolitionists in the North, were in print attacking the South through its "peculiar institution," slavery. To Grayson the very integrity of genres in literature was in danger from the misuses of fiction by propagandists. It was Grayson's objections to what he regarded as propaganda in Harriet Beecher Stowe's *Uncle Tom's Cabin* (1852) that led to *The Hireling and the Slave* and to his use of neoclassical pastoral to vindicate the agrarian South and to denigrate industrialization in the urban North. He enjoyed unleashing eighteenth-century invective against Mrs. Stowe; but he structured his criticism according to his models, Pope and Dryden, fashioning a neoclassical poem in heroic couplets and defending slavery by evoking a pastoral vision for the life of the slave and implying a Dantesque hell for the "hireling," the wage earner in the industrial North.

In his autobiography Grayson makes no claims for *The Hireling and the Slave* (1855) as the work for which he wishes to be remembered. Rosengarten has located it accurately as "a rejoinder to Uncle Tom's Cabin."[5] It did achieve instant local success in the Charleston area, going quickly through two printings; but it is remembered today more as William P. Trent characterized it in his biography of Simms, as an example of the insensitivity of the Southern slaveholder than as a poem or as agrarian criticism of industrialization. Nevertheless, two significant modern critics have had something positive to say about the poetry: Edmund Wilson on the pastoral poetry, in *Patriotic Gore: Studies in the Literature of the Civil War* (1962), and, surprisingly, the liberal Jeffersonian, V. L. Parrington, in his *Main Currents in American Thought* (1920-1927).[6] Both acknowledge that Grayson defends slavery against its attackers; but they also note that he admits the possibility of imperfections and even acknowledges a few specific abuses. Grayson also decries what he perceives as the hypocrisy of the North about the system. Northerners "made the system and enjoy the profits. Now they can no longer carry on the trade, they slander the slaveholder of their own making." He champions the agrarian way as the best way of life for this nation, and slavery as the form that this has taken in the South. It is definitely not to be abolished for the time being, while it should not necessarily be expanded. Grayson never envisioned, as George Frederick Holmes did, a utopia or a Baconian renaissance in the South; nor did he advocate, like Henry Hughes or Thomas Dew, slavery in the South as an exemplar for the rest of the world.[7]

There is nothing original in Grayson's apology except that he expresses it in verse. As a social critic Grayson was one of several Southerners, who, like the best known of these apologists, George Fitzhugh, argued that the hireling in the industrial slavery in the North is worse off than the slave in the South.[8] The difference is that Grayson's most effective social criticism of industrialism comes not from his logical argument but from his pastoral images of an alternative life style, drawing more on his memories of the Sea Island life of his distant boyhood than on the realities of plantation life in the 1850s. Like the Presbyterian theologian, James Henley Thornwell, Grayson believed that what was actually owned in slavery was not the person but his labor, for which duty the slave received full care and protection. He was convinced that this was a better arrangement than the hireling had.[9] In his view of the institution of slavery he was not as Calvinistic as Thornwell, but he too believed that it provided a means for improving the condition of the slave and for providing an education in Christianity. He frankly assumed racial inferiority, at least in the present state of the slave; and he mentioned

Hammond's "mudsills" theory as probably accurate, while admitting that it was a cause for "offense."

Grayson not only had an extreme agrarian distaste for industrialization and the industrial state but also a rationalist's fear of the anarchy that could result from class strife. In his most detailed defense of slavery in prose, a review in *Russell's Magazine*, he expressed fears that the conflicts in industrialization, especially the exploitation of the worker, would lead to socialism, communism, anarchy.[10] In a second edition of *The Hireling and the Slave* Grayson combined his pastoral of the slave with a defense of the Indian, *Chicora*, to publish the *Hireling and the Slave, Chicora, and Other Poems* (1856). His next book of poetry, *The Country* (1858) was pure late eighteenth-century pastoral extolling the virtues of rural life. In his role as reviewer for *Russell's Magazine* prior to the war he occasionally responded to attacks on the South and on slavery. Continuing the defense of slavery, however, was not one of the major purposes of his autobiography, for he was now writing in the midst of a war that he had already warned would inevitably destroy slavery.

In response to Paul Hamilton Hayne's invitation to contribute regularly to *Russell's Magazine*, Grayson saw as his mission to defend all the traditions of the South that he found under attack, including neoclassical traditions in literature. His exchange with Timrod was a modern version of the old argument of the ancients and the moderns, applied to traditional neoclassicism and the new Romantic views. Grayson was eager to do battle with a view of poetry that threatened to break down genres and to promote generic anarchy: the concept that "poetry becomes prose and prose becomes poetry." Poetry is dependent on a poet's maintaining a generic distinction and on giving form and order to his words. "Poetry must be defined...from the form in which these words are arranged." It is "the expression, by words, of thought and emotion, in conformity with metrical and rhythmical laws."[11] He intended to attack Romanticism as mistaken literary theory and practice, and he specifically sought to promote in the literary environment of Charleston in the 1850s a fair critical reception for poetry in the style of Johnson and Pope. It had always been there earlier, but a new generation of Romantic critics now tended to denigrate verse in the neoclassical style as something less than poetry.

Timrod believed that Grayson had read Coleridge too casually, not being fully aware of his distinction between poem and poetry.

The real question, as he saw it from a Coleridgean perspective, was "what are those operations of the human faculties, which when incarnated in language are generally recognized as poetry."[12] The younger poet shared Coleridge's concern with poetry not merely as an arrangement of words but as the product of a faculty of the human mind, "an imagination more than usually vivid," as it employs language "natural to men in a statement of excitement." He was infuriated by Grayson's description of Wordsworth as a "verse-making machine" whose poetry "was plagued by a characteristic matter of factness." To Timrod, Wordsworth was the very poet whose poetry was almost perfectly illustrative of the character of the poet Coleridge had described.

In a later essay, "Literature in the South," Timrod was unmistakably continuing his attack on Grayson and those he represented in Charleston: "Here no one is surprised when some fossil theory of criticism, long buried under the ruins of an exploded school, is dug up, and discussed with infinite gravity by the gentlemen who know Pope and Horace by heart, but who never read a word of Wordsworth or Tennyson. . . ."[13] In his autobiography Grayson draws on his essay, "What Is Poetry?," but he also makes an effort to rebut Timrod by documenting that he had read Coleridge and Wordsworth. He did not object to Timrod's associating him with earlier ideas because his image of himself was that of a man of reason from a better time, who advocated order in an age which had come to value emotionalism and demagoguery both in its literature and in its politics. I have stressed this exchange between Grayson and Timrod because it was one of the more interesting critical debates in antebellum literary history.

When war came, Grayson turned to biography, writing, on request from Benjamin F. Perry, a biography of William Lowndes, the manuscript of which was apparently lost in the great Charleston fire of 1861. His next and final effort was undertaking accounts of two lives that had been set against the direction the South had taken, his biography of Petigru and his autobiography. He began the autobiography first but generously put it aside during the last year of his life to write the life of his late friend. When Grayson died at his daughter's home in Newberry on October 4, 1863, he left behind these two manuscripts, plus a brief attempt at a war diary. The biography of a man known for his antisecessionist stance was publishable immediately after the war, but the autobiography of an

antisecessionist who had also written a book defending slavery was
not.

II

It was writing an essay for the *History of Southern Literature*
(Louisiana State University Press, 1985) on Southern literary magazines and an article on Grayson for the *Dictionary of Literary
Biography* volume on Southern critics that called to mind that Grayson's autobiography was still unpublished in book form.[14] Consequently, I was enticed by a fellowship in Southern Studies to the
University of South Carolina in Columbia to edit the manuscript. I
had also become aware of the recent scholarship by Drew Gilpin
Faust and Michael O'Brien acknowledging the complexities of being
an intellectual in the antebellum South.[15] After a minor search that
at first produced only a typescript, the manuscript was found in the
South Caroliniana Library, bound inside a ledger used by Grayson
when he was in charge of the customs office at Charleston. He had
unfortunately glued his manuscript pages to the pages of his ledger,
and, since these pages were wider than the pages of the ledger,
some of the edges had begun to crumble away.

There is evidence of four prior readings of the manuscript. The
first was by Grayson's wife, who added a few marginal notes on the
Christian character of her husband. The second was by Robert Bass,
who transcribed the manuscript for his 1933 University of South
Carolina dissertation in English. After his reading, a few edges
apparently broke away. The third reading resulted in a WPA-spon-
sored typescript of the manuscript (1941), a smudgy carbon of which,
not the original, is in the South Caroliniana Library. The fourth, by
Samuel G. Stoney, resulted in his printing most, but not all, of the
manuscript in *The South Carolina Genealogical and Historical Magazine* (1947-50). Stoney depended heavily on the transcript made by
Bass, and he omitted the literary criticism in chapter 11 as well as
several other shorter passages.

I also observed that Grayson had made many additions to his
manuscript, at first in ink and later in pencil, often making longer
insertions on the backs of preceding manuscript pages. Bass footnoted
many of these as alternative readings, including both what Grayson
had marked out and often what he had written in. The WPA typist
did the best job of including Grayson's revisions but was at a loss

to figure out where some of the insertions were to go, since Grayson had not always consistently marked the spot.

In his edition, Stoney had properly assessed the autobiography as history, finding Grayson to be a surprisingly objective recorder at a time when objectivity was a difficult perspective to maintain. He does not, however, seem to have recognized the benefits of publishing an antebellum Southern autobiography written by a man of letters who had the vantage point of knowing both the South and the North. Viewed rigidly as an historical account, the manuscript must have been disappointing except for graphic descriptions of such events as the clash in Congress between supporters of Jackson and supporters of Calhoun, the great Charleston fire, or the firing on Fort Sumter. Unmistakably, Grayson was less engaged in recording events than he was in dramatizing his own ethical awareness of what he had lived through. The events where themselves important to Grayson; but, in autobiography, his assessments of these events are even more significant.

I believe that it is important to publish this little known autobiography it its entirety for several reasons. Even if this were a lesser work than I believe it to be, publication would be appropriate because autobiography is at last recognized as a significant literary genre, one in which Southern literature, if Mark Twain is excluded, has not been exactly rich. Southerners kept diaries and journals, but they are not known for their autobiographies. I believe that Grayson's autobiography is a noteworthy addition to Southern literature. First of all, it is discernibly important because of who he was. Grayson was acknowledged by his contemporaries as a political figure of some importance, as a man of letters, and as an engaging representative gentleman of the old school. He was a conservative critic who could comment on the latest fashions in poetry and in criticism. He was a writer respected by Simms, who recommended him to Duyckinck for inclusion in his *Cyclopedia* as "an old friend of mine, a fine prose writer."[16] As a man of letters he knew the literature of his age, and in his knowledge of classical and English literature he was the nearest thing in Charleston to a successor to the learned Hugh Swinton Legaré. Even more important, he knew something about the craft of biography and of autobiography.

Grayson never belonged to what Drew Gilpin Faust has designated a "sacred circle" of intellectuals — William Gilmore Simms, James Henry Hammond, Edmund Ruffin, Nathaniel Beverley Tucker, and George Frederick Holmes—who felt like exiles in their region and wrote jeremiads in explanation of the South's shortcomings. But he was a regular among an erudite group who met to discuss literature in John Russell's bookstore, featured by Paul Hamilton Hayne years later in his essay "Ante-bellum Charleston."[17] This group included literary figures like Paul Hamilton Hayne, Henry Timrod, and William Gilmore Simms, with whom Grayson would have differed on Romanticism in literature. But it also included professional men, more likely to have shared his views, such as his friend James L. Petigru; Basil Gildersleeve, after the war, the great classical scholar at Johns Hopkins University; Dr. Samuel H. Dickson of Charleston Medical College; Patrick Lynch, Roman Catholic Bishop of Charleston and classical scholar; William Taber, editor of the *Charleston Mercury;* local physicians John Dickson Bruns and F. Peyre Porcher; and Judge Mitchell King. These men were contributors to *Russell's Magazine* (1857-60), the best magazine in South Carolina and, along with *The Southern Literary Messenger,* one of the very best in the antebellum South. Timrod, enthusiastic about the latest in the theories and poetry of the Romantics, may have recognized Grayson as of "the old fossil school" still active in Charleston, but Hayne acknowledged him as one of his closest friends and recognized that his literary opinions were still representative of those of the conservative professional man in a region that protected its traditions.

As one whose special interest is Southern literature, I would expectedly stress Grayson's autobiography as a significant literary text; but I would not slight the historical import, because he was also a public figure, professionally active in the mainstream of Charleston life during an important era in Southern history. There has been great interest in Mary Chesnut's diaries of the Civil War viewed from the perspective of a woman and in Theodore Rosengarten's publication of the journal, along with a biography, of Thomas B. Chaplin, plantation owner and slaveholder.[18] Grayson's perspective on the time that occasioned that war was much broader—that of a lawyer, politician, and government official, who, from experience, grasped the politics of his time and who, temperamentally, rarely suffered fools. As a political figure he had friends at both extremes. Despite political differences, he exchanged letters with James Henry Hammond, and in the support of the Union he corresponded with Benjamin F. Perry.

What Grayson regarded as the most important thing about his autobiography should be stressed. Nothing was more decisive to him than responding to his time and his place from the perspective of his self image as a gentleman. The indispensable essay for understanding the standards Grayson set for himself and for others in his autobiography is his "The Character of the Gentleman," a long review of a published address given at Miami University by his friend Francis Lieber, a distinguished professor and kindred spirit at Grayson's own South Carolina College.[19] Grayson makes it clear that what the gentlemen exhibits is a character distinguished by "liberality in thought, argument, conduct." He applauds Lieber's stress on "veracity" and on never indulging in abusiveness of others. To these virtues he adds "forbearance in using any advantage, not only towards friends and acquaintances, but strangers also and enemies." In temperament Grayson was different from his son's close friend, Thomas B. Chaplin, or from James Henry Hammond. His autobiography should be of interest, not for any sensationalism but for its delineation of a man of reason, who tried to live by his code of a gentleman at a time of increasing unbridled emotionalism.

It was a complex fate being an American writer in the nineteenth century; it was a burdened one being a Southern writer. Grayson's life also confirms that even a gentleman of reason, seeking to exemplify "liberality in thought" in the South in time of sectional conflict, could find himself emotionally trapped in contradictions. As a participant in the controversies of his time Grayson exemplifies the Southern intellectual who criticized emotional positions held by other Southerners but who also defended slavery from attacks outside the South because he, like nearly all intellectual Southerners, had accepted it as a "peculiar institution" into his own logical system. In the 1830s he had supported nullification; by the 1850s he was an outspoken antisecessionist. He defended slavery; but, possibly influenced by the agricultural expertise of his friend William Elliott, he assailed the cotton economy that had made slavery seem a necessity to most Southerners. He was right about cotton. Any hope of regional self-sufficiency needed for secession to work vanished when the South turned from varied agriculture and modest manufacturing to a preoccupation with cotton. What Margaret Mitchell imagined Rhett Butler saying to Southern romantic hotheads about the South's deficiencies as they celebrate the coming of war in *Gone With the*

Wind, Grayson long before had apprised the imagined reader of his autobiography.

If Grayson has become only a footnote in literary history as a defender of slavery in verse, his autobiography should earn him recognition in Southern history as a bold opponent of the idea of secession. In the 1850s Grayson used his pen to defend the South from Northern demagoguery when he thought it necessary but also to criticize Southern demagogues whenever he thought it essential for the survival of the Union. He took more published risks than his better known antisecessionist friend, Petigru; and he experienced the consequences—the loss, through local political pressure, of his job as collector of customs in Charleston. Yet as an antisecessionist he is barely known outside histories of South Carolina, not earning even a footnote in an older standard work, Carl N. Degler's *The Other South: Southern Dissenters in the Nineteenth Century.* John McCardell in *The Idea of the Southern Nation* perceives Grayson only as a South Carolina poet who "eagerly took up" George Fitzhugh's arguments in defense of slavery.[20] The situation is little changed even now. I transcribed the manuscript of Grayson's autobiography in a room with two historians beginning work on antisecessionism in the South. They did not know Grayson.

Once the South was at war, Grayson chose publicly to be a patriot, loyal to the Confederacy; but, privately, in his autobiography, he continued to be realistic as to the problems that plagued the South and would provoke defeat in war. In war, as previously in peace, men of little reason and great demagoguery were in control. Grayson's autobiography is not a chronology of the events of a life but a register of the perceptions of a Southerner, proclaiming the history of a region that had come to a tragic circumstance. To Grayson it is clearly tragic: the greatest experiment in the history of man's political life, the Union, was dissolved and, he believed, gone forever. It is this honest sense of loss, expressed at a time most Southerners thought they had found their national identity, that makes this work uncommon. Grayson's autobiography is also his jeremiad, his lament for agitation that had come "out of the North" and for the disrupting forces that had responded in like fashion in the South.

Grayson's autobiography is a political document but he intended more than that. In preparation for his own life he wrote for *Russell's* extensive reviews of biographies, Parton's *Life and Times of Aaron Burr*, John C. Hamilton's *History of the Republic of the United States*

of America as Traced in the Writings of Alexander Hamilton, J. W.
De Forest's *European Acquaintance, being Sketches of People in
Europe*, and Simms's *Life of Nathanael Greene*.[21] He even made a
dry run at biography when he prepared the manuscript of his biography of William Lowndes. It is my judgment that his autobiography was to be a serious literary endeavor in this genre, a life
study similar to, but also different from, two models he mentions —
Boswell's *Life of Samuel Johnson* and Rousseau's *Confessions*. He
begins his autobiography with a quote from Johnson on the old
Horatian purpose of literary writing:

> There are few lives, Dr. Johnson remarks, of which the narrative
> could fail to amuse and instruct if faithfully and judiciously written. . . .
> It may be so, since every life has its lesson and romance. All that is
> necessary for the writer is to tell the story in a fitting manner with
> a just regard to truth on the one hand and a decent reserve on the
> other.

Grayson's admiration for Johnson is as pertinent to his choice
of point of view as is his concept of the gentleman. He must have
seen himself as a Charleston Samuel Johnson, born a century late
into the last stages of an Age of Reason and living into what was
an age of irrationality and emotional conflict. Like Johnson he will
speak with veracity, troubled by his belief that the South, as well
as the North, bears responsibility for the tragic dissolution of the
Union and the chaos of civil war that resulted. But he will maintain
his personal stability through reaffirming his sense of self-identity.
The chaos in society need not be reflected in chaos of soul.

It was this personal reserve that he knew would make his
autobiography distinct from Rousseau's or from Boswell's biography.
It is the affirmation of the integrity of his own life that will have to
offset the tragic errors of the age.

III

I can only make suggestions for reading Grayson's text as autobiography. Though Grayson's is clearly a lesser achievement, I
would cautiously risk a comparison of his Southern first-person autobiography with a famous later third-person de facto Northern one,
The Education of Henry Adams. The education of William J. Grayson,
with its stress on reason and order, was in many ways as inadequate

a preparation for chaos and rebellion in the South as Adams's was for the multiversity of the twentieth century.

Grayson begins his autobiography with an account of his education. Before he left home for college preparation in the North, he had developed a love of reading: "I had hung over a torch light in the chimney, a candle being unattainable. . . . I had laughed over Don Quixote until the old lady (Mrs. Ann Joyner) would become impatient to know what I laughed at and why I did not read aloud that she also might enjoy the jest." Formal education at school was not equal to reading at home. He complains:

> But on Long Island my mind was deprived of all nourishment and starved for want of food except what a free intercourse with nature gave it. At a period of life, from twelve to fifteen, when the intellect hungers and thirsts after knowledge, I saw no books. I could have devoured a library. But if Mr. Todd had books, as I suppose he had, they were tabood to the boarders of the family school.

His second school, with Uzriel [sic] Ogden at Newark Academy, was "a place of immense pretension and very small performance."

His best preparation back home was under the tutelage of Milton Maxcy, who prepared him for college and for his brother, Jonathan Maxcy, president of South Carolina College. He found his fellow students in Columbia concerned not with their studies but rather with the French Revolution.

> . . .the French Revolution was the popular sentiment. . ."The Rights of Man" and "The Age of Reason" were the great books of the day. Their author was the most admired genius. Men who had never heard of Shakespeare or Milton were deep in the pages of Paine.

From a perspective of half a century later Grayson comments on the lack of preparation his college had provided for life: "If its alumni succeed in life they succeed not in consequence of college influences but in spite of them." He found college to be "a sort of hybrid between the English high school and the University with the advantages of neither." The influence of upper classmen was not exactly conducive to the education of the lower classman.

> He makes rapid advances in smoking, chewing, playing billiards, concocting sherry cobblers, gin slings and mint juleps, becomes adept at whist and. . .champaigne and hot suppers to say nothing of more

questionable matters and takes degrees in art and sciences about
which his diploma is altogether silent. . . . What he learns in the regular
college course is learned so imperfectly that it is forgotten in a year
or two.

His own education equipped him only to be a schoolmaster or
a writer, not for a feasible profession in the South. As to his fellow
students, most were more suited to a trade school, an education that
Grayson contends is needed. He utilizes Pope ironically: "What peerless cobblers are in college lost." The view of South Carolina College
presented here is at variance with the general praise he gives it in
his review in *Russell's* in 1857 of La Borde's *History of South Carolina
College*.[22] In his review he is more explicit on the learning of some
of his professors and the actual talent of many of his classmates. In
his autobiography his purpose is different, stressing the inadequacy
of preparation.

Grayson does not sustain for long a straightforward chronological
account of his life. His autobiography communicates effectively to its
reader for the same reason that Adams's masterpiece does. We are
willing to be led along by the author's sharing with his reader his
sense of the way things were in the past from the experience of the
author's present. Janet Varner Gunn has defined truth in autobiography as a matter not of the "facts of the story itself" but of "the
relational space between the story and its reader."[23] My other authority, James Olney, has said that literary autobiography is an
attempt by a writer to trace "that creative impulse that was uniquely
his."[24] Grayson's creative impulses were grounded in values of the
eighteenth and early nineteenth centuries, and the life he traces was
styled on reason, on ethical common sense, and on the conduct of
the gentlemen; but it was lived out in a time of increasing sectional
emotion culminating in the irrational act of disunion. The autobiographer is also concerned with defining self; and, as Gunn also
makes clear, the "question of the self's identity becomes a question
of the self's location in the world."[25] When Grayson is satisfied that
he has accomplished this definition and relocation, without compro-
mising his own integrity, his autobiography is completed.

Most writers on autobiography also agree that this is ostensibly
the least literary kind of writing. The art is often deceptive. So is
Grayson's. He is seldom dramatic, putting himself on exhibit as an
actor in events. The structure comes from the author's rereading his

past from his privileged vantage in autobiography from "a point in time...located on the lifeline of the writer somewhere beyond a moment of crisis." Janet Gunn also proposes a description of autobiography that I would use for a description of Grayson at his best — "the poetics of experience."[26] This sense of rereading a life from experience is central to Grayson's autobiography: experience divulges the errors of the past. He aspires to interest his reader both in that past and in his assessment of that past from some point after the exigencies. We do not know exactly Grayson's distance from that past until his last chapter, when he reveals that present as the chaos of wartime Charleston.

As autobiographer, Grayson can vary his point in time according to the effect he wishes to achieve. He often gives the impression of being close in time to the events that led to disunion. On the other hand, when he recalls simpler times, he can distance himself from both the present and the past, evoking a sense of something valuable as lost by employing the pastoral genre chosen for all his own major literary efforts. Lore Metzger has recently affirmed in his fine study, *One Foot in Eden; Modes of Pastoral in Romantic Poetry,* that the microstructure of pastoral "has at its centerpiece a stylized landscape, which readily assimilates allusions to a golden age, paradise, Eden or Arcadia."[27] Grayson may not nostalgically evoke a golden age, but he can recapture a better time back in an agrarian past. Metzger also finds the large macrostructure of pastoral often expressed in terms of "antitheses between nature and art, country and city, happiness and melancholy, communality and alienation, past and present."[28] Grayson's antitheses are between past and present, between country and city, and, to some extent, between the happiness resulting from the sense of communality evident in the early days of the century and the alienation generated by the divisiveness of the present.

For Grayson the pastoral garden persists in his memories of the Sea Island country of his boyhood. He writes: "At that time and before, people lived on their plantations and all useful and pleasant things flourished accordingly. Now plantations are cotton fields rearing a crop for foreign markets and little more." Against the dark of the autobiographer's present, Grayson summons forth a specific pastoral garden from the past — the plantation of Mrs. Ann Rippon, which he visited as a boy. Viewed from the 1860s, it makes for a fitting contrast between past and present, pre-fall and after the fall.

Her plantation abounded in all good things. Her garden was excellent, producing every fruit and vegetable. Oranges were plentiful, figs without number. [But now] peaches and pomegranates formerly seen everywhere are seldom met with, figs are scarce and small. Few planters have a good peach or strawberry; worms destroy one and weeds choke the other. Formerly they were cultivated under the owner's eye and flourished accordingly. The planter's whole attention now is absorbed by his cotton crop.

A major cause of the decline of the plantation, the serpent that despoils this Garden, was in his judgment the cotton economy. He informs his reader early in his autobiography that the "cultivation of a great staple like cotton or tobacco starves everything else." Furthermore, it was their blind faith in the international importance of the cotton economy that led many Southerners into the false belief that the South could secede and maintain its independence in a war because its cotton was essential to the textile mills of England and France. Near the end of his autobiography, in the midst of war with Charleston under blockade, Grayson banishes any hope that England and France will come to the aid of the South rather than lose their imported cotton. England will produce her own cotton in Egypt and India. The author of *The Hireling and the Slave* knows that she will never rescue "the royal house nursed by slavery," coming to the aid of a region that requires slaves for its economy.

Publicly, after war was begun, Grayson made no further political statements; but, privately, to his anticipated reader in the near future, he expresses his misgivings about the capabilities of the South to fight a war, about the qualities of the South's leaders, as well as about the possibility of England and of France as allies. In his autobiography Grayson is realistic about the South's capabilities, and he fears that the South is to be abandoned to her fate by the rest of the world. In his war diary he also confides his distrust of the wartime leaders of the Confederacy. It is this private frankness and open fairness that Theodore Rosengarten noted as distinguishing Grayson's autobiography from his public rejoinders, *The Hireling and the Slave* and the essays Hayne requested for *Russell's*.

Yet Grayson's approach to the past does not represent it as all of one hue. Not all was golden in his boyhood; the Southern past had its dark as well as its golden and fertile green garden. His life had its anguish as well.

My father died when I was about ten years old. I remember very little of him. He was reserved in disposition, I think, and I was shy and sensitive. The association of father and child at so early an age is not commonly a very close one. I retain indeed but few memories of any kind relating to the period of my life anterior to his death. Of these few not many are pleasing. It is common to talk of the happiness of childhood, but I cannot remember much of mine. If childhood had joys for me, the joys, for the most part, are forgotten. I can remember the pains more. . . .

One of his memories is as dark as anything found in Mark Twain's autobiography. A great plantation then, but planted only in potatoes and cotton now, was that of Major Hazzard, his father's cousin. A memory that Grayson could never repress was the horror of the slaveholders' violent response to rumors of a slave insurrection.

The ringleaders were seized a few hours before the time. They [the slaves] were tried without delay and a dozen condemned to be hanged. Their heads were cut off, stuck on poles, and set up along the highway leading from Purysburg, the place of trial, and to Coosawhatchie, the judicial capital of the district. The sight was so disgusting that some of the younger people refused to bear it. They so far disregarded the majesty of the law as to take down the hideous butcher's work and bury it where it stood.

Both the pastoral and the horrible are sheltered in his memory. On the one hand, he recalls Major Hazzard as a magnificent specimen of the low country planter, whose gardens were renowned, "roses in endless profusion of every variety and bulbous roots not unworthy of tulip fanciers in the United Provinces." On the other, he cannot dismiss the memory of the boy's horror at the slaveholders' violent suppression. The adult offers an explanation: "This mutilation of the dead was a barbarous practice borrowed from our English forefathers among whom it flourished especially of the Stuart Dynasty." He concludes: ". . . my memories of the hall and the hospitable master are still pleasant crossed though they sometimes are with visions of the ghastly black heads once seen in the neighbourhood and of the savage justice of our ancestors."

If Grayson locates the lost garden of the past in the plantations of his Sea Island home, he also idealizes village life, South and North, early in the century. The Long Island of his boyhood school days "was very Dutch and very primitive," in his memories clearly a pastoral scene. Yet, that too has been altered when he revisits it years later with his wife. All is changed, and the reality does not measure up to idyllic memories.

> I told her extravagant stories drawn from youthful memory of the beauty of Long Island and the attractions of the Dutch village. We found the Country without a charm. It was very dry; the dust covered the trees by the road. My wife laughed at my Dutch paradise and I could say nothing in its defense. . . . It was one of life's illusions dissipated by time and experience, such illusions as attend us from boyhood to old age and unable to stand the test of time and experience.

To safeguard his memories from the actualities of the present, Grayson determines not to revisit his New Jersey home, the scene of his adolescent love with Miss Kate Kearny, remembered as "very pretty, very lively, and very agreable," since the "picture of fancy or memory has not been displaced there by rude reality." He also witnesses the power of memory: "even in the other case, the old impression has resumed its place and I think of the scene rather as I formerly knew it, at fourteen, than as I found it at thirty. The colours in the picture of boyish fancy are indestructible; those in manhood's have already faded."

If Edmund Wilson could find words of praise for Grayson's pastoral poetry, I would, like Simms, who admired his prose style, and Benjamin F. Perry, who judged him the finest prose writer in the state, be an advocate for the prose of his autobiography. There is striking descriptive writing when he contrasts things as they were then with the way they are now altered. He details not only places as they used to be but activities as they were enjoyed then. His account of drum fishing in Beaufort Sound echoes in miniature his friend William Elliott's classic account in *Carolina Sports*.[28] He also relives the joys of travel in the old days, back before the steamers took over, recalling the small schooners that traveled the Sea Islands, and, even earlier, the canoes of six, eight, ten or twelve oars, "in which planters were accustomed to visit in the city." In those days passengers leisurely stopped often to prepare dinner and to await the ebb and flow of the tide.

> The oarsmen kindled a fire on the shore and cooked their victuals under the trees. In the evening and morning the kettle was boiled, coffee was made, and the passengers enjoyed a sort of lying picnic,

made pleasant where, as often happened, two or more boats came together and made the voyage in company.

But nothing could match the beauty of the voyage itself.

In still night when the weather was fine the full moon shining and the rivers and broad sounds calm and unbroken except by the dip of the oar or the wake of the boat where the agitated water gleamed with phosphoric light, the passage was full of enjoyment. Nothing in the gondolas of Venice watering on her dirty canals or more open and airy Lido would surpass it. Nor was the accompaniment of music wanting. The songs were not so refined as passages from Tasso, which are said to be common with the Venetian gondoliers, but they were interesting in their way and sung as joyously.

Grayson savors again the excitement of longer sailing voyages, sailing up the Delaware River back in 1818 to Philadelphia or sometimes finishing with a race against time with another schooner back to Charleston or, simply, the glory of a day at sea.

The day was brilliant; the wind fair and moderate; the orchards as we glided past them were in full bloom; the shores freshly green and exceedingly beautiful. It was one of those days that to live is a joy and to look on the flowers and fields, the valleys and hills, abundant happiness.

Before the advent of industrialization, in simpler days, the North was different too, more pastoral in appearance. Before "steam cars" induced "multitudes to travel," when he journeyed to Washington to take his seat in Congress, Grayson remembers it as a better time prior to the changes generated by industrial capitalism.

The North had not yet reached the riotous period of enormous wealth and the presumption that comes of it. The glare and glitter of the newly made rich were rare. The glories of the soap boiler and tallow candler, the shoemaker and hat manufacturer grown into million-aires, were as yet in Chrysalis State. . . . The manners of the day were tame and rude, those of old families of moderate fortune. Forty years have made immense changes. Now the American rich from the Northern States encumber and perplex the gentlemen ushers in every court of Europe and flutter like moths over every watering place in their own country.

From the privileged position of the autobiographer, engaged in a rereading of his experience, Grayson is sanctioned to give his reader a contrast between complexities of the present and a simpler agrarian and village life and to infer a quality of life that has been lost. When he was a boy the men of the Revolution lived, often rough in demeanor but honest and open in character.

> During my boyhood many men of the revolution were still alive. And they were a jovial and somewhat rough race, liberal, social, warm hearted, hospitable, addicted to deep drinking, hard swearing, and practical joking, and not a little driven to lose language and indelicate allusions.

He is also adept at character sketches that individualize what has been lost. Old General Pinckney was representative of the integrity of the old order in the South. In the North it was John Adams, whom Grayson visited in 1811 at the invitation of the ex-president's former private secretary, Mr. Shaw. More than forty years later, Grayson reminiscences:

> There are few incidents in my life to which I look back with more pleasure than my visit to Quincy and its venerable inmates. . . . The nerves of the old man were so tremulous from age that it was necessary to place a small table before him. On this he rested both arms to steady his hands in raising his cup to his lips. But however feeble his frame his mind was clear and strong. His conversation abounded with anecdotes of Revolutionary times and men. They were told with simplicity and ease and we listened to them with delight.

Three signal events which Grayson witnessed are integral to what little narrative structure there is in his autobiography. He must in some degree narrate: (1) the crisis between Jackson and Calhoun and its effect on the South Carolina delegation in Washington; (2) the battle over nullification, which he supported then but thinks less significant now; and (3) the fight between secessionists and anti-secessionists in which Grayson, the defender of slavery in *The Hireling and the Slave*, was an ardent participant as a devout Unionist. He devotes considerable time and space to all three pivotal moments. What he reports has been told before but not from Grayson's perspective as one who had been both with and against the majority in his region. He describes what happened then, but equally important, rereads the issues from the present of wartime.

Grayson begins the narration of his presence on the scene in Congress from his omniscient position of knowing now what was to happen to the national government he had become a part of back in 1833. He relives his elation on his first glimpse of the Capitol on his journey to Washington to take his seat in the Congress, but adds from the sobering perspective of a quarter of a century later: "I little thought that so soon the madness of knaves and fools, of political black legs and puritans more selfish than their mates would prostrate the incipient fortunes of its people and blast all their hopes of future greatness." No passage is more basic to Grayson's purpose in his autobiography. His anguish comes from the knowledge that, in secession and civil war, this country "would be imitating the mad follies of Mexico and South America." Grayson had reasoned that North Americans would never stoop to such follies as revolution and secession if only the course of reason could be sustained. He had attempted to do just that. Now he can only deplore.

When Grayson focuses on the powerful men of his time in Congress, he is distinctive in his characterizations and surprisingly candid in his judgments. But then, he knew the art of the character sketch from eighteenth-century literature and, in his concept of the Southern gentleman, veracity was a cardinal virtue. The extraordinary event of his first term in Congress was the crisis between President Andrew Jackson and Vice President John C. Calhoun. His own role was more that of an observer than an active participant. The conflict, Grayson characterizes shrewdly, was due as much to their common Scotch-Irish heritage as to their political differences.

> There were some resemblances between the two men—the President and the great South Carolina Senator, once friends, now implacable foes. They were of the same Scotch Irish stock and exhibited its characteristic traits. In both were seen the long face, the hollow jaws, the thick bustling hair, the tall gaunt erect figure, which belong to the race. Each of them had great strength of will and force of character. There was one feature of their common ancestry in which General Jackson was probably superior to his opponent. He was the best hater. But even here the resemblance was not lost. It is said of Mr. Calhoun that he tolerated no political heresies and broke down in his own State and never forgave the politician who opposed his opinions. He made many enemies in doing so.

Grayson was also a discerning witness to the best exhibitions of the great orators of the day. He not only individualizes them in action, but also dissects their strengths and weaknesses. He recounts, in one of the best descriptions of John C. Calhoun as orator that we have, that he

> was not a pleasing speaker. He was exceedingly angular in phrase as he was in figure. His manner was abrupt. His sentences were often incomplete. He cut them short in the heat and hurry of his utterance. His ideas appeared to outrun his words and leave them limping in the rear. His delivery was stiff and without grace, but it was impressive from its intense and eager earnestness. There was a glare, a fire in his eye, the fire of a soul that seemed to burn within him. It fascinated the beholder and riveted his attention. Mr. Calhoun's argument was always vigorous, subtle and clear. In all his refinements you understood him perfectly as a skillful debater, not a declaimer or rhetorician.

He characterizes the artfulness of Henry Clay in political oratory:

> an orator, long and carefully trained, and of imposing manner, his figure tall and commanding, his voice powerful, flexible, musical, and under perfect command. He had more action with one exception perhaps than any speaker in the Senate.

Grayson concludes his triumvirate of orators with an account of the most renowned of all, Daniel Webster, whom he and other Charleston Whigs later honored at a dinner in Charleston in 1847.[29]

> The speaking of Mr. Webster, on occasions, was heavy and uninteresting. But when roused by a subject worthy of his great intellect, he poured forth magnificent sentences of perfect English, so round, clear, vigorous and musical as none could equal or imitate.

On the other hand, there was one congressman, Davy Crockett, whose subsequent reputation baffled Grayson, restricted, as he was, to what he had heard and seen at the time. He recalls the man Crockett as the most unhumorous person he had ever met. Having known the man, Grayson was astonished by the legend.

As a partisan of neoclassicism in literature, Grayson is not only adept at character sketches but also at satire. He chronicles the change that takes place when the politician fresh from the country recognizes the privileges of office in Washington. The satirist who wrote *The Letters of Curtius* cannot forego narrating the corruption of the American democrat once he experiences the gratifications of power:

> The congressman goest to Washington with his country experience and is amazed to find how important a man he has become. Great is the deference shown him in various quarters. Pages and door keepers bow down before him and do his errands. He is a power in the city. He is the dispenser of the body corporate. It depends on his vote whether the city debts are paid, its streets and avenues improved, its public grounds enclosed and planted. His power comands respect. Society is open to him. He is no longer the man he was in his native village. There he played Sycophant to his people. Here he is small divinity with his altars and offers of incense.

A full review of the nullification debate does not suit Grayson's purposes in autobiography. He never believed that nullification inevitably led to secession. Still, when he turns to a critique of the secessionist movement in the 1850s, his judgment is harsh and Miltonic on the nullification movement he had supported in the 1830s: "It led to debates among politicans as interminable as the deliberations of Milton's fallen angels in which 'they found no end in wandering mazes lost.'" Even his greatest claim to fame as a Southern partisan, *The Hireling and the Slave*, viewed from the perspective of war, is not as pertinent to his autobiography as his antisecessionist literature was in an attempt to forestall the tragedy that happened.

In his autobiography Grayson also resumes his role as literary critic, continuing his quarrel with the advocates of another form of disorder, Romanticism in literature. He discloses that his young friends in Charleston, no doubt Timrod and Hayne, are of newer persuason while he holds to the old principles.

> My select friends are now of the new schools. I adhere to the old masters and their followers...My taste is too antiquated to fall into raptures over the metaphysical sentiments of Shelley, or the renovated pagan deities of Keats, or the Hindoo mythological monsters of Southey.

What is even more apparent here than in his earlier essay on poetry in *Russell's* is that, though Grayson prefers Pope and Dryden to Wordsworth and Coleridge, perhaps in response to Timrod's contention that he did not understand Coleridge, he intends now to demonstrate that he knows the works of the very Romantic writers he disavows. What he writes on Coleridge on the imagination anticipates what was said much later in greater detail by some of the Chicago Neo-Aristotelians in their quarrels with the New Critics, whose concept of the imagination the Neo-Aristotelians contended was derived from Coleridge. Grayson concludes:

> The last notion of Coleridge confounding poetry with the poet identifies the art with the faculty which produces. But imagination is not to be identified with one art any more than with another. The imaginative faculty belongs equally to all the arts as their common source.

I am confident that if the literary criticism in his autobiography had been published Grayson would have been looked upon as a more important antebellum Southern critic. It is a far more exhaustive account than in his essay "What Is Poetry?" I do not believe that Edd W. Parks in the standard study of antebellum Southern critics ever read this chapter, available to him only in Robert Bass's 1933 South Carolina dissertation. He remarks only that Grayson "devoted one chapter to literature. No doubt this seemed a reasonable proportion to a man who had spent his life as a distinguished lawyer, state legislator, Congressman, Collector of Customs at Charleston, and plantation owner."[30] By failing to include the autobiography in his account of Grayson as critic, Parks excludes Grayson's best critical essay and misses entirely Grayson's wit, as when he comments on what he sees as Coleridge's limited view of poetry: "... he is like a musician who plays on one string of his viol. We may wonder at the dexterity of the performer but with the conviction that he would give us better music from the whole instrument." What Parks neglected to regard and what Stoney failed to appreciate is that this chapter on poetry was intended as a major chapter in the autobiography. If what happened to the republic is Grayson's major concern, what was happening to literature was also of consequence. In his preface Grayson had made it clear that a major purpose in his writing *The Hireling and the Slave* was to revive the style of Dryden and Pope by using it for a political purpose that would attract attention. After all he reasoned: "May we not imitate the poetry of Queen Anne's time as well as the tables and chairs?" Grayson was by the standards of a new generation of critics in the 1850s a literary reactionary, as Edd Parks portrays him; but the views he still speaks for in his autobiography were, as Timrod witnessed, in Charleston not his alone. Again, Grayson reminds us that the South was never exclusively Romantic in literature or in politics.

The final segment of Grayson's autobiography covers the struggle of the antisecessionists and the secessionists. It is in a sense his jeremiad, a tale of tragic consequences for those who like Grayson and Petigru lost and knew what they had lost and for those who won and did not know what the South had lost. Grayson, measuring up to his standards for a gentleman, once again reports both sides charitably and generally without rancor. He even recounts, with good humor, the debates in the back alleys of King Street that erupted when the two groups happened to meet after their respective meetings in nearby buildings broke up. But he also makes explicit the tragic consequence of the victory of the secessionists: "The great event of the age—the dissolution of the North American Republic. I witness the death of the great Republic with sorrow. I was born with it and I survive." What does Grayson distinguish as the reason for this triumph of irrationality, for this folly of a great country behaving as foolishly as a small Latin American country? To a neoclassical rationalist the villain is surrender of the will to emotionalism and irrationality. "It is thus become the lot of our Country from whatever cause to exhibit to the world another example of human folly and madness."

Who is to blame? Grayson asks his question and answers it with customary fairness and objectivity, exhibiting a rather remarkable magnanimity in a manuscript written in the midst of a war which his reason told him would be lost by the South.

> Are these men without blame on the South side any more than on the North side of the Potomac? The verdict of impartial history will be that of "guilty" for both. . . . But is the North alone culpable? Is the South altogether blameless? I say we are but I doubt it.

On the back of this sheet, where Grayson occasionally wrote longer additions to his text, he scribbled several versions of what he apparently wanted to get utterly right, perhaps intended as a further comment on all those, including Southerners, even Grayson himself, who because of moral vanity cannot see their own wrong. He began his autobiography with references to Rousseau's *Confessions* and Boswell's *Life*. He now implies their moral vanity as perceived by those who read them, perhaps unknowingly, from a position also of moral vanity.

It was the moral vanity only of Rousseau and Boswell that arrayed revelations of their vice and meanness to the world. They see the relevancy of vice and meanness by R and B from nothing but moral vanity and they feel for the violaters no sentiment but contempt.

By further implication the same judgment might be made of those in the North and in the South who judge the guilt in Grayson's time. At such moments, all is vanity for those who judged and are judged.

Although when war came Grayson endeavored to be patriotic and to praise the courage of heroes, it is clear from his private comments in his autobiography that he abhors war as a savage, irrational act. War to Grayson, the rationalist, is the ultimate in chaos and in denial of humanity.

It is hideous in all its aspects. It demoralizes as much as it destroys. We never think of the inhuman ferocity, the field strewed with dead and wounded, the mutilated bodies and human eyes to look upon.

In his war diary he tallies the losses for both the military and the civilians even while recounting and respecting, as part of his day-by-day reporting, individual acts of courage.

Grayson's final chapter focuses on the burning of his letters in anticipation of the capture of Charleston by Union forces and in preparation for moving to his daughter's home in Newberry. While performing this act he returns to the past evoked by the letters, to memories of the people he had corresponded with, to voices from the past; most important of all, to the letters of Petigru, for whom he must now halt the account of his own life to take up that of the dead friend. His act of burning is symbolic of the destruction of that past, leaving alive only the memories. He can now fall back only on his neoclassical sense of moral order and on his concept of the values lived by the gentleman, consoling himself that "virtue even in this world is happier than vice." He has characterized his own life as rational—having been lived, as much as is possible, according to principle in a time when the values of community and government were abandoned. It is on this note that the autobiography ends. Grayson seems satisfied that, in such times, he had lived according to his own sane standards. It is all that he can demand of himself as consolation for the failure in society that has produced secession and war.

I offer William J. Grayson's manuscript, here published complete for the first time, as a document in literary autobiography, granting its readers, as autobiography should, an assessment of his life and a judgment of the historical context in which it was lived. It is seemingly artless but, nevertheless, penned with considerable art. It is, in part, pastoral prose poem; in part, social and literary criticism; in part, jeremiad. Janet Varner Gunn cautions that the integrity of autobiography can be threatened by ideology, raising the question of "whether or not the self can make the move from inside to outside, from private to public, from silence to speech without sacrificing its essential integrity."[31] It is Grayson's sense of fairness that prevents this from happening. His purpose is not ideological, a defense of slavery once more. His perspective is not taken from the customary nineteenth-century idea of progress but becomes a more tragic Southern avowal of loss. Writing in wartime, he sees his task as an occasion not for celebrating the birth of a new nation but rather for lamenting the loss of the greatest experiment so far in government, "the North American republic."

Grayson is certainly not guiltless of defending the South and of assailing those he regards as its enemies, but he has written at a difficult moment an often fair and unexpectedly objective account of a life lived from a time of union and disputation to a time of disunion and war. Eugene Genovese has made a strong case in his *Political Economy of Slavery* for secession as the natural consequence of the efforts of a slaveholding elite to save its civilization based on slavery.[32] Grayson speaks in his autobiography not entirely alone, but for a class of professional gentlemen—lawyers who contributed to the defense of slavery, but opposed secession.

Two recent books edited by Michael O'Brien reinforce a view that there were Southerners who dissented from the majority view, and John McCardell has recently suggested that the majority, early in 1861, may still have hoped that sectional rights could be maintained in the Union.[33] It is a minor point in Southern history, perhaps; but utter bitterness of feeling was not the sole characteristic of the relationship between the North and the South. There were those who did not see all Northerners as their enemies or accept secession as a practical or rational act. I became aware in the 1950s, when I first worked on Southern literary magazines, that there were men like John Reuben Thompson, editor of the *Southern Literary Messenger*, who was known for his fairness, even on the verge of war, in "all matters literary" in his dealings with the North. When Thompson was attacked for this by fellow Southerners, as far South as

Charleston, Paul Hamilton Hayne came to his defense, declaring: "A true literary spirit is essentially liberal."[34] Hayne's venerable friend, William J. Grayson, in his autobiography exhibits a good measure of this same fairness and objectivity, the liberal spirit and unabusive veracity of the gentleman, in a difficult time to display it—in a time of war. Fortunately, Grayson's autobiography survives the threat of the prejudiced ideology the poem he is remembered for could not survive. The question of the self's identity in autobiography becomes a question of our understanding of the self the author reveals as it locates itself in its world. In the brief coda that is his conclusion Grayson seems to be at peace with himself because he has performed that duty. He has fought honorably and lost but preserved his sense of self by not surrendering to the forces in his time he has judged as harbingers of chaos.

IV

In this edition I have included as part of the text what seem to be Grayson's latest corrections, added first in ink and later in pencil, occasionally written on the back of the sheet, usually with the place of insertion clearly marked. In almost all cases the additions make for a more interesting reading. I have not footnoted deletions, as Bass did, because they are clearly marked out, and I want a readable text. This intention has also guided my decisions in making corrections in the manuscript. I have corrected what are obvious errors, or what appear to be inattentive errors; and I have even made a few changes for aesthetic reasons. My rationalization is that Grayson had little time for a final careful proofreading and that this is not a diary but a literary autobiography. For the textual purists I have left a few peculiarities in spelling whenever a pattern emerges or nineteenth-century usage permits. I have left his punctuation untouched except for consistency in indicating titles. Punctuation in his century was often a personal matter and often in a much freer style than is customary today. For titles Grayson sometimes used quotation marks; on other occasions, nothing at all. I have opted for consistency by using quotations marks for all titles.

Unfortunately, there is a gap in the last chapter, with three or four pages missing from the manuscript that I can do nothing about but to suggest that a reader may, if he wishes, go to his memoir of Petigru for another account of his friend's life. It may be in fact that these manuscript pages were removed to use in the other life.

What is important is that this is the first publication of Grayson's autobiography in book form and the first complete publication in any format. I have added Grayson's war diary as an essential extension of the autobiography, the raw materials for what might well have been restructured in the autobiography had he lived through the war. I have edited it, adding passages which were unfortunately omitted in the only previously published edition. I believe I have provided, with some effort, the only complete text and the one that permits the best understanding of Grayson's purposes.

When was Grayson's autobiography written? No dates are given, but I suspect it was written over a rather short period of time. Robert Bass contributes an account of Grayson's working on his biography of William Lowndes during 1860, confirmed by Benjamin F. Perry, who had requested it. That year we know that he also wrote a privately published reply to Professor Alexander Hodge, who had contended in the *Princeton Review* that the Union was not dissolvable. Grayson's reply, as one who had long contended that it should not be dissolved, was to the effect that all this was now after the fact: citizens "owe obedience so long only as they are citizens when their state secedes." In print he could accept his defeat on secession with loyalty to his state; but he was also ready, as Bass remarks, to "take on the tone of a Jeremiad" in his "lamentations for the country at the time of whose founding he had been born and which he had now outlived."[35] Sometime after the great fire of December 11, 1861, he began expressing his feelings about what had caused the present state of affairs by revisiting the past through the act of writing his autobiography. Bass notes that he does not mention the trip he made to Newberry and Anderson on July 30, 1862, suggesting that writing on his autobiography had stopped before that date. We do know that on May 10, 1862, he began his diary, persevering until January 31, 1863. So, the best educated guess is that the autobiography was written during 1862, most likely continued until some time before July 30, or even halted before May 10, when of necessity he turned his attention to keeping a record of the present in his diary rather than to a remembrance of the past.

The advantage of the autobiographer is that he knows so much more about how he lived his times than anyone else. The dramatic irony here is that the reader knows the denouement, something that Grayson, as privileged as he was in his knowledge of the past, did not even suspect of the future—the survival of the great North American republic.

The Autobiography of William J. Grayson

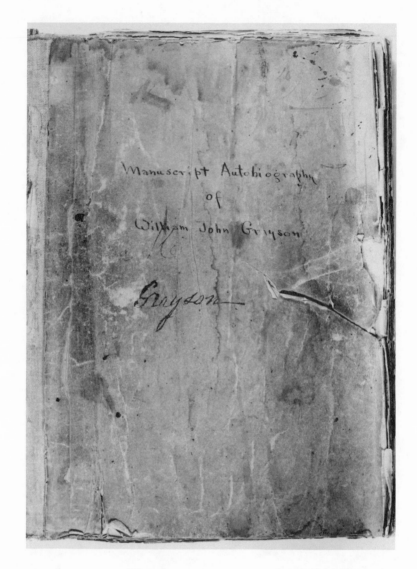

Title page of the autobiography. *South Caroliniana Library, University of South Carolina.*

Chapter One

There are few lives, Dr. Johnson remarks, of which the narrative could fail to amuse and instruct if faithfully and judiciously written. It may well be so, since every life has its lesson and romance. All that is necessary for the writer is to tell the story in a fitting manner — with just regard to truth on the one hand and a decent reserve on the other.

In every such narrative truth should be carefully respected. The story professes to be a true story not a fictitious one. But although the witness should be exact in saying what he knows, he must not say all that he knows. He should tell the truth only, but not the whole truth. To tell the whole truth is hardly possible and if it were possible it would not be advisable. The exposure of human infirmity that must follow such unreserved revelations could neither satisfy the reader's taste nor commend itself to his judgment. It would disgust not gratify. Even truth in its disclosures must be guarded by a modest reserve.

The occasional violaters of this sober rule have few imitators. The example of J. J. Rousseau warns not invites. Not many men are willing to be the heralds of their own infirmity or infirmities. If not able to abstain from doing a bad act most men are modest enough to be ashamed of it. They are not so base as to proclaim their infamy to the world. Boswell in his "Life of Johnson" reveals much of his own. He is always presenting himself in the most pitiable plight while he glorifies the wit or wisdom of his illustrious friend. He crawls in the dust to elevate his hero. He is glad to be contemptible if it elicits an oracle from his idol. His book, Macaulay says, is the best of biographies, "It has no second."[1] Yet Macaulay would not have imitated the biographer's self abasement to surpass his work. Rousseau and Boswell are moral suicides. For Boswell we feel some kindness notwithstanding his meanness; he honoured virtue and venerated genius after his fashion. Rousseau is detestable — an impersonation of selfishness and sensuality with no one redeeming quality; without the natural affection that brutes themselves entertain for their young. Yet even these men Boswell and Rousseau have, no doubt, kept back from public view some secret places in their hearts which they had not hardihood enough to expose. As far as they have gone their example is not alluring. It warns, not invites.

A life then to be fully written should be written with some reserve. The frankness of the narrative must be kept within the bounds of a reasonable decorum. The human heart will not bear to be shown to the proper world divested of all drapery. It must be veiled like the body in decent clothing. In some such way it occurred to me in an idle hour to test the truth of the saying that any one's life may be so told as to impart instruction or amusement. I may confirm the adage or disprove it by relating mine.

I was born in November 1788, in the town of Beaufort, South Carolina. The town is situated in the Southern Corner of the State, on Port Royal, in a parish of islands. It was on one of these islands that Ribaut attempted in 1562 to establish the French Colony whose story is so disastrous. To Port Royal the Lords Proprietors ordered the expedition under Sayle in 1670. The colonists arrived in safety but afraid of Spanish hostility they abandoned the noble bay and its islands in a few weeks for the safer banks of Ashley river. Again in 1682 Lord Cardross began a settlement of Scotch adventurers in this beautiful portion of the State. They were assailed and dispersed by the Spaniards from Augustine in 1686. The country was nevertheless too inviting to be neglected and emigrants from the South Western counties of England soon found their way to its shores. They began the town of Beaufort in 1712 and once more, in 1716, Port Royal was desolated with the country around it. In the Spring of that year the Yamassee war broke out. The Savages killed many of the whites and drove the rest to seek shelter in Charleston. During the revolution of 1776, British troops occupied the luckless place and now in 1862 Northern invaders have seized the town, plundered the islands, demoralized the slaves and are occupied in drilling them for servile war. The marauders come as friends to restore peaceful relations by fire and Sword. They have union on their lips and confiscation in their hearts. They are missionaries of union and the constitutory of confiscation and blood shed.

The little town has not increased as American towns are accustomed to do. It is remarkable for the conservative property of standing still. Its population is no greater than it was fifty years ago and its condition as to all material advantages is very much the same. It has always been on good terms with itself nevertheless and for better reasons than usually accompany self complacency. It is quiet, healthy, religious, dresses well, is of good manners and morals and not a little addicted to mental cultivation. It has been eulogized moreover in the geographical works of Jedediah [*sic*] Morse.[2] In the early editions of his book he praises Beaufort for its intelligence, hospitality and refinement. The account of Mr. Morse was written before the days of the modern Apostles that now flourish in New York and Boston and while Paul and his contemporaries were still authorities in all Christian churches amicable relations too existed in Morse's time among the States. The friendship of the Revolution had not yet been superseded by the hatred that now prevails between North and South. Subscriptions for various purposes were received and praise duly administered by New England travellers in the Southern States. It was a pleasant traffic for the Northern visitor and he was never weary of pursuing it. There was always something craved for a book, or a church, or a college, and money was never refused to those who asked it. Contributions are now lured in a different manner, by armed bands and ships of war. Courteous solicitation is changed into robbery and the eulogy of old into libel. And yet the virtues of the ancient town have gone on steadily increasing. It has become more and more remarkable for intelligence, piety and good works while those who praised it formerly now occupy it as enemies.

My father, John Grayson, was an officer of artillery in the continental army during the Revolutionary War. My father's father was an Englishman, a native of Yorkshire. He had carried on commercial business in the West Indies and afterwards in Carolina and Georgia. An old field near Satilla river in the last state still bears his name. He married the daughter of Col. Thomas Wigg whose father had been among the earliest emigrants from England to Port Royal. Col. Wigg dying in 1760 left five children, three daughters—Mrs. Hazzard, Mrs. Heyward and Mrs. Grayson—and two sons. One of the sons left a daughter, the mother of Captain John Rivers of James Island, the other had a son who died in early manhood without issue. The name so common at one time as to comprise a majority of the vestry in St. Helena parish is now confined to Mr. William Wigg and his family, lately residents of St. Lukes parish.

My father entered the army at the age of seventeen as a lieutenant of artillery in Roberts' regiment — Beckman's. He was one of the garrison in Charleston when it was surrendered by Lincoln after a brave defense to the British forces in May 1780. After the surrender the officers, prisoners of war, were placed in cantonments, at Haddrel's point, over against the city, where Mount Pleasant village now stands. While there the young lieutenant was forced into a quarrel, with a brother officer, a Frenchman and professed duellist.[3] Although no longer able to fight the enemy the prisoners, it seems, were at liberty to fight each other. It relieved the tediousness of captivity in a way conformable to the Soldier's pursuits. The cause was trivial enough, but not smaller than is common in "affairs of honour." It was as weighty, perhaps, as many that have produced long conflicts among States and Nations. To help out their scanty rations while prisoners, one of the combatants raised chickens, the other cultivated a garden. The chicken of the poultry breeder made marauding expeditions on the cabbages of the Gardener. It was a very natural proceeding and in the spirit of the times. But the chicken raid gave occasion to high words and high words led to challenge and a duel. The Revd. M. L. Weems, formerly pastor of a church in Alexandria and Chaplain as he called himself of General Washington, made the affair a subject of one of the curious pamphlets of which he was the author and vender.[4] He called them by quaint names the gambler's looking glass, the drunkard's looking glass, the duellist's looking glass. These pamphlets with histories of bloody murders, psalm books, testaments, his life of Marion and of Washington, he carried through the country in a light wagon, for sale, fiddling as he went and preaching when invited. His favorite text was "God is Love" and his favorite topics for illustrating God's goodness to man-kind were George Washington and Langdon Cheves. His fiddle, like Goldsmith's flute when the poet travelled on foot through Europe, made the eccentric traveller welcome wherever he went. His custom was to give his old horse the reins and as the horse walked the road slowly the master amused himself and cheered the way with the sounds of his violin. Whenever night overtook them, he was sure of a welcome at a farm house or cabin and of hospitable entertainment for man and horse. The old traveler was returning from one of these periodical circuits when he was seized with a painful disease and was landed from a passing steam boat on the wharf at Beaufort in a destitute and deplorable condition. There was no hotel. While many citizens passed by on the other side of the way and the city authorities were deliberating what to do with the unfortunate stranger, a good Samaritan, the Rev. Benjamin S. Scriven, took him to his house.[5] Mr. Scriven's excellent wife tenderly nursed the poor old itinerant bookseller and chaplain of Washington thus picked up by the way side and at his death they buried him in the graveyard of the Episcopal Church. His grave is unmarked by any memorial. Mr. Weems is entitled to a place among the earliest cultivators of literature in the Southern States. His "Looking glasses" were tracts for the times — moral lessons in the shape of stories founded on facts. They were popular, widely circulated in the country, and useful in their day. His "Life of Marion" and of Washington were narratives of a higher order. Even they were not ambitious in their aim, and belong to the class of gossip and anecdote rather than exact or elaborate history. Yet it is to the life of Marion partly that the partizan hero owes his early and wide spread fame with the American people.

My father died when I was about ten years old. I remember very little of him. He was reserved in disposition, I think, and I was shy and sensitive. The association of father and child at so early an age is not commonly a very close one. I retain indeed but few memories of any kind relating to the period of my life anterior to his death. Of these few not many are pleasing. It is common to talk of the happiness of childhood, but I cannot remember much of mine. If childhood had joys for me, the joys, for the most part, are forgotten. I can remember the pains more distinctly — petty disappointments, mortifications from angry words or heedless acts of others, the brutality of a teacher who threatened me at six years old with a dark closet and a long knife, the petulance or sneers of friends, a very small thing to the older parties, as small as the stoning of frogs by idle boys may be to the boys, but a serious affair to the subjects in either case of such attentions. These early sorrows were not all selfish. I can recollect almost nothing of a younger brother who died when seven years old except his little disappointments and griefs. One incident of the kind I remember as if it were of recent occurrence although it belongs to the last century. My father had appointed an afternoon for sailing in the harbour and my brother and I were to be of the party. It was necessary to submit to certain maternal manipulations before we were ready. I got away in time. My brother was kept too long and as we sailed to and fro before the town I saw him on the shore very disconsolate with his hands at his eyes too late for the promised pleasure.

The chief pleasures I remember of my early boyhood are those I enjoyed in the house of my father's mother. I spent my holidays of Easter and Christmas at her plantation on Parris Island. I was a favourite child, the son of a favourite son and was petted accordingly. How well I remember the eagerness with which I looked forward to the months of April and December; how I regreted the rapidity with which the days passed by; how much I enjoyed them; how reluctantly at their close, I returned home to school and its troubles! My grandmother was an admirable specimen of loveable old age. I still see the dear old lady, at seventy, actively ordering her household. The white muslin cap with the broad black ribbon around it, the ample folds of the same material covering her neck and bosom, the clear blue eye undimmed by age, the grave and gentle expression of countenance, the fair and delicate features, all rise up before me as of yesterday. I never had from her a harsh word or angry look at my boyish mischief. All my memories of respecting her are of unmixed reverence and love.

She had a neighbour Mrs. Ann Rippon of her own age whose plantation lay on the opposite side of the island, on the Broad river shore, about three miles off.[6] The brother of one of the friends had married the sister of the other and a son, the only offspring of the marriage, bound the two old aunts together in a closer intimacy. I was a frequent and willing guest at Mrs. Rippon's. Never was hostess more devoted to the comfort and enjoyment of her friends or better pleased at having a house full. She was wonderfully managing, always bustling, scolding and unwearily devoted to the callers. The finest hams of her own curing, the fattest turkies of her own raising, the choicest fish and oysters and puddings and pies and dainties without number were marshalled on her dinner table in suitable order. How she insisted on one's eating! There was no escaping. No knife and fork were ever active enough or sufficiently persevering at her table. If you eat never so much, she earnestly pressed you to eat more, not for form sake or imaginary politeness, but with an air of absolute distress to see you, as she would say, so delicate in your appetite or so little satisfied with her fare of her table. Should there be a dozen guests at her table her eye appeared to be on every one. If she saw the smallest falling off in the enjoyment of her dishes, she became at once restless, fidgety and unhappy at having nothing that could please you. Her plantation abounded in all good things. Her garden was excellent, producing every fruit and vegetable. Oranges were plentiful, figs without number, peaches and pomegranates in profusion. At that time and before people lived on their plantations and all useful and pleasant things flourished accordingly. Now plantations are cotton fields rearing a crop for foreign markets and little more. The fruits have almost disappeared. Oranges are rare, pomegranates formerly seen everywhere are seldom met with, figs are scarce and small. Few planters have a good peach or strawberry; worms destroy one and weeds choak the other. Formerly they were cultivated under the owner's eye and flourished accordingly. Even the fish and oysters of the coast and inlets were better of old or better looked after. They have become less abundant like the deer of the woods and the small game of the fields, or the people are less diligent in seeking them. The planter's whole attention now is absorbed by his cotton crop.

The cultivation of a great staple like cotton or tobacco starves everything else. The farmer curtails and neglects all crops. He buys from distant places not only the simplest manufactured article his brooms and buckets, but farm productions, grain, meat, hay, butter, all of which he could make at home. What is obtained in this way is sparingly consumed. If grain and hay are bought, horses, mules, cattle suffer from short supplies. Success or failure in the crop for market makes little difference in the supply of food. If the crop is short everything is put on half rations; if it succeeds, the planter seeks an additional enjoyment, a jaunt to the North, or a voyage to Europe, and mules, pigs, and cattle, fare little better than before. This is true in a greater or less degree of the whole cotton growing region. It is especially true of the low country planters in Georgia and Carolina. They devote themselves to their cotton fields. They buy their corn from North Carolina, their meat from Kentucky, their hay from New York, their butter from farmers a thousand miles away in a climate that makes it necessary to house and feed everything six months in the year. Under this system the country that might be the most abundant in the world is the least plentiful. The beef is lean, the poultry poor, the hogs a peculiar breed with long snouts and gaunt bodies, toiling all summer to keep themselves alive with partial success, and in the winter making a slender and uncertain return for the damage they have wrought to fields and fences. The planter buys salt butter from the North when he might enjoy home-made fresh butter all the year round. It is said he has no grasses. He may have green pastures of rye or oats through the winter and in summer make ample supplies of roots and hay. He neglects them all. With a hundred head of cattle he is without milk for his coffee. The practice is to turn the cattle out in November that they may take care of themselves among the woods and swamps. They are driven up in May, the calves marked, the cows milked, and butter made for a few months of summer. Twenty cows will then produce what a good dairy cow yields in England. It never occurs to the planter to keep up a few cows and feed them. He goes on year after year buying salt butter and drinking coffee without milk. A friend of mine, in a sudden emergency, fell on a singular device to obtain milk which may illustrate the system that produced it. My friend and cousin, Mick O'Brien, was an Island planter, on a large plantation, with a fine stock of cattle. He did with them as his neighbours were accustomed to do; he turned them out in the winter to feed as they might about the woods and marshes. He had no milk, but he was alone and liked his coffee as well without it. One day however a family in a boat overtaken by bad weather stopt at his landing and claimed shelter and entertainment. Mick was the son of an Irishman and as generous as the day. He received them with warm hospitality. But in the family was a young child needing milk. What was our host to do? His cattle had been for months in the woods and were wild as deer. To hunt them up, pen them, milk them in the usual way would require a long time. The occasion was pressing. A brilliant idea suggested itself. He ordered his cattle minder to mount a horse and drive the cattle through the woods, posted his hunter at a convenient place and instructed him to shoot the best cow with a young calf that should pass in the herd. The order was obeyed, the cow knocked over, and speedily milked as she lay disabled on the ground; the child received its food and the calls of hospitality were answered by an improvement in dairy management not discreditable to the genius of the old Country and suggested by the customs prevailing in our own.

During the holiday times that I spent in the Country I learned the arts of fishing and shooting at an early age, as all boys do in Carolina. At first my fishing was confined to catching minnows with a pack thread line and pin hooks. Attended by a retinue of little negroes, I caught in the shallow creeks of the marshes, mud fish and sometimes an eel which we ran away from, thinking it a snake. Next I attempted yellow tail and whiting. In due time I became

initiated in the noble sport of drum fishing. Port Royal, or Broad
River as it is locally called, is the favorite haunt of the drum. It is
a large heavy fish, weighing fifty or sixty pounds and sometimes
more. It makes a singular noise, in Spring of the year like the tap
of a drum, which explains its name. The sound is heard distinctly
from the bottom of the river at a depth of five or six fathoms. The
fish afford excellent sport to the fisherman and no bad dish for the
table. Among sea or river delicacies the roe of the drum is an
unsurpassed dainty. The fish bite only in the Spring of the year but
seem never to leave the rivers in the vicinity of Port Royal. It is
supposed that like many other productions of the Country they are
not so numerous as formerly. The largest number ever caught, as
far as I have heard, was caught a half century ago. In this great
success it was my fortune to have a share. With ten lines, from half
ebb to low water, we took ninety six great fish and when the sport
was at an end the fish were biting as rapidly as before. Our bait
gave out and we rowed away from the ground, in our loaded boat,
unsated with the day's sport and eager to continue it. It was a
beautiful day, a bright sky, a gentle South wind just sufficient to
ripple the green sea water of the bay and moderate the warmth of
an April sun and the landscape around us with Hilton Head and
Parris Island and Saint Helena and the single palm tree on Dawes'
Island looked out through the pure atmosphere, in all its beauty,
clearly and distinctly defined. In the eagerness of competition through
the day we lost a great number of fish after hooking them. The hook
tore out, or the line broke, or the hook, or strap gave way and the
mortified and impatient fisherman was obliged to stop and repair
his tackle while his companions were catching more fish by his side.
Since the great achievement of ninety six, I have never known more
than forty drum caught in a day's fishing and that but seldom. It
has become common to coil a whole tide and take only two or three.
The drum is not confined to Port Royal. They are found as far North
as New York and they are common on the coast of Florida, but no
where except in Port Royal sound is drum fishing an institution and
a jubilee cultivated and enjoyed by old and young, white and black,
master and slave.

But I have anticipated events and gone beyond my story. Before
I had been made free of the corporation or grand craft of drum
fishing, fortune or education carried me a long way from its scenes.
A great change came over the dreams of my boy life. I was borne.[7]

Chapter Two

Northern Schools, Utrecht, Newark

About a year after my father's death my mother married again. Her second husband was a kind and social man, active in business, a substantial planter, and highly esteemed in the community. He was a widower with four children; my mother had two. The newly married pair began their matrimonial partnership therefore with six children. Another was in due time added to the number. The increasing household or the supposed advantages of a Northern School which then and since have beset the imagination of Southern parents, induced my friends to send me when twelve years old to the North under the charge of Mr. Solomon Saltus of New York.[1] Mr. Saltus had a brother living in Beaufort with whom he was accustomed to spend the winter season. In the early spring of 1801 I went with him on his return home to be placed at school somewhere in his neighbourhood. The passage was long and boisterous. The age of steamers or clipper ships was not yet come, and we were three weeks going from Charleston to New York. It was too early in the year for travellers and the passengers were not numerous. One of the number, a Scotch merchant, astonished me with the breakfasts that he seemed to delight in. His favorite dish was a plate full of soft hominy stirred up with London porter. The corn grist was a substitute, I suppose, for the more acceptable but unattainable oat meal. I was never tempted to try the virtues of the compound but our fellow passenger appeared to find it wholesome and palatable. During the voyage I got to be on friendly terms with the first mate of the ship and our arrival in New York I remained on board in the dock for a week or more, the ship guest of the kind hearted sailor. We went to market every morning and I have pleasant memories of the fresh cod and other dainties of the Fly market dainties made more acceptable by the long voyage and sea fare. Even the cooking I have not forgotten. My entertainer cut his fish across into slices of an inch or more for frying a mode of cutting up and cooking that I recommend to epicures. The sociable old mate invited me to visit him at his farm on Long Island. But although willing enough to go I never went. My indulgent guardian had not forgotten me. My time was come — the hour and the man — the last in the shape of an elderly Scotch schoolmaster who kept what he was pleased to call a family school for a select number of boys at New Utrecht on Long Island.[2] We set out from New York on a fine afternoon in the early part of May. We crossed the ferry to Brooklyn. The ferry boat was the ancient Dutch invention, an undecked Schooner with flat bottom, straight sides, and huge lea boards. The city of Brooklyn was at this time a mere village with houses scattered along the river and on either side of the main road running up from the East river into the interior of the Island. The Dominie's tight waggon with two good horses carried us with my bedding and baggage. We arrived at the little Dutch village before sunset. I was a newcomer. It was the first evening. I was introduced into the family part of the mansion and permitted to take tea with the master's wife and daughters. We had very nice white bread and fresh butter. I thought the beginning a very good one. But it was the last time I ever saw wheat bread or tea in the household. The next day I was turned over the school side of the house, to brown bread and chocolate. The chocolate was not indebted to cocoa for any of its properties and the brown bread was of rye, very dark but wholesome and palatable enough for hungry school boys. The school had the reputation of being a select family school; we never saw the family. The family side of the mansion and the school side were separate communities. A close partition divided the house into two tenements. The south end with a long piazza on the West and a shorter one on the East constituted the family residence. A small shed or "Stoop" that covered a door on the North end of the building formed the entrance to the rooms occupied by the pupils. On the first floor, at opposite sides of an entry or hall, were the school room and eating room; on the second floor were four chambers that afforded accomodation for fifteen or sixteen students. The house stood back from the road about fifty yards and the lawn or lot was surrounded with large lombardy poplars at that time a favorite tree in all parts of the Country.

The village of New Utrecht was very Dutch and very primitive. The road coming from New York or Brooklyn on the North turned West at a right angle near the school leaving it on the outside or East of the bend and on the West or inside the elbow, the village Tavern bearing as a sign the image of Schuyler or some other Dutch worthy. In the school house corner of the road lay a shallow pond where horses were watered, where in due time I sailed my boats and cut my feet on the fragments of bottles thrown into it from the neighbouring tavern. My wounded feet got well as they might; they received no attention from the matron of the house who left all such cases to spontaneous cure, never intermeddling with the medical skill of nature which she wisely judged was better than her own. On each side of the green street or road stood houses at wide intervals. They were generally of stone rough hewed, one story in height, with gardens, fields and orchards extending behind them. About a half mile up the road from the school, and in the middle of the way was the Dutch Church built of stone, an octagon below with a roof of sugar loaf Shape crowned with a belfry. There the village girls took lessons in the evenings from itinerant Yankee teachers of psalmody. We sometimes attended as lookers on and thought the girls very pretty and the singing as charming as older amateurs think a fashionable opera. At intervals along the wide road from the school to the Church were huge trees of buttonwood or sycamore. The village stands about a mile from the Narrows and from the Sandy beach of the bay below over which Sandy Hook and its light house are distinctly seen. The Country about the village is level and well cultivated. It abounded in orchards for the fruit of which the great city afforded a ready market. Late in May or in early June, the Country glowed with the bloom of innumerable fruit trees, apples, pears, cherries, plums, surrounding the farm houses and imparting to them attractions that did not belong to their homely architecture. The limit of our rambles to the West was the rocky and precipitous Narrows. On the East the country ran into sandy wastes, salt marshes and mill ponds in which we caught crabs and bathed occasionally in Summer. It was a desolate region and hardly seemed to admit of much improvement. On the South the bay and sea were our limits.

Our teacher's name was Todd. He was an easy tempered man, slovenly and slouchly in gait and dress. His small scraggy wig was always awry. During school hours he carried a quill in his mouth and chewed it industriously while the saliva at times ran down from the corners of his lips. He had been educated for the church but a slight impediment in his speech induced him to exchange the pulpit for the school. He was a man of learning and irreproachable in his domestic relations. He was somewhat of a public man too and played the part of chairman at political meetings in the Dutch tavern when party spirit ran high between Federalists and Republicans in the times of Hamilton and Burr. The parties and their purposes gave us of the School so little concern that I am unable to tell which side received our Dominie's support or which was victorious.

The discipline of the establishment was not rigid. The scholars came from remote parts, from the Southen States and the West India Islands. Their parents were too far off to be exacting. Commercial agents were not as diligent and solicitous about the sons of their distant friends as about the sugar and coffee in the warehouses sent to them from the same quarter and an easy way of getting along was naturally the policy of the school. In this family institution as I have said, we saw nothing of the family. It consisted of Mrs. Todd, three daughters and two sons. One of the daughters was grown up, an accomplished young lady, and married a business man of New York thus drawing what for a village belle was a prize in the matrimonial lottery. But except with the sons and the venerable old Dominie at school hours, we had no intercourse with the household. To its females we were outside barbarians.

For those who were disposed to learn our teacher was not an incompetent instructor. He was willing and able to impart knowledge to those who desired to obtain it. But it was very much a matter of free will with the pupils. There was no confusion. I remember one of his astronomical lessons which in the absence of globes and orreries was not badly conceived. At any rate it made an impression on my memory which has never been effaced. He closed the windows and darkened the room, put a hoop on a table, placed a lighted candle in the centre of the hoop, suspended a ball to a string and set the ball spinning. He then carried the string with its spinning ball slowly round the hoop. The candle was the sun, the hoop the earth's orbit; the ball carried round the hoop represented the annual course of the earth, the spinning, its diurnal motion, the sides alternately dark and lighted by the candle, the changes of day and night, while a slight inclination of the hoop gave a better than a hundred lectures of elaborate descriptions or printed explanations committed to memory. It never failed to command attention.

In the quiet village of New Utrecht, with this kind but somewhat careless teacher, I remained a year and a half. We roamed the Country far and wide. In the warm season we dispensed with shoes. We cared little about hats or caps. They were incumbrances to the freedom of our movements. We lived whole summer days in the surf on the sea beach. We skated in winter on the ponds and got rides with the Dutch farmers into whose sleighs we jumped as they passed our gate at a rapid pace. We helped the fishermen to draw their seines on the sea shore, in the shad season, of March or April. They encouraged our exertions with liberal encomiums, calling us collegians by way of compliment, but they offered us no fish. It was the approved Northern mode at that time of dealing with their Southern neighbours. The North took all the profit and the South the praise. Yet the draughts of shad were sometimes so large that liberality would have been easy. On one occasion it became necessary to run a smaller seine within the large one and scoop out a portion of the fish for fear the great net might be broken by the multitude. There was also caught along the sea shore a great quantity of a bony fish which the Dutch called manhadden. These fish were used for manure. At a short distance from the beach, heaps of them slightly covered with sand putrified and gave odours which differed widely from those of roses or violets. But they fertilized the land and were therefore not ungrateful perhaps to the farmer's nose.

We made raids, in the proper season, on the apples and cherries, the plums and pears, of the neighbourhood. The old farmers took it in very good part. They sometimes gave chase to us as to any other mischievous wild animals. But they made no complaints to our Dominie. On our part we regarded the raid as no robbery. We should have treated any such charge with scorn. It was the spirit of adventure. The monopolists of orchards were our natural enemies. We spoiled the Egyptians. We assailed the Spanish galleons. It was of no moment to us, in our free democracy, what strainers at gnats and swallowers of camels like our Dominie's old masters and mates might think, of our adventures. We were living under the old primitive law and everyone took fruit where he had the power and eat it with no scruples of conscience. Was it not the gift of nature, of her sun and showers, to her children, the younger ones especially including ourselves? One of our neighbours more benevolent or more sagacious than the rest compromised with the juvenile commonwealth. He threw out of his enclosure one row of his cherry trees for our use with the understanding that we should respect the rest of his orchard. We were put on our honour and the confidence was never abused. We were more honest than our Northern partners with whom a large concession of privileges and advantages commercial and political served only as inducements to steal the whole. We broke no faith and encountered no secession ordinances.

While at the Long Island School I became an expert and bold swimmer. I learned with many falls to skate. I gave vigour to my constitution by abundant exercise, during all seasons, in the open air. But I had no access to books. Before I left home I loved reading. I had hung over a torch light in the chimney, a candle being unattainable, to shed abundant tears at the story of Paul and Virginia in the house of Mrs. Ann Joyner—the widow of Capt. John Joyner who commanded the frigate, So Carolina, a vessel purchased by the State during the Revolution—, I had laughed, over Don Quixote until the old lady would become impatient to know what I laughed at and why I did not read aloud that she also might enjoy the jest. But on Long Island my mind was deprived of all nourishment and starved for want of food except what a free intercouse with nature gave it. At a period of life, from twelve to fifteen, when the intellect hungers and thirsts after knowledge, I saw no books. I could have devoured a library. But if Mr. Todd had books, as I suppose he had, they were tabood to the boarders of the family school.

My school mates were, for the most part, from the West Indies. They were pleasant and amiable companions, but nothing more. Two of them made exceptions to the rest as to temper and talent. One nearly a man grown was ill natured and tyrannical. His petty oppressions are not among the agreable memories of the school. The other exception was Richard Dyott of the Island, of Barbadoes if I remember rightly. He was the only one of the school who learned Latin and Greek and was the favourite and show pupil of our teacher. He was a lad of brilliant parts with that kind of versatile talent that does everything readily and well. He rose, I believe, in time to distinction in his native island.

Whatever small annoyances may have attended on our New Utrecht School ended in a few months. Our worthy Dominie during a short vacation paid a visit to some friend at New Port in October 1802. The fish of New Port are abundant and fine. Our master feasted imprudently, and was carried off by a sudden attack of cholera morbus. The school died with him. The scholars were dispersed and I returned to the house of my old friend Mr. Saltus in New York.

Saltus and Sons were dealers in ship chandlery. Their large warehouse was on Front or Water street, the residence, in Pearl Street near Broadway. The old lady was a daughter of one of the ancient Dutch families. The city had not yet been overun by New England adventurers and foreigners from all quarters of the world. The "Collect" was still a pond where boys skated in winter and sailed boats in summer. Brooklyn City was in embryo only. The Hudson was without a steam boat, almost without a ship. It was navigated by river and coasting sloops having huge masts standing straight up and down with great mainsails to suit. Ships were confined to the East river. They were of small tonnage. One of seven hundred tons was a monster which every one went to see as they, not long since, went to see the great Eastern. She was an East Indiaman called the Manhatten.

My old friend Mr. Saltus was grave and quiet. The old lady had all the love of order and neatness that belong to her race and which conduce so much to the well being of a house though sometimes troublesome to its inmates. Her dress was never soiled except by occasional particles of snuff which she used profusely. Many a six penny worth I bought for her at the neighbouring grocer's round the nearest corner. The division of labour was not so great then as now among shopkeepers and snuff was sold with sugar and candles. The old couple had two sons and a niece living with them. The eldest son, Francis, was a steady, silent, somewhat austere man of affairs. In the advanced age of the father he was the man of the firm. Nick, the younger son, was easy and chatty, inclining to be somewhat of a dandy, particular about the cut of his coat and fit of his boots, and more suited apparently to become a beau than a man of business. Nick, nevertheless, died unmarried while the solid man of business found favour with the ladies. The niece was a charming little lady not at all inclined however to play the lady's part exclusively but industrious and useful in the management of the household. In those primitive times of sixty years since, the customs differed widely from those now prevailing in wealthy households. Miss Maria helped the servants through the day with bustling activity and at night we might see her very handsomely dressed for some ball or other entertainment.

After a short interval of time I went to a school at Newark, New Jersey. It was not a family school this time for a few select boarders to be treated as parts of the master's family whom they never saw. I lodged with the Rev. Uzriel Ogden and went to the Newark Academy, a place of immense pretension and very small performance. The Academy building was a large one of brick.[3] The pupils were numerous, male and female. In the lower rooms of the institution Mr. Findley taught. In the upper, with much more pomp and circumstance, Dr. Woodbridge presided over the female department.[4] He received boys also in one of his rooms. I was for some time one of these and the Doctor lives in my memory as a portly pedagogue formed by nature and improved by art to predominate over half-fledged intellects male and female.

I remember having learned one thing at the Long Island school, but I have no such memory of the Newark Academy. . . . The mode of teaching geography may serve to illustrate the general method of instruction. It was taught without maps or globes. Morse was the text book of the school. We learned by committimg to memory large portions of the book, the boundaries of countries, the names of rivers and mountains, of cities and towns and their descriptions. But it was left to the pupil's fancy entirely to give position to the names. We might have learned by rote the whole of the worthy Jedediah's volume and yet have had very indefinite notions of the where about of cities, states or empires. They were a confused jumble in the pupil's memory without local habitations.

The house of the Revd. Mr. Ogden stood near the Episcopal church of which he was the pastor. Newark, at that time, was a town of one long street. The church was built in the middle of the Street which widened before it into a sort of common or park. Before the South door of the Church grew a double row of unhealthy locusts. On the North side a shallow pond afforded us in winter the amusement of running over its half thawed surface at the risk of breaking through the ice. It was no place for the skater. The pastor's house was an old, low, rambling, mansion of wood with all sorts of additions to the back part of it. The house stood on the east side of the street over against the Church. To the South a garden extended. On the back of the garden an apple orchard covered a larger space. The master of the house was a grave and imposing personage, tall, stout, and dressed in rusty black. He wore a huge wig white with powder, knee breeches, dark worsted stockings and shoes with large silver buckles. He had lost his voice at a fire where he took cold from over exertion. Although he continued to preach, it was impossible for the best ears to hear him distinctly. With the management of the household he had little to do. He appeared at table and said grace. Except at such times he was shut up in his study and rarely seen by his boarders. The government of the house devolved on the wife. She was a very large woman, tall and stately, one who bore sway with a commanding spirit, resolute to stand no nonsense and always prepared to enforce obedience to established rule.

In Newark, I learned nothing. I read nothing. The art of keeping a school at the North seemed to consists in making the most money with the least annoyance to teacher and scholar. The great and only important inquiry was, are the bills regularly paid by the scholars' friends. If they were, all was well. The art appeared to be thoroughly understood in Newark. I continued to some extent in New Jersey the kind of life I had led on Long Island. I skated on the ice bound Passaic in winter. I swam across it in summer. I made one of boating parties to New York and elsewhere. On one of these occasions we went to the home of one of the party, on the banks of the Raritan. We sailed down the Passaic across Hackensac bay, between Staten Island and the Jersey shore, round Amboy, to the farm of David Cotheal's parents. The old folks received us with great kindness, entertained us with delicacies of the Country, with new laid eggs, fresh butter, sweet milk and the fruits of the season and mollified our sun burnt faces with newly skimmed cream. Cotheal is the only Northern school mate whom I have met with in after life. I saw him in Washington in 1834 and was at his house subsequently in New York.[5] It was a large and handsome mansion in one of the new streets. He had become a successful merchant which in New York implies large fortune. When we met, the rambling school boys had grown into grave men with the burdens of life on their shoulders, troubles not to be removed, like those of our voyage, by simple means, many of them past cure by any medicine. We looked curiously at each other unable to recognize the boy in the man.

More than once while at Newark I walked to New York on a visit for the day to my old friends in the city. The distance across the Passaic and Hackensac bridges was ten miles. I went early in the morning and returned in the evening. Jersey City was not yet in being. There was a tavern at the ferry place and a few houses in various directions that had not yet attained the dignity of a village. The only wharf was where the ferry boat lay. The boat was of the ancient Dutch fashion. The Hudson river on the New York side gave births to river sloops and coasters only. The foreign shipping was confined to the East river.

At Newark School life was not so rude and semi savage as at New Utrecht. We made no marauding expeditions after fruit. We were not totally cut off from all female care and supervision. Mrs. Ogden was not so exclusive as Mrs. Todd. We were subjects of the Newark lady's supreme authority. She presided at the table where we eat with the family. At the Academy too the young ladies of the town were seen at least once a day. I even made some acquaintances among them and fell in love with one. It was a passion of fifteen, a mature affair compared with an earlier impression five years before. At ten, I had been the devoted admirer of a lady of five and twenty, engaged to be married to a man of her own age. I took as much pleasure in sitting near her looking at her and talking with her as we see people take on similar occasions. I suppose the case was analogous to that of a man of eighty becoming enamoured with a girl of fifteen. Miss Kate Kearny of Newark was very pretty, very lively, and very agreeable.[6] Her family lived above the bridge, beyond Ogden's mill pond, some distance up the road and outside the Northern limits of the town. Her mother was a widow with three or four children. I sometimes endeavoured to entertain Mrs. Kearny with accounts of my own home. I may have wished to make a favourable impression on the young lady's imagination. I told of orange trees bearing abundantly in the open air, — trees as tall as her apple trees, — full of fragrant blossoms in the spring and of golden fruit in autumn. But it was evident that my stories were regarded as apochryphal. The old lady quietly intimated that the oranges she supposed were produced in hot houses. I am afraid I was not successful in opening her eyes to the truth and in vindicating my claims to veracity. She thought there was some mistake on my part, or that I was exercising a traveller's privileges. Some years after my return home from the North I heard that Miss Kate was happily married and comfortably settled in New York, where I hope she continues to prosper. But I have never heard.

In 1803, I returned to Carolina with Mr. Saltus and arrived at Charleston early in November. The old city has grown greatly since that time. In 1803, Tradd Street was to the retail trade of the place what King Street is now. The Carolina Coffee house at the corner of Bedon's alley and Tradd Street was a distinguished hotel. Public balls and dinners were given there. The private boarding house where we lodged for a few days stood on the South side of Tradd Street a few yards from East Bay. On the West and North the city was greatly within its present limits. Creeks and marshes occupied a large portion of the beautiful public walk and garden that now adorn its Southern extremity. But I had little time to make acquaintance with the town's topography. As soon as the wind served we sailed for Beaufort in the Schooner Delancey, David Bythewood master.[1] Our vessel was the only packet between the two places. Our Captain was an old, experienced sailor. He had crossed the ocean many times in command of large ships and had never lost a spar or anchor. He had now retired from long voyages at sea to command a humbler craft between Charleston and Beaufort. He was slow but sure in his movements. His practice was to go from plantation to plantation along the creeks and rivers, gather a load of sea island cotton, drop down to the entrance of Coosaw river and in a snug harbour, behind Otter island or in Parrot creek, to wait a fair wind for Charleston. Sometimes the wind came in a day or two; sometimes it was delayed for weeks. If he had passengers their stores were exhausted as well as their patience. They were obliged to send a boat to Beaufort for fresh supplies and to nurse their patience as they might. Nothing moved the anchor until the proper wind blew. The old Captain's care and judgment, if slow and sometimes annoying, commanded nevertheless the confidence of all his employers. It was one of his rules never to entrust his helm to any hand but his own— an excellent rule not only for the minor voyages but for the more important voyage of life. Our veteran navigator was as exact and vigilant in the greater as the smaller adventure. He was not willing with all his care to rely on his own skill and sagacity only. He was an earnest Christian and when too old to carry his neighbours to port in their temporal expeditions he strove to guide them in the long and final voyage that ends in another world. He became a preacher in the Baptist Church and died in his ministry at an advanced age. The old fashioned coasting trade ceased as he abandoned it and the Schooner was displaced by the Steam boat when the "Lovely Keziah," the Captain's last vessel, disappeared from the creeks and rivers of St. Helena and Port Royal sounds.

The event was attended with other changes. The modes of travelling were altered. The canoes of six, eight, ten or twelve oars, in which planters were accustomed to visit the city from great distances were no longer used. The spacious steamer took their place. It is more expeditious and comfortable than the small boat, yet the steamer was not free from discomforts. Greater facilities multiplied travellers. The dinner table was sometimes too short. The crowd scrambled for places as they do at the tables of fashionable watering places. It was amusing at times to see a provident candidate for a good place take his seat a long time in advance of the dinner hour and patiently wait for an expected dish. But the rule was—place for the ladies, and they were sometimes so numerous as to drive the reluctant squatter a long way from his post and its anticipated pleasures. Frequently the crowd was so great that a bed was unattainable either in the berths or on the cabin floor. For those well provided with a good boat having a close awning, the primitive mode of travelling was not without its attractions. You stopt occasionally, at stated intervals, to wait for the tide. At one point you stayed for the flood at another for the ebb. The oarsmen kindled a fire on the shore and cooked their victuals under the trees. In the evening and morning the kettle was boiled, coffee was made, and the passengers enjoyed a sort of flying picnick, made more pleasant where, as often happened, two or more boats came together and made the voyage in company. In the still night when the weather was fine, the full moon shining and the rivers and broad sounds calm and unbroken except by the dip of the oar or the wake of the boat where the agitated water gleamed with phosphoric light, the passage was full of enjoyment. Nothing in the gondolas of Venice whether on her dirty canals or more open and airy Lido would surpass it. Nor was the accompaniment of music wanting. The songs were not so refined as passages from Tasso, which are said to be common with the Venetian gondoliers but they were interesting in their way and sung as joyously. The singers were the negro oarsmen. One served as chief performer, the rest as chorus. The songs were partly traditionary, partly improvised. They were simple and inartificial consisting of one line only and the chorus. The singer worked into his rude strain any incident that came in his way relating to the place of destination, the passengers on board, the wife or sweetheart at home, his work or amusements by field or flood. There was sometimes a playful humour about them; sometimes compliments were introduced to the master or mistress more hearty than polished. The voices were generally good, the tunes pleasing and various, sometimes gay, sometimes plaintive. They were sung con amore and imparted fresh vigour to the sturdy crew. "Cantantes minus via ladit." Light is the rower's toil that song relieves. Other stimulants were not wanting. The planter in those days carried with him his case of square bottles well filled and the rowers shared the contents from time to time with the master. Sometimes a race varied the scene. Then, mile after mile, the toiling crews stript of jacket and vest urged each other to desperate exertions, while the sweat rolled from their faces and the speed of the boats was quadrupled. At the end of the race the victorious oarsmen boasted of their exploits and taunted their defeated antagonists. In the race, the song, the scenery, the night bivouac with its broad contrasts of fire light and darkness, its busy faces and social enjoyment, there was material for both the painter's and poet's art.

On land too along the coast country the mode of travelling has changed. In former times the planters made their journeys to and from the city on horse back or in their carriages. The roads were bad. The rivers in the winter were sometimes impassible. The traveller was delayed. But abundant hospitality awaited him on every side. On every plantation the master hailed the guest coming as a boon. Good cheer was abundant and the longer the stay the greater the pleasure imparted to the host. The spirit of hospitality is not as cordial as formerly. The country is not so plentiful. The planter who, sixty years since, raised grain, hogs and poultry in abundance starves every thing now for the cotton field. To feed many horses has become a serious tax to the hospitable. For this or other causes the traveller is not so sure as formerly of a welcome in a chance visit. I have known an old gentleman to retreat from his piazza when he saw a visiter approaching, betake himself to bed, and have it announced that he was too sick to receive a guest. Howitt tells a similar story of his Australian experience. His approach to a station on one occasion drove a whole family to their beds.

My young life was early enough in the State's history to note other transitions. I have witnessed changes in manners as marked as those in the modes of travelling. During my boyhood many men of the revolution were still alive. They were a jovial and somewhat rough race, liberal, social, warm hearted, hospitable, addicted to deep drinking, hard swearing, and practical joking and not a little given to loose language and indelicate allusions. If "immodest words admit of no defence" the veterans of the war were very often defenceless. They were fond of dinners, barbacues and hunting clubs. The abundance of deer in the Country led to associations for sport in every neighbourhood. They met monthly or oftener to hunt and dine. Afterwards when deer became less numerous, the club assembled to eat drink, and talk of politics and planting only. At these festivals no men was permitted to go home sober. It was contrary to good manners and good manners were observed so rigidly that force was used if necessary to secure a just attention to them. Drink round and off with your heel taps were fundamental rules. No man was permitted to disregard them. I have been told of one exception only. In my younger days I heard an old friend, himself one of the set, relate that it was customary with a member of the Beaufort hunting club, a distinguished man in social and political life, to throw himself on the generosity of his companions. He would appeal to them by saying "gentlemen if I drink when you drink and as you drink, I shall be disabled before the day is half over. I shall lose a great part of the conversation and enjoyment. Allow me to drink as I please. I pledge my honour that I will be as drunk as any of you at the close of the meeting, but let it be in my own time and way." It was impossible to resist a proposition so equitable and altogether reasonable from so elevated a quarter. The privilege claimed was yielded accordingly and was never abused. The pledge was always fully redeemed.

My old friend was accustomed to tell another story of barbacue law and its requisitions. It related to Mr. Robert Brown.[2] He was for many years a merchant in Charleston where he died not long since at a very advanced age. When quite a young man and lately come from Scotland in pursuit of fortune in America he was engaged in mercantile business with Mr. Mair, a brother Scotchman, in the town of Beaufort. The young stranger was invited to club as all strangers were. As the drinking went on and reached what Mr. Brown thought a reasonable limit he refused to drink any more. The laws were expounded to him by the venerable pundits of the club. He still refused. They insisted. The dispute waxed warm. At last a compromise was suggested by some Harry Clay of the company. In the spirit of that boisterous practical joking which like the drinking was in character with the manners of the age, in consideration too that Mr. Brown was a stranger ignorant of the rites and ceremonies of the society, it was proposed that the result should depend upon a race. Mr. Brown was to have five yards start. If the club could catch him he was to submit to the laws; if he outran the whole barbacue posse he was to do as he pleased. The distance to be run was about a mile, from the barbacue house to the town. The five yards were measured. The parties were posted, Mr. Brown before, the whole club behind. The word was given and away they went like the foot racers in the games that the pious Aeneas celebrated on the coast of Sicily in honour of father Anchises.[3] It was much less of a race however. The young Scotchman having perhaps a drop or two of Highland blood in his veins outran his pursuers without trouble and evaded the penalty of the law. The most surprising part of the whole affair is that a young man from the land of Burns should have run away on such an occasion. It is very certain that the poet would have done nothing of the kind, and fled as little from good liquor as the Muses.

Other races were run. A veteran of the war undertook to beat the fastest runner of the club, the challenger to have a start of fifty yards in a hundred to carry on his back the fattest man of the company and to smoke his pipe during the race. The race was lost and won by a few feet only but which racer was victor I am not able to remember.

The practical jokes of the times were sometimes mischievous and sometimes worse. On one occasion at the club it was proposed to sit in a circle on the ground, to sing a song and, with the chorus at the end of every stanza, to beat the ground with their hats. It was put to vote. The majority ruled. The song was sung and the hats battered. The joke of this boisterous merriment was in the fact that one of the party, a raw member or guest, wore a new beaver of which he seemed proud while the rest of the company brandished their old hats that were none the worse for the sand or the beating. An another time a foreigner very timid about insurrection made one of the meetings. It was the period when the horrors of St. Domingo were in every mouth. An alarm was given, every one pretended to be frightened, the stranger took to the woods; guns were fired and yells and other noises kept up during the night. The next morning, the victim was found in a tree half dead with fear and shivering with cold. He was consoled by being told that the attempt had failed and that they had escaped the threatened danger. Many more similar tales of the old campaigners in the seven years war I have heard related byone who had taken no inactive part in the sport. (Capt. Detreville)[4]

At this period it was customary to lock the door at dinner parties in the city. No man was permitted to leave the room. The close of the feast found the weaker vessels under the table. The stronger heads staggered or were assisted home. It was to escape from one of these potations that Marion, it is said, leapt from a window during the siege of Charleston and broke his leg. The accident compelled him to leave the city and was the means of giving his partizan services to the State. We may infer from the incident that there happened occasionally other revolts besides the great Revolution against legitimate authority.

During the prevalence of these customs of the good old times I can remember seeing the veterans of the day, after dining with one of the party, going the rounds to each others houses, as long as they could walk, drinking and breaking the wine glasses and tumblers. In addition to the drinking and swearing there was much laxity of morals appeared in various ways. Religion was very little regarded. Church going was for the most confined to the women. They are always better behaved than their lords. Sunday was a day of boat-racing, foot-racing, drinking and fighting. The negroes from the country assembled in town and broils were common among them. It was not much better with the lower classes of whites or with any class. Quarter-races and cock-fighting were popular amusements. Licentiousness prevailed everywhere. Many exceptions were to be found, excellent people, moral and pious and the more worthy of commendation from the temptations and offences abounding around them. But they were the exceptions; the rule was the other way. Seven years of war and licence had not strengthened self denial or led to the controul of appetites and passions whatever effect they may have had in promoting the exercise of other virtues.

There was one evil custom which the war had served specially to promote and which time and increasing civilization have greatly modified and lessened. Duelling was common. For many years after the close of the Revolution, the professed duellist was a popular member of society however mischievous his influence.[5] He was the incarnation of cool, systematic, deliberate homicide. Expert at the pistol he kept his hand in by assiduous practice. He was usually detested by the better part of the community but was everywhere tolerated. It has been said that the practice is beneficial to society. It is opposed to all laws human and divine, yet it is supposed to polish our manners. We are told that it restrains the wrong doer. So does any other mode of assassination. The man whose insult or injury may provoke a knife at a corner or a musket shot from a hedge row or thicket, will reflect before he ventured upon injury or insult. So far from promoting refinement, it is irreconcilable with it, and becomes less prevalent everywhere as refinement increases. It is the product of a barbarous age and flourishes in proportion as the manners of the people are coarse and brutal. It is the natural attendant of a drinking, swearing, licentious people. In Ireland, in the times of Sir Jonah Barrington, it was almost as common to fight a duel as to blaspheme or get drunk.[6] Ireland was not remarkable for civilization at that time. In England as manners have improved, duels have become rare. Perhaps having been once established in a community the custom of duelling may never cease entirely any more than stabbing or poisoning. They proceed from the same causes from hatred and revenge and will continue while the causes endure. The professed duellist, the necessary offspring of the custom, is little better than a professed assassin. I have known a half dozen such men in my time and they were all bad citizens, the dread and reproach of society.

A duel that happened fifty years ago in my little town of Beaufort illustrates the spirit and nature of the custom. At a public entertainment a slight disturbance took place. Mr. S—— interfered to restore order. Mr. U—— sitting at a distance and looking on remarked to one near him that Mr. S—— was officious. The word that Johnson applies in affectionate commendation to his deceased friend Levet—

> Well tried through many a varying year
> See Levet to the grave descend

Officious, innocent, sincere,
Of every friendless name the friend.[7]

— this word of praise to the dead was judged to include such heinous meanings when applied to the living as to demand the exposition of blood. The expression was reported to Mr. S—— by some kind friend. Such friends are never wanting on these occasions. A message was sent forthwith to inquire whether the expression was used as reported. Mr. U—— had forgotten the trifling incident and denied having made the expression. But a friend assured him that he had. It was accordingly admitted. At the time party spirit ran high in the village. The two young men belonged to different factions. They were made champions. Neither party would permit its adherent to recede. The dispute was urged to a challenge. The parties fought, were both shot at the first fire and died a few hours after. The affair in all its progress was known to the oldest, the gravest and most prominent men of the town. Nobody interfered except to promote the quarrel. The young combatants were remarkable for good temper and quiet deportment. There was no anger or animosity between them. They were victims to a brutal custom used for party purposes by the evil passions of the community. It was a double homicide of which the most influential men were aiders and abettors. The youths were members of large families and the distress produced by their death was widely diffused. But their honour was preserved unstained and the passions of their parties were gratified.

The comparative rudeness of manners in the time of the Revolution and immediately after, may be illustrated from another point of view — from an incident exhibiting the barbarity of judicial proceedings in the good old times. In the early part of the century I happened to be near the scene of a negro conspiracy. It was arranged not far from the plantation of Major Hazzard on the Euhaw.[8] Major Hazzard was the first cousin of my father, their mothers being sisters, and he had taken me, a boy of sixteen, on a visit to Hazzard Hall. While there I saw a neighbour of the Major's, ride up to the house, late in the day and hold a whispered conference with my host. The visiter went away in a few minutes and that night the guns were taken at bed time from the parlour to the chambers. It was not a common proceeding. I heard the reason for it the next day. There was a rumor afloat of a threatened insurrection among the slaves. But like almost every other plot of the kind, the scheme failed.[9]

Information was given by one of the negroes wiser or more timid than the rest. The ringleaders were seized a few hours before the time appointed for the outbreak. They were tried without delay and ten or a dozen condemned to be hanged. Their heads were cut off, stuck on poles and set up along the highway leading from Purysburg, the place of trial, to Coosawhatchie, the judicial capital of the District. The sight was so disgusting that some of the younger people refused to bear it. They so far disregarded the majesty of the law as to take down the hideous butcher's work and bury it where it stood. This mutilization of the dead was a barbarous practice borrowed from our English forefathers among whom it flourished near the close especially of the Stuart dynasty. Hundreds at that time were hanged, drawn and quartered, in the Western counties, and the air infested for miles about market towns and crossroads from the stench of carcases suspended near them by the merciless brutality of Jeffries and his master.[10] I don't know that the custom has yet ceased in Great Britain. In 1840, Frost and two others were sentenced to be hanged, beheaded and quartered, the head and quarters to be subject to her majesty's disposal. What her majesty would do with the commodity thus thrown by the law upon her hands, she was not obliged to decide. A technical objection was made to the trial of weight sufficient to substitute transportation for death. In Carolina, since the time I speak of, justice has assumed no aspect so ferocious as far as I remember.

My host, Major Hazzard was a magnificent specimen of the low Country planter. He was tall and of portly proportions with great courtesy of manners and dignity of address. His sister used to say of her brother that nature intended him to be a nobleman and that his figure and bearing would do honour to a Queen's drawing room. No drawing room, I am sure, ever held a gentleman of more friendly and hospitable nature. His modes of thinking were in keeping with his person. His plans were large. When his neighbours were content with a garden of a few roods, he required one of twenty acres. It contained every goodly tree and beautiful shrub and fragrant flower. There were avenues of orange trees, beds of Gardenias, roses in endless profusion of every variety and bulbous roots not unworthy of tulip fanciers in the United Provinces. My old friend had not yet built his house and lived in the humbler mansion of his father. The plan nevertheless was ready. It was suitable to the garden. But fortune rarely favours the liberal and the design was never executed.

The Major's ideas were equally aspiring in other matters. He talked in well rounded phrases of his agricultural projects and advantages. His land was more fertile, his forest trees of statelier size, his cotton of larger growth, his corn more productive, his potatoes bigger than those of his neighbours. His flocks and herds too were choice and numerous and all about him was in accordance with the physical and mental endowments of the master. On the first evening of my visit, he showed me an immense double barrel gun manufactured and imported for his own use. It was fatal to every buck or doe that came within its range. The horns of numerous victims nailed on the large live oak that stood near the piazza of the house attested its power and the owner's skill.

His family removed with his sister, Mrs. Waight, to Georgia, and are living on or near St. Simons Island. Hazzard Hall has passed into other hands. The magnificent garden has disappeared. I have seen cotton and potatoes growing in its squares. But my memories of the hall and its hospitable master are still pleasant crossed though they sometimes are with visions of the ghastly black heads once seen in the neighbourhood and of the savage justice of our ancestors.

A long time subsequent to this period, I met in Washington with Mr. Goodrich better known as Peter Parley to the book making world. The conversation turned on the good old times, on the degeneracy of the age from the Revolutionary standard of public and private virtue. Mr. Goodrich listened to the conversation or some time and said to me at last—Confine your attention to your own neighbourhood as it was forty years ago, compare its condition then with what it is now, and tell me which you think best, the manners and morals that prevailed formerly, or those of the present time. I recollected the manners and morals of "sixty years since."[11] I compared them with those prevailing in my parish at the time of the conversation and was compelled to confess that the change for the better was immense. Religion had revived. The churches were filled. Sunday was kept sacred. Schools on that day were established. Temperance prevailed. The riotous sensuality of the old times had disappeared. If immorality existed it was at least deferential enough to conceal itself from the public eye. My experience is that of every man whose memory runs back as far as sixty years, when every public day was a day of drinking disorder and fighting throughout the country.

I replied to Mr. Goodrich by saying that so far as my own people were concerned I was obliged to admit that the improvement of the present times over the past was incalculable. He said that he had put the same question to a great number of persons, in every part of the country, and had received the same reply everywhere. It was a fair case of inductive reasoning and there was no denying that the good, wise, virtuous, old times were to be found in imagination only. There was no reason to deplore the degeneracy of the country in manners, morals or religion. And as we have since seen, there is surely no falling away in devotion to the country's supposed welfare or in the sacrifice it involves.

A similar conclusion is equally sound in reference to the intellectual improvement of the country, its classical attainments and colloquial talent. It is a common notion that they were greater at or immediately after the Revolution than they have been since. It is a mistake, I think. There was sixty years since a sort of dinner table society of greater hilarity and heartiness than any existing at present. The men were more jovial and talked louder as they drank deeper. There was much singing of songs. They gave toasts and indulged in a noisy vivacity. But the wit was of no high order. It was of that kind in which Sir Robert Walpole indulged at his table among his parliamentary and other friends and was in fashion for the same reason, it was the only sort of wit readily and generally understood or appreciated; every guest could relish a smutty allusion. As with the wit so was it with the learning. The knowledge of the day was not deeper than it is now and not so widely diffused. The few educated men were prominent because they were rare. They were tall because the mass were diminutive. The sources of improvement since then have been vastly multiplied. The general intelligence has increased accordingly. Even if we confine our attention to the few distinguished intellectual leaders of former times, I believe that we can find their equals or superiors of a later date. I greatly doubt if any Revolutionary worthy was as deeply read in classical learning as a contemporary of our own in the Charleston College or that any diner out was the equal of Hugh S. Legare in colloquial ability or brilliant and various attainments. In the combined threefold character of scholar writer and orator Mr. Legare has been perhaps the most accomplished man produced by the State.[12] His attainments in classical learning, in a full and exact knowledge of the Latin and Greek writers, were such as are rarely reached in our imperfect American Schools. He conversed, spoke, and wrote, with an equal command of harmonious language and copious knowledge. He was superior to Webster in range and accuracy of information and the equal of the New England orator in force and beauty of style. Perhaps we may say of Legare what Porson said of Gibbon, that he spun the thread of his verbosity somewhat finer than the staple of his argument. The fruit of his eloquence was sometimes hidden by the exuberance of the foliage. His rhetoric was rather Roman than Athenian in its character.

In private life Legare was a pleasant companion. His disposition was social. His manners were frank, cordial and refined by a large intercourse with the world. Yet his temper was fastidious and marked often with an impatient tone that seemed to indicate some standing cause of discontent. There was a cause of discontent. Nature had given him much, but he wanted more. He was sensitive and unhappy on the score of personal disadvantages. His physical gifts were not in keeping with his mental endowments. His figure was badly proportioned. He had a large head and features, a long body and short legs, so that, sitting, he seemed a tall man, and, standing, a short one. There was a stiffness too, from nature or disease, about his arms which gave an awkward appearance to his gait. These things annoyed him as they have done other men of even greater genius. They soured his temper and marred his happiness, yet his success was great. He died in the prime of life, while Attorney General and acting Secretary of State, on the threshold of what promised to be a brilliant career. He must have taken a high place at the bar of the Supreme Court and nothing could have prevented him from playing a great part as Statesman or diplomatist, unless it were the lack of a stronger will and greater decision of character. Perhaps, in view of the unstable position held by American politicians, Mr. Legare died fortunately, while his fame was high and rising and his place an exalted one in the country's councils before the inevitable ebb that awaits the politician sooner or later and wrecks his fortunes.

The change in Society of which I have spoken began about the time when I returned home from my Northern School. There had been a great awakening of religious sentiment among the people. One of the most efficient instruments in producing it was the Rev. Joseph Clay of Savannah.[13] Mr. Clay had been a distinguished lawyer. He became an earnest Christian and, zealous in diffusing religious truth, exchanged the bar at once for the pulpit. His high social standing, the purity of his life, the eloquence of his discourses, all conduced to give great weight to his ministry. He was supported by others. An immense change followed. As it went on, the Baptist Church in Beaufort became too small for the number of worshippers. At a subsequent period the Episcopal Church required enlarging from a similar cause. Both Churches now double their former size are better filled than when of humbler dimensions. There is no doubt that all was not gold that glittered in these religious revivals. There was some self deception and some deceit. Many perhaps were swayed by sympathy rather than led by principle. A few may have been crafty self-seekers only. But much was genuine. There is no passion that holds the heart in a stronger grasp than the religious sentiment and its influences certainly are not to be mistaken. It subdues every other emotion of our nature. I have known it to reconcile old enemies, stop impending duels and overcome inveterate bigotry. It is never fairly excited in a community without producing ample, genuine, invaluable fruits. I have witnessed two of these religious revivals and never without manifest advantage from them to the moral condition of the people.

The influence of the religious feeling produced by the preaching of Mr. Clay extended to the rugged veterans of the war whose camp lives had witnessed very different scenes. Many of these became exemplary members of Christian Churches. Among them the most remarkable was Col. Robert Barnwell one of the revolutionary brotherhood of whom I have spoken.[14] Col. Barnwell, son of Col. Barnwell of Colonial history, was among the youngest of those who took part in the Revolutionary war. After the war he rose to great eminence in the State as an eloquent speaker and politician. In the convention assembled in Charleston to ratify the constitution of 1787, Col. Barnwell although still a very young man, was among its most able and efficient advocates. He was afterwards distinguished as an orator in the State legislature and in the Congress of the United States. His natural powers of elocution, the flowing, copious, gift of speech, which no labour can acquire, have been seldom surpassed. He was fond of discussion and always ready for it in all places public or private. During his whole life he maintained a sort of intellectual dictatorship in our society which no one was disposed to dispute. The phrase with which he usually prefaced his expression of opinion—I think myself—became a bye word among his juniors. In the latter part of his life, under the influence of those religious changes which I have attempted to relate, Col. Barnwell became an active and devout member of the Church and frequently, as lay reader, occupied the pulpit in the Independent Church on the outskirts of the town where the Rev. Benjamin Palmer officiated as pastor before.[15]

Other religious movements followed of a similar kind. The last was in the year 1832. Its most active and energetic promoter, the Revd. Daniel Baker of Savannah, came to us from a like scene in his own Church.[16] He brought with him a depth and fervor of devotional feeling that diffused itself from parish to parish among many congregations. The effects were curious and interesting, and well worthy to excite the attention of adepts in human nature. The philosophic observer who may have attended to watch effects would have been in danger of being carried away by the torrent of evangelical ardour. Very few persons were able to resist its influence. It broke down conventional distinctions; the poor and rich were united as brothers. It erased the lines of sectarian division; the churches of various creeds joined in the same services, sometimes in one place of worship, sometimes another. It opened all hearts and houses; the town was a great family to a certain extent having all things in common. Political party spirit ceased. Party purposes lost their attraction. The hardest natures were softened. Ancient quarrels were reconciled. The lion and the lamb lay down together. Strangers brought by these events from adjoining parishes found all doors open to them with hearty welcome. The town became a great congregation of Christians bent on objects apart from their ordinary pursuits.

These events produced a variety of comments from abroad. They were ascribed to fanaticism, to the contagion of excited emotion or passion, such as sometimes maddens a mob or a people with very different purposes. This was the solution of those who are unwilling to see anything in the world not dreamed of in their philosophy, who substitute for the immediate government of the supreme being, or a special Providence, a certain immutable order of events alike invariable in the moral as in the material world. I do not see what is gained by the substitute. It only removes the difficulty of explaining the world's government a single step. It is like the Hindu device that places the earth on the back of an elephant and the elephant on the back of a tortoise. Nothing intelligible comes from the Hindu or European philosopher. The regular sequences and immutable laws of moral change are the elephant and tortoise in the philosopher's theory of God's government. These philosophic speculations are founded on imperfect or apparent analogies. Their inventors regard the world as a machine like a watch or steam engine subject to certain laws imposed by the maker and operating independently of his immediate care or presence. They compare two things about one of which nothing is known. They compare the finite with the infinite, the power limited in itself and bounded by exterior existences with the power that is unlimited and unbounded by exterior existences with the power that is unlimited and unbounded; the force which is easily exhausted with that which acts forever and without an effort. We know nothing and can know nothing of the absolute or unconditional. We cannot establish analogies between things known and things unknown. We are driven at last to rely on the deep instinctive convictions of the human heart. These convictions teach us that God rules the world by his immediate influences. If it be a necessity of the human mind to infer a creator from a creation, it is equally a necessity to infer a special Providence from passing events. We can as little conceive of a world's continuing to exist without the immediate active energy of the Supreme Mind as of its beginnings to exist. In this innate conviction we must rest with the certainty that if helped by philosophers and we attempt to go beyond it, we shall miss our way.

But whatever weight it might have with others the solution of the philosopher could not satisfy the Christian. If the Christian believes what he professes, he must believe in the immediate influences of the Divine Spirit on the human heart. If this Spirit exercised its power over the minds of individuals and of multitudes in former times, why not now? Shall we doubt its presence in a religious revival where the results are lives of true, enduring, piety? If it be said the effects are transitory at times and the reputed convert returns to his former vices, what then? It is a repetition only of what happened in Apostolic times. The sower's seed, formerly as now, fell on stony and thorny places as well as on spots of fertile soil, yet the sower and the seed were always the same.

I was present, during the progress of the religious excitement at a council held by the pastor of the Church, the Rev. Joseph Walker, and the great revival preacher of the day, and was amused at the suggestions of the veteran as to the order and arrangement of the services for the better attainment of the end in view — for exciting and moulding the feelings of the congregation.[17] I said to myself here is something like stage trick; the innocency of the dove seems to be guided by the wisdom of the serpent. I was disposed to look suspiciously on the proceeding. But the suspicion was unjust. To use all legitimate means to attain a proposed end is in all things the condition of success not less so in spiritual than in temporal things. There was nothing improper in the means proposed any more than in preaching a sermon or singing a psalm.

In all instances of great results from these religious revivals some preparatory measures and moral conditions seem to precede them. The preparation in the case to which I have referred was the faithful and diligent services of the resident clergyman. His devotion to his pastoral duties for many years had made the ground mellow and ready for the sower's seed. The harvest was great accordingly. The beneficent effects of the labours from the excellent men engaged in this extension of Christian faith were evident, extensive, and permanent. Many members were added to the Church. Some of these have been active instruments in the diffusion of truth. Dr. Fuller of Baltimore and Bishop Elliott of the diocese of Georgia are among the most remarkable.[18] They both left the bar for the pulpit. There were many others who changed their pursuits to engage in the ministry, some to instruct masters, others to teach slaves, all to live lives of active usefulness and genuine piety. There can be no mistaking the character of the tree which produces so much valuable fruit.

It is the nature of these religious revivals among the churches to appear at long intervals. They are the comets of the religious planetary system. They come and go periodically. They are not less essential portions of the system than its planets, the regular Church services, that move in more regular, or less eccentric, orbits, and all no doubt have their ordained parts to perform beneficent and important to the whole.

About the time when the first of these religious revivals took hold of the popular mind, the old temple dedicated to good cheer where the race was run, where unmeasured quantities of ham and turkey, of beef and mutton, of old Jamaica and gin and wine and punch were consumed — the ancient rustic shed consecrated to hospitable rites and good fellowship was prostrated and destroyed. It fell in the great hurricane of 1804.[19] The storm desolated the coast of Carolina and Georgia, tore up whole forests, drove the sea water over a great extent of land never reached before by the highest tides, overwhelmed plantations, and laid in ruins the venerable barbacue house where generations had feasted and made merry. It was never rebuilt.[20] The pious may have construed its fall into an omen of moral change. The overthrown temple of Bacchus was fortunate at least in one respect—it was not without a poet. There had come with me from the North in 1803, a teacher in pursuit of employment. He was an Irishman, named Findlay, and was induced by ill health to seek business in milder climate.[21]

On his arrival at Beaufort Mr. Findlay opened a school on the bay in the upper part of a long building of tapia the lower story of which has been a place of merchandise from before the Revolution. He was a good teacher, had published an excellent treatise on arithmetic, and was a pleasant and instructive companion. He was a poet besides. When the barbacue house was blown down he wrote a copy of verses on its fall. The poem was published in the Charleston "Courier" on the first of November 1804 and was generally admired. The Editor of the "Courier" expressed the hope that the writer would not wait for the fall of another barbacue house before he resumed his pen. It was never resumed. In a few months the penman had gone the way of the subject he celebrated. The place that had known him knew him no more. His verses are his only remaining memorial.

At the time that the poem was written the "Courier" was in its second year only. It was published then by A. S. Willington, as it is now by A. S. Willington and Company. Mr. Willington had come South in the winter of 1802 with Loring Andrews, from Massachusetts to establish a daily paper in Charleston. They found there W. Cullen Carpenter, an Englishman, intending to do the same thing. Their friends advised a combination of forces and the "Courier" was the consequence. It was published at Craft's South Wharf by A. S. Willington for Loring Andrews and was edited by Carpenter who was part proprietor though his name does not appear on the paper. The first number was issued on the 10th of January 1802.[22] It has been remarkably prosperous—a striking illustration of the power exerted by united industry, integrity, and intelligence. Although his sight has failed the veteran Journalist still takes an active interest in his old enterprise. He has had many aids and partners, from time to time in his long career, but the success of the paper must be ascribed mainly to his steady energy. It furnishes now for almost sixty years the most valuable materials for the future historian. Among its stores of minor value I have searched for and found Mr. Findlay's poem. Mr. Carpenter praises it as a good specimen of the mock heroic the invention of which he ascribes to Philips the author of the Splendid Shilling.[23] The invention, it seems to me, belongs to a much older date than that of the Splendid Shilling although Carpenter appears to borrow the opinion from the authority of Johnson. I think my readers will thank me for introducing them to my old teacher's poem. I have taken the liberty with it of omitting a line or two and of changing a word occasionally but very rarely.

The stately pile to which the writer refers as erected by "patriot worth to the Muses to be their safe retreat" was the Beaufort College. Our "Sacer Vates" however successful as a poet has utterly failed in the character of prophet. The safe retreat is as prostrate as the Barbacue house that stood near it. The whole fabric has disappeared like an unsubstantial pageant. The materials have been devoted to other uses. The remains of lime and shell of which it was built may enable one who knows its history to fix its position. But the stranger who walks over the spot would with difficulty believe it to have been so recently the site of a building of solid materials, one hundred and twenty feet long, fifty wide and three stories in height. Although a temple of the Muses it has found no poet to lament its fate. It has not been so furtunate as its neighbour, the frail old shed of humble architecture and slender materials devoted to other gods.

About 1804 my dear old grandmother died at the age of seventy four. She left me a few negroes and a third of her plantation on Parris Island. The family gossip assured me that I might have had more for the asking. But family gossip has the slight defect of being founded generally on very slight foundations. I was the eldest son of the eldest son. My grandfather entertained English notions of landed property. He had dropt certain expressions in relation to his wishes. But the land was the wife's inheritance and at her disposal and he could express his wishes only. The venerated testatrix had two living sons to consult who held opinions not at all identical with these of their father. Yet she desired to know when making her will, whether I was satisfied with its provisions. It was not for me to say no. If there was a question of casuistry in the case it was not my part to solve it. I was willing to assent to whatever was agreable to her. Indeed I never thought much about the matter. It was more ignorance than disinterestedness. I was at the happy age when money and property have but little value. I was not yet aware of the disadvantages of dividing land into small tracts. The plantation was a good one as a whole; it was converted into three and was of little value to anybody. With such an argument to countenance selfishness

I might have been if aware of it, more worldly wise in giving an answer.

Such divisions have been so often injurious to plantations in the State that if may be doubted whether the abolition of the primogeniture law has been a sound policy so far as land and negros are concerned. In a report of Col. Blanding to the South Carolina legislature respecting the survey of a canal line through the swamp lands in St. Paul's parish,[24] he ascribes the abandonment of the inland swamp plantations in part to the repeal of the primogeniture law.[25] At the time of the Revolution, the swamps of St. Paul's included one hundred and twenty eight settled plantations; at the time of Blanding's report they were reduced to eight. A large quantity of land had been thrown back into a state of jungle and morass. The lands are fertile and durable. But the whole swamp must be cultivated systematically to be cultivated at all. The leading canal must be kept in order. The division and distribution among many heirs of the negroes on one plantation of the swamp led to its desertion and was enough to derange the whole plan of management by drawing away the requisite labour from a part. The abandonment of one plantation thus led to the abandonment of all the swamp. Where so many productive fields existed eighty years ago very few, a half dozen perhaps, are now under cultivation.

This perpetual subdivision of estates is detrimental to the masters, to the slaves, to the land and therefore to the State. A dozen sons look forward to the partition of the parental property with exaggerated notions of their future fortunes. Each one of them expects to live on a part of the property as the father lived on the whole. Their energies are never roused or directed to other's employments. They are to be planters. But the fragment of the estate fails to support the inheritor. It is too late when he discovers this to betake himself to any other pursuit and he sinks into a class who live on the memories of the past and rest their claims to consideration on the virtues of a name. They are not willing to see that a name in social life is, like a cypher in arithmetical calculation, naught if standing alone, whatever it may be when associated with something else of positive value. They become component parts of the only aristocracy in America — that described by General Foy as composed of men willing to live without working, to consume without producing, and to occupy all public offices without fitness for any of them.[26] The effect of dividing estates is as bad for the slaves as for their masters.

It breaks up their homes and scatters them among strangers. The land suffers also. It is made liable, by being broken into small tracts, to injudicious clearings that strip it of timber, to the multiplication of fences and houses, to imperfect cultivation. The farms are too small for good stocks of cattle. Without cattle there is no manure and without manure there can be no crops. The effect of the distribution of estates in slaves is obvious about Charleston. If the slaves had remained on the plantations the country might have remained a garden as it was of old. The slaves have been dispersed and it is a desert. Laws that are beneficial to countries which have no slaves may be little suitable to those that have. Their polity should be conformed to their condition. But whether the condition itself is a desirable one to the white is another question.

Chapter Four

College

My instruction hitherto had been confined to a little French and to what is called an English education. At sixteen I became ambitious of learning to read Homer and Virgil in their own language. About this time two brothers of Dr. Jonathan Maxcy the first President of the South Carolina College opened a school in the town of Beaufort.[1] One of them, Virgil Maxcy, soon moved to Baltimore, rose to distinction at the bar, married a lady of fortune, was some time minister for the United States at Brussels and was killed with Secretary Upshur and others by bursting of Stockton's famous new gun called "the peace maker" of which a large party were witnessing the trial of a steam ship on the Potomac.[2] Milton Maxcy remained in Beaufort during his life, practised law, became politician and member of the State legislature and married a lady of family and fortune.[3] Of the two brothers Milton had the finer and better cultivated mind; Virgil more force of character and greater ambition. Under Milton's instruction I read the ordinary Latin authors, made some progress in Greek and at the end of eighteen months became a candidate for admission into the sophomore class in Columbia College. I was examined by the Rev. Doctor Maxcy. The examination was not half so formidable as I had supposed. A letter from his brother had smoothed and macadamized my way. I constructed an ode in Horace. The Doctor made a few critical remarks on the exquisite beauty, the curiosa felicitas of the poet's diction and the work was done. It was almost as summary as the examination of Mr. McKibben for admission to Chancery practice as the author of the "Carolina Bench and Bar" describes it.[4] "What will you charge a client for filling a bill asked the Examiner," Chancellor Thompson. "Fifty dollars was the ready reply." "You are admitted," said the Chancellor. "You understand the science exactly and are fully prepared for practice."

Before my formal initiation, during the first night of my arrival in Columbia, I was introduced by an acquaintance to the mysteries of college life. In one of the recitation rooms we found an assemblage of students engaged in a scene of great jollity and good humor. Some were singing; some talking; some mounted on benches and making set speeches; some interpolating critical remarks on the orators, while the young freshmen performed the part of silent and admiring auditors. George Davis of whom Mr. Petigru speaks so warmly in his address, and John M. Davis were conspicuous actors in the play.[5] At this period a rage for the French Revolution was the popular sentiment. It had convulsed the Republic during Washington's administration and was still prevalent in the Country. The Gallic propagandists of liberty were all patriots and heroes. The "Rights of man" and the "Age of Reason" were the great books of the day. Their author was the most admired genius. Men who had never heard of Shakespeare or Milton were deep in the pages of Paine. On the night of my introduction to the social life of Alma Mater the song sung was one in celebration of the French Convention and the rights of man. It announced that in America these rights first began and a noisy repetition of "viva les" for the convention, the rights of the race and America, closed every stanza and was shouted out by all voices in full chorus. The scene differed as much as possible from that of the pale student the midnight lamp and classic page.

The professed design of the legislature in establishing the South Carolina College was to enlighten the minds of the people and better fit them for the task of self government. When it was proposed at the beginning of the Century to revise the constitution of the State and extend to the interior a due share in the powers of government proportionate to its increase in population, the proposal was objected to from below. It was said that the people of the upper, or back, country were too ignorant to be entrusted with a larger participation in the toils or privileges of ruling. The means of instruction were almost as scanty below as above and education was every where imperfect and superficial. This however was only another reason for the college. It was established after much opposition from those chiefly who were thought to be most in need of its aid. The work of imparting knowledge to the benighted was successfully begun under the auspices of Dr. Jonathan Maxcy. Few men were better fitted to pioneer a way for intellectual progress. He possessed a controul over the hearts and minds of his pupils that no one of his successors had equalled or approached. His influence was that of genius, moral worth, tact and commanding eloquence. His eloquence was irresistible. No youth however rough his training could withstand its power. Its force felt by others. When on one occasion the trustees of the College came to the conclusion that President Maxcy had been negligent in his duties and arraigned him before the board, they were so overwhelmed by his defence that they dropped the charge without another whisper of discontent.

The great merit of the South Carolina College is that it has tended to make the State one people. At the Revolution and for some years after it, the Upper and Lower country were two communities with little intercourse and less sympathy with each other. I remember hearing a lady of Greenville expressing in Columbia an angry impatience at the increasing intrusion of the low country people when forty years ago they began to find their way to the mountain region. Their coming she thought had enlarged the price of eggs and chickens to the housekeeper with no corresponding advantages to the people. She considered their advent a nuisance which she would gladly abate. The traces of these former differences between the two portions of the State are still discernible in their civil division and their names. The lower or older part is a region of parishes and saints; the upper, of Districts and less holy men. Below we find spiritual chiefs, St. George, St. John, St. Peter, St. Paul above, secular worthies only, Sumter, Pickens, Pendleton and Anderson. But the real differences of which these names are signs were removed or weakened by the influence of the College, by its establishing cordial and enduring friendships between the young men from every part of the State. The College associations became so strong as to regulate the disposal of State Offices in the legislature and to excite the jealously of those who were not free of the corporation.[6]

One of my classmates was James L. Petigru of Abbeville District.[7] We were intimate companions, talked together with the ambition of undergraduates, read to each other Horace and Rabelais, Pope and Bacon, and were admitted by all parties to be the two best scholars of the class. He wrote verses in College, but was compelled by the law to forswear the company of the lighter Muses. He has been distinguished through life for many exalted virtues, generosity, devotion to friends, the undaunted defence of the oppressed and the vindication of truth and right at every hazard. He rose to great distinction at the bar and was for many years and continues to be its head and ornament. The friendship begun between us in the rooms of college has never ceased. At the end of more than a half century, it remains unchanged. The fact may illustrate the general effect of college companionship in amalgamating the two sections of the State.

My roommate was Thomas I. Dupont of St. Luke's parish South Carolina.[8] There never was a man more worthy to be loved for the gentleness, liberality and frankness of his nature. He was one of those who redeem our race from the contempt or aversion we are sometimes tempted to feel for it. He studied medicine after leaving college and practiced his profession in the neighborhood of Bluffton before Bluffton was yet a village. In the same tenement with us were Thomas Gaillard, James Dent, Robert B. Campbell and Alexander Bowie.[9] Gaillard moved to Alabama and has written a book on the history of the Church. Dent I have lost sight of. Campbell has been a member of Congress from the Marlborough district more than once. He was some years Consul for the United States at Havanna and subsequently at London. He has maintained in every position the character of a gallant and chivalrous gentleman and man of the world. Bowie has been a successful lawyer. He removed to Alabama and became a judge, adding one more to the number of distinguished men given by the college to the younger sister of So Carolina.

Notwithstanding the direct and incidental advantages secured to the State by her college, the institution, it seems to me, may be made more practical and useful. The whole system of American collegiate education is defective. It does not answer the end proposed. If its alumni succeed in life they succeed not in consequence of college influences, but in spite of them. Distinguished men have been educated in our colleges it is true, but their progress has not been more rapid than it may have been under other auspices. Eminent men indeed are independent of circumstances. It is the mass of students that must be considered and provided for. For them our college system is an inefficient contrivance. It is a sort of hybrid between the English high school and University with the advantages of neither. In the English high school boys find discipline and diligence; in the University young men enjoy ample accommodations and thorough scholastic aids. With us, young boys are sent to college where they are subject to little restraint and the senior, a man grown, lives like the freshmen in lodgings and with scanty aids in his studies and no social advantages.

The end of education is to improve the manners, morals, and mind of the Student. Our System operates lamely for these purposes.

To refine the boy's manners he is taken from the guidance and restraints of home and placed in rude barracks with boys of his own age, removed from the checks imposed by female society and by older persons of his own sex and left entirely to their boyish devices. He sees his professors for an hour or two only every day. There is no social relation between them. The student herds with boys alone and if he escapes from becoming a bear in his habits he will owe his good fortune to his stars and not at all to the influences of college life. What a charming school for manners, the steward's hall afforded where greasy bones were hurled about and joints of meat badly cooked thrown under the table! Perhaps the cooking is better nowadays or the disapprobation less emphatic on the student's part.[10]

Collegiate provisions for imparting or preserving good morals are quite as remarkable. The raw freshman is subjected to the influence of companions a little older than himself. He is ambitious to emulate the high spirited example of his senior. He makes rapid advances in smoking, chewing, playing billiards, concocting sherry cobblers, gin slings and mint juleps, becomes an adept at whist and "old Sledge," in champaigne and hot suppers, to say nothing of more questionable matters and takes degrees in arts and sciences about which his diploma is altogether silent.

The mind of the young pupil fares no better than his manners or morals. What he learns in the regular college course is learned so imperfectly that it is forgotten in a year or two. Nineteen times out of twenty the graduate of thirty is unable to construe an ode in Horace or to demonstrate a proposition in Euclid. He acquires in College habits of intellectual idleness, of light reading, of superficial thinking. His knowledge is shallow and loose. He forgets probably much of what he had learned in the preparatory school. Should he undertake a profession he must begin anew. He has acquired nothing from Alma Mater to assist his progress, very much perhaps, in his idle habits to retard it.

For the student of a higher grade who has the ability and the disposition to acquire knowledge, who would make learning the business of his life, who is formed by nature to excel in letters, no help is necessary that a college affords which he cannot procure better elsewhere. It was otherwise five hundred years ago. Then books were rare. Men of learning were few in number. Both men and books were collected together at certain points and students gathered around them. The universities then assumed their present forms. They were under the control of the few who monopolized the learning of the age. But books now are abundant everywhere. The youth who is really disposed to learn has no need to leave home for the purpose. All appliances are around him. He requires nothing but the will to command them. The gathering together of disorderly masses of professed students is no longer necessary. Nevertheless we adhere to an imperfect imitation to a shadow of an obsolete system. We go on riding in the old stage coach and sailing in the old packet ship when rail roads and steamers are within our reach when the multiplication of books and scholars makes the college superfluous.

It may be doubted then whether our collegiate system for educating boys be particularly well fitted to promote good manners and morals; whether it be not a hindrance to those who would pursue professions, and superfluous to the man of genius who seeks learning for the love of literature. But this is not all. The system brings about a waste of ingenuity that would be valuable to the State if properly cultivated. In college it all goes to waste. Among the thousands who take diplomas without learning anything how much excellent mechanical talent is thrown away; how many good carpenters, turners, tinners, joiners, have been spoiled!

"What peerless cobblers are in college lost." Men who could have learned to make a lady's slipper like a Parisian artist are prevented by our absurd system of education from ever touching a last. The undeveloped genius has been lost to the world. Pope's line may be adapted to every trade as truly as to the cobbler's, and with more propriety perhaps than it could claim in its original application to Lord Mansfield.[11] "How sweet an Ovid was in Murray lost," had more courtly compliment than honest truth in it.[12] It is not permitted to humanity that it should combine the faculties which make a great poet with those necessary to consitute the eminent Statesman advocate or Judge. Cicero, it is said, wrote indifferent verses; Richelieu was not more successful and the verse of Frederick exposed him to the derision of Voltaire. Lord Mansfield would have done no better probably than either of these illustrious candidates for poetical honors. The faculties that frame an elaborate degree are not those that express passion or describe nature.

In consideration of this waste of mechanical talent, a waste so injurious to the parties themselves and to the general welfare, which politicians talk about so much and care about so little, would it not be well to make it a part of the college course that every boy should learn a trade. What a blessing it would be to college graduates when they have failed at law, or physic, or divinity, or planting, or playing lecturer, or professor, or politician, or poet, or gentleman at large, if they were able to make a hat, or a shoe, or a cart or a bureau, or a pair of pantaloons, or any other article of ordinary use. It might save them from begging or borrowing. It might give dignity to labor and elevate handicraft employment in public estimation. It might establish the important truth that the industrious mechanic is superior to the idle gentleman. It might assist genius and learning in securing an independent life safe from "the patron and the jail." It is a rule of the rabbis that every man should learn a trade. The celebrated Benedictus Spinoza in obedience to this law acquired the art of grinding glasses for telescopes. He supported himself by it through life. Wealth was offered to him by friends but he refused it. Professorships in universities were pressed upon him but he preferred the free life that was sustained by the work of his hands. The superiority of such a man over the loiterer whose education has taught no means of winning his bread is as great morally as intellectually. His life teaches more than his books.

But supposing the college system of education to be never so efficient and valuable for the few it does nothing for the many whose purpose in life is to follow some handicraft calling for support. For the instruction of this great and important part of the people our system of education makes no provision at all. What farmer or mechanic is ever taught any thing at school appertaining to his intended future vocation. The only schools for instruction in mechanic arts are the penitentiary and the apprentice system. The objection to the penitentiary school is obvious. It is a close corporation and its franchises belong exclusively to rogues and rascals. It is only when men violate the laws that the State is so kind as to teach them a trade. The apprentice system was established, no doubt, when labourers were serfs; it makes the boy more a servant than a pupil. He learns to be a drudge before he becomes a proficient. His advancement in his trade is a secondary consideration with the master. The first is how much service the master can get out of the servant. Why wait until a man is a burglar before he is taught a handicraft? Why make a boy a menial before he is trained to a trade? Why should not the State establish schools to teach youth the various mechanic arts according to the genius of the boy or the wishes of his friends? Would not such schools be as benificial to the people as those that give lessons in Latin and Greek? Are they not as much required by the general welfare?

In the ancient schools of Persia, the curriculum, or course of education for the people was to shoot with the bow, to ride, to speak truth. Let us substitute the rifle for the bow, add a trade to the course, and we should have a system of education for general use superior to any pursued at present. The department in the old Eastern scheme which relates to telling truth has lost none of its importance. If we judge from the unlimited lies, public and private, North and South, that are put daily in circulation, we must conclude that to tell truth is a lost art and that we cannot attempt too soon to rediscover it by steady persevering efforts.

At the time of my college life, Columbia was a rambling, ill built, village. It contained but two private dwellings of brick, those of Mrs. Dinkins and Mr. Ben Waring. The college buildings were the President's house, the Steward's house and the two old colleges. The central building of the North College was not yet finished. The principal hotel or tavern was Dr. Green's near the State house.[13] It was a long, rough, wooden house with poor lodging and worse fare. The Doctor in addition to his professional avocations was post master, tavern keeper, steward of the College, and a general authority with his neighbours on all subjects ordinary and extraordinary. He was a man of singularly simple manners and modes of speech, as far removed as possible from the pomp and phrases that are common on public occasions. The last of these in which the old doctor took part was a meeting caused by the death of Lafayette. A large number of people assembled and Dr. Greene was called to the chair. Mr. James Gregg, the father of the Brigadier whose death at Fredericksburg has made his name illustrious, rose to propose the resolutions.[14] Mr. Gregg's manner was remarkable for gravity and abruptness. "Sir," said he, addressing the chair, "Lafayette is dead." "Dear me. Is it possible," the chair remarked. "Yes, Sir," the speaker went on to say, with still greater emphasis, "Lafayette is dead." "What a pity" replies the chair "I am very sorry to hear it, what was the matter with him?" The gravity of the meeting was somewhat disturbed but that of the chairman and speaker was imperturbable. The chief merchant of the place was Ainslie Hall.[15] He carried on a large and profitable business at the corner of the main street and the first cross street North of the State House. Among the inhabitants and neighborhood were two of the famous partizan chiefs of the Revolutionary War Colonel Thomas Taylor and Colonel Wade Hampton.[16] He became General Hampton in the War of 1812. They were prosperous, wealthy, and remarkable, among other meritorious acts and qualities, for sometimes inviting a number of the college lads to take part in their good cheer. Their dinners were a great contrast to those of our worthy steward whether at the steward's hall or in his own house where bacon and "long collards" constituted the standing dish. We gave our kind entertainers the most convincing proof that we appreciated the difference. Col. Hampton's table was adorned not only with dainties and dishes of substantial excellencies but with magnificent cups and vases of silver won by his horses on the turf and set out in compliment to his young guests. He was uniformly courteous to them all and made the day pass very pleasantly. His plantation a few miles below Columbia was the scene of the feast. Col. Taylor was not less cordial in his welcome though plainer in his mode of giving it.

Columbia was not at that time a city of gardens as it has since become a place of abundant fruits and flowers. Dr. Benjamin Waring was the first, I believe to plant a garden and fruit trees on a large scale. Mr. and Mrs. Herbemont followed and set the example of cultivating the grape for making wine.[17] When a member of the legislature and invited with others by the urbane and kind hearted cultivator to test the virtues of his manufacture I thought the wine very pleasant. But not so my more experienced colleagues, adepts in old Madiera and sherry; they held the home article in very slender estimation. They thought it, as they said, a good wine to keep, and were content that it should be kept accordingly. The making of wine however has not ceased and from this small beginning is gradually extending in various parts of the State. Some centuries hence our State may be as famous for wine as for cotton or rice.

I graduated in 1809. During the last summer of my stay in College I fell ill and was obliged when convalescent to leave Columbia without attending the final examination or the ceremonies of commencement. I had no claim therefore to the honors of the class. They were assigned to James L. Petigru and Alexander Bowie. The authorities sent me a diploma without the required examination. I became a bachelor of arts with the usual inaptitude of the tribe for any definite or useful employment. I was fairly launched on the great sea of life with no acquired skill to buffet with its waves. Nature had given me no special ability for the work. She sends three classes of men into the world—one that can neither advance alone nor be helped to success; another with ability to go out without the necessary strength of will to impel them; a third of clear perceptions and resolute purpose who are able to run the race without aid or a voice even to encourage their efforts. My friend Petigru belonged to the last class of adventurers on the World's ocean and I to the second—to those who are not fitted to make the voyage alone but who are able to sail it well enough under the pilotage or impulse of a more vigorous and decided spirit. But the impulse and pilotage were wanting. My relative with whom I lived was the best of men but altogether unsuited for the post of philosopher and guide however excellent in that of friend. He had too much deference for my opinion to attempt to direct them. I had a great reputation with him for talent and he was more ready to be ruled by my judgment than to offer his own. And yet my old friend Mr. Joyner was well versed in the world's affairs.[18] I never met with one who had seen more of them. He was the most social of men in his temper and habits. He knew everybody and had a memory supplied with inexhaustible stories relating to his numerous acquaintances. He had the faculty too—by no means a common one—of never missing the point of an anecdote. He was not like another old acquaintance, Mr. Joseph Longworth of St. Luke's who always enjoyed a joke greatly but never could carry one in his memory.[19] A neighbor met Mr. Longworth one day riding home from court at Coosawhatchie and laughing as he rode. "What is the matter" inquired the neighbor. "A joke," was the reply. Dawson came into the courthouse yard in a coat ludicrously short. Everybody laughed at it. The wearer of the queer garment bore the laugh with great good humor and at last turning to the company said very gravely, "You may laugh at my coat, if you please, but it will be a long time before I get another." "Why," said the neighbour, "I see nothing in that to laugh at." "Very true," Mr. Longworth replied, "I see nothing myself as I tell the story, but it was a good joke enough as I heard it." Dawson's remark was, "You laugh at my short coat, it will be long enough before I get another."

Mr. Longworth was one of the ill fated passengers on board the new steamer Pulaksi, when on her way from Charleston to Norfolk with a crowd of passengers, she was destroyed in the night at sea by the explosion of her boiler. A few escaped with shattered nerves and memories haunted by the terrors of the scene. Mr. Longworth was never heard of.

My old friend Mr. Joyner would have made no mistake in transmitting a joke like the one I have related. His memory was tenacious to a hair. He had a story to tell of almost every remarkable man of the Revolution in South Carolina and I have often wished that I had kept a record of what I heard so frequently. Like all narrators of stories and anecdotes he told the same tale frequently but his stock was so large that after years of intercourse I sometimes listened to what I never heard before.

I dawdled through three or four years of life without a purpose. I read a great many books for no definite end and acquired much miscellaneous knowledge without method and with no view of applying it to any particular use. I had the benefit of a lesson in botany at his own house from the accomplished naturalist and writer, Mr. Stephen Elliott.[20] He pulled a flower to pieces for my especial advantage and initiated me in the mysteries of petals, pistils and stamens.

If a science could be made alluring by the character of its Professor, botany in the hands of Mr. Elliott would have been irresistably attractive. He combined the manners of a refined gentleman with the most exact and comprehensive acquirements in natural philsophy. His work on the botany of the Southern States obtained for him a European reputation. He was not only profoundly versed in Natural History, but was also a general scholar and a vigorous and polished writer. His zeal strove to stimulate into activity the literary talent of the Northern people and for this purpose he established and conducted the "Southern Review." Its first number was issued in 1828. While under his supervision the "Review" enjoyed a reputation higher perhaps than any similar work in the United States. His own contributions were always admirable and he was able to command the support of the best ability in the Southern States. The success of the periodical seemed to depend on his influence and genius. However ably conducted after his death its reputation was no longer the same. It struggled on for existence, during some years, with various fortune, in different hands, first under the guidance of Stephen Elliott Jun, now bishop Elliott of Georgia, then of Hugh S. Legare, Whitaker, Simms and Dr. Thornwell in succession.[21] But neither refined taste, nor classical learning, nor trained and laborious skill, nor energetic and practised ability of the highest order, nor dialectic depth or subtlety, has been able to preserve the "Review" from the fate that seems to await all American periodicals those especially of the Southern States. There is something wanting among us. We need in the South a large publishing house with its business and financial resources, a wider circle of cultivated readers, more numerous contributors and money to pay them for their contributions. For a Quarterly Review in the South there are other difficulties. It is a head without a body, a portice without a temple. It is not Hamlet without the Ghost, but the ghost without Hamlet. We have little to review. He might exercise his skill, it is true, on the voyages, journeys, histories, biographies and poetry of other countries besides his own, but they come to him already reviewed by both friendly and hostile critics. They have been dug into and turned over and sifted as thoroughly as the gold fields of Australia by indefatigable diggers. There is nothing left for a new hand. It is reversing the natural order of production to begin a Country's literature with a Quarterly Review. We should begin with books to be reviewed. It may be doubted then whether in any hands, a Southern Quarterly could be more, for any length of time, than a vehicle for politics or theology, a denizen of the shifting sands of party disputation or the bog of controversial divinity.

But notwithstanding the opportunity so tempting of obtaining knowledge from so distinguished a quarter as the great Southern Botanist I soon found that I had no vocation for natural science. I was content to look on nature's face without investigating her nerves and muscles. I prefered knowledge of a practical nature and therefore improved my skill in billiards, one of the sciences I had acquired in college and which I found more attractive than the tribes of monogynia or decandria. I ran no small risk of acquiring other accomplishments that commonly fall to the dot or billiard players. The town could boast of many examples inviting imitation and I had full opportunity to follow them. My ideas of life and its requirements were shadowy and indistinct. I had grown up with some vague notion of having a place already garnished for me in the fragment of an inherited estate. The necessity of task work had never been inculcated on my mind. I had no adequate conception of the importance attached to the objects which men pursue most eagerly through life. We can hardly rouse ourselves to toil after what we neither covet nor value. I saw nothing to seek eagerly in power, or great riches, in large houses or gorgeous furniture, in showy equipages, or dress, or jewels, or broad fields, or immense harvests, or in the admiration and subserviency which great wealth secures to its possessor. Why should I strive to acquire those things for which I cared nothing? Let those toil for them who prized them. I did not. So partly from indifference, partly from the want of training, I sought no occupation. I pursued no profession. Our system of education had taught me no lessons for practical life. I thought my little property enough for my moderate wants and became a loiterer in the high ways and bye ways of the world. My friends were very far from imputing my proceedings to a philosophic disregard for the world's advantages. They decided unanimously that my philosophy was sheer indolence. Perhaps it was. Yet inaction does not always spring from indolence. Indolence may be more an effect than a cause. The inactive life that ends in idle habits may arise from a sensitive and fastidious temper averse from the rough contentions necessary to obtain honors and offices and intolerant of the arts which others practise without reserve in seeking them. The man who is eager after the objects of general pursuit comprehends in the loiterer one cause only for absence from the field of strife. Not to be importunate in seeking what so many covet is imputed, in their judgment, to the only cause they can understand. They regard as indolence what may be indifference for their practices and pursuits. At any rate this is a comfortable mode of viewing the matter for those who have failed in life's battle and are seeking for a reason that may satisfy their self love for something better.

Among my acquaintances at this idle period of my life not the least agreable was Henry T. Farmer afterwards D. Farmer of Charleston.[22] He was the nephew of Mrs. Baring, the wife of Charles Baring of Pon Pon. Mr. and Mrs. Baring were in possession of a large estate on Combahee river. Farmer with his family lived at the plantation in the winter and in Beaufort during the summer. Mrs. Farmer's two sisters, Miss Coates and Mrs. Shepherd, very agreable ladies, spent the summer with her. Farmer was among the most hospitable of men, with a little more taste for expence than was altogether consistent with strict economy. He indulged in private theatricals, dressed his servants in livery, kept a yacht, and gave excellent dinners with good wine. He had taste and talent, sung a good song and was addicted to poetry. His theatricals he reserved for the winter and the country. The only attempt at acting that he made in Beaufort was in passing himself off as a brother divine and a young clergyman just arrived from one of the middle States. He called on the stranger, introduced himself under a feigned name and discussed their logical subjects with him for an hour with great solemnity. Farmer announced to us that his personation of a brother was complete. The clergyman intimated to me many years subsequently that the suspected deception and that his visitor's theology was of very indifferent quality. Farmer's favorite songs were the "Maid of Lodi," from an opera fashionable at the time, the heroine of which dies for love, and another beginning with the line "Why does azure deck the sky?"[23] The same question is put in the song respecting everything beautiful in Nature and it is always answered in the same way. The sky is blue, the rose is red, the stars sparkle and the flowers are sweet to resemble the eyes, lips, glance and breath of the poet's mistress. Farmer not only sung poetry but wrote it. The only poem from his pen of this period that I remember was written on the ruin of Sheldon Church in Prince William's parish. The Church had been burnt in the Revolution and the walls and pillars formed the very rare thing in America, a beautiful ruin. It was mantled completely with the luxuriant wines of the Country and "bosomed high in tufted trees, that grew around it." It has been repaired since then and changed from a beautiful ruin into an ugly Church. At the time of Farmer's writing his poem, Scott's poetical reputation had attained its zenith and octosyllabic verse was the favorite measure of the rhyming fraterinty. The poet compared the old church to an aged warrior,

> A chieftain gray, of many years,
> Whose armour hacked and rent appears
> Whose shield is pierced with battle spears![24]

Church and chieftain had fought their battles of spiritual or temporal strife and were alike, battered, broken and disabled.

A few years after this time Farmer's, the poet's fortunes became prosperous. He removed from the scene of his gay and pleasant avocations, studied medicine in New York, was graduated, practised in Charleston, betook himself in the intervals of business as all Americans do, to an active participation in politics. He wrote in the city journals on behalf of his favourite faction which ever that was of the two that divided the city. He had published previously a small volume of poems the longest of which was a spirited eulogy on New

York in general, but especially on Halleck, who had attained about that time some considerable local celebrity by his Satirical poem called the "Croaker." Farmer tells his readers that the City is "unrivaled as a trading town" and "immortal for her Croaker." The trading has gone on to increase immeasurably but the immortal verse is no longer remembered. Halleck threw away his genius on topics of temporary interest as many have done before him. The topics are forgotten and the poem has shared their fate. I made a visit to Charleston about this period and for the first and only time saw the old general of the Revolution Charles C. Pinckney.[25]

About this time I had an opportunity of seeing Mr. William Lowndes, one of the most prominent among the distinguished men of the Country. He was a member of Congress for the election district of Beaufort and Colleton and was on a visit to his constitutents in St. Helena parish. I dined with him in a large company at the house of Mr. John Porteous in Beaufort. I ventured to suggest to Mr. Lowndes' attention a passage in Eustace's classical tour, a book lately published and at that time of some reputation. The passage refers to the hymns of some length in honour of the virgin, the words of which are usually Latin and Italian. One begins with these lines. He took up the suggestion as if [he] had received a favour. Mr. Lowndes was familiar with the subject and discussed it with a readiness, intelligence, and interest that would not have been easily found with any other political leader of the day. At an earlier period while in college, I had an opportunity of hearing Mr. Lowndes deliver a speech in the House of Representatives on which he was a member from St. Bartholomew's.[26] His mode of speaking was marked with great purity of taste in language and diction. It did not belong to the vehement order of oratory so much the fashion in our country. It was only persuasive, effective—such a mode as I suppose is acceptable and popular in the British house of commons; he caught and retained the ear of his audience without apparent effort and never failed to leave a deep impression on all who heard him of the thorough sincerity of the speaker as well as of the audiences. Mr. Lowndes was not only a distinguished representative of the people in public affairs but he was eminently remarkable as a representative man of the Society in which he lived—a society composed of landholders, owners of estates cultivated by negro slaves. There was something of this form of society in New York and New Jersey before the revolution of 1776. It is now confined in N Amer to the Southern States.

Such a Society will necessarily resemble that of a landed gentry in other countries. There is about it the sure sense of superiority in landlord or master; the same call for protection of dependents; the same claim from them for attention and kindness in sickness and want. In the slaveholder these circumstances will be even more efficient in their influences as the comparative position of the master over the slave is higher than that of the landlord over his tenant and the bond between master and slave is more intimate and enduring. Accordingly the slaveholder in reference to his personal dignity is more tenacious and sensitive; more prompt to protect his dependents from wrong not only by resort to law but by an appeal to arms; and he ministers to the wants of his slaves habitually in sickness and health to an extent and with an interest unknown among landlords. A nice sense of personal dignity produces courtesy in social intercourse. Courtesy is a keeper of the peace. What is exacted it readily yields. Refinement of manners is the natural consequence of a guarded intercourse. It is attended with hospitality generally and liberal dealings. The views of the slaveholder are not generally avarice or niggardly selfishness. He is too proud to be mean and if sometimes too profuse to pay his debts and too careless to be exact in his affairs, he is never dishonest. This is a courage that belongs to a dominant class, with respect exaggerated sometimes to undue sensitiveness. Integrity, refined manners are the natural characteristics of a slaveholding country. Of this society in its highest forms Mr. Lowndes was a perfect example. His manners were marked by a quiet dignity and easy courtesy. There was no coldness of condescension about them. He placed himself on a level with his companions of the moment as if expecting to receive as well as to impart information and pleasure. He was in this respect a contrast to an illustrious contemporary who was always prepared to give but never seemed to expect or desire a return and whose talk, deeply interesting as it always was, took the form rather of monologue than conversation. I have been so much impressed by the finish and completeness of Mr. Lowndes' character and manners; for this reason I have thought a sketch of his life more extended than I had intended would not be unacceptable to the public.

Chapter Five

Life:

Its Duties. Matrimony. School Keeping.

But my time for careless observation of men and things and of idle speculation on them soon passed away at five and twenty. I was placed in opposition and gave the usual hostages to fortune. I added one more recruit to the ranks of matrimony as it becomes every Christian man to do, and have no cause to rue the adventure. It has imparted to my life all the happiness which true and constant affection can bestow. In January 1814 I married Miss Somarsall, daughter of Thos Somarsall of Charleston. He had been a merchant in the West Indies trade, one of those whose fortunes had fallen a sacrifice to French rapacity and whose money has since been fraudently pocketed by the Federal government after being refunded with long delay but that of France. My wife's maternal grandfather was Col. Daniel Stevens of Charleston. He held with credit many offices of the city and State; was major; Colonel of the ancient battalion of artillery; and chairman many years of the Orphan House Board and the Board of fire masters. He filled also the place of United States assessor, (what was then styled supervisor of the Revenue) under Washington's appointment and held it as long as the office was continued. But among all the old gentleman's claims to consideration, of which he was not a little proud, he valued more highly than any other his descent from Cotton Mather, the great Puritan divine, the foe of prelacy, heresy and witchcraft.

Men who pursue knowledge for its own sake only and who are suddenly awakened to the necessity of seeking their own bread betake themselves commonly with one of two pursuits. They become authors or schoolmasters. But the South, fifty years ago, offered no field for authorship. I turned to the remaining resource. I obtained a place in Beaufort College, as assistant teacher. The Rev. Dr. Brantly was head of the institution. He was a graduate of the South Carolina College in the class of 1809 and minister of the Baptist Church in Beaufort.[1]

Dr. Brantly was one of the most distinguished approved preachers of the sect to which he belonged. He had beyond most men the gift of a vigorous mind in a vigorous body. His knowledge was extensive, his sermons always forcible and often eloquent. Few preachers of any church were more impressive and in his own he had no superior. His manner acquired more unction as he advanced in life and his last ministrations were just preceding the paralysis that prostrated his strength and soon terminated his life were remarkable for the depth and fervour of their piety. He was liberal in his sectarian view and refused to exclude from his communion members of other Churches whom he recognized as fit candidates for the communion of another world. From Beaufort, Dr. Brantly removed to Augusta, subsequently to Philadelphia, and finally to Charleston, where he was President of the College and pastor of the first Baptist Church. Dr. Brantly had the misfortune to fall into some differences with the board of Trustees. The cause was a trifling one. Some young gentlemen of the College had come to the conclusion that the manners of the President were not courtly enough to suit their tastes. They were not treated by him in the decorous mood that was their due. He was not a professor of demeanour. He had probably called them dunces on some trying occasion. There are such in all schools. They arraigned their teacher before the Trustees. The board entertained the charge and called in the President to defend his manners against the criticism of his scholars. The trial was too great for his sensibility and paralysis and death were the result.

During his ministry in Philadelphia I was much in his family and had an opportunity of witnessing some of those terrible baptisms that are peculiar to his sect. The rite was performed in the Delaware river, during the winter season. It was necessary to break the ice to enable the minister and candidates to reach the water. Members of the Church stood in the river with hooks on poles to protect the pastor from the floating ice. The garments of the baptised froze on their limbs. The teeth of the spectators chattered as they looked on. They found it difficult to understand how the parties could escape death from the exposure. It is a favourite tenet with the Baptist Church that no ill ever came from such ministrations. I hear complaints of rheumatism from the Doctor and from some of his most zealous members but the rheumatism no doubt proceeded from other causes. The ceremony has not a pleasing tone. It served to remind me of those ascetic practices in various quarters in which physical suffering is made to do the work of spiritual devotion. It does not appear to be in accordance with the Psalmist's declaration where he tells us that the Lord is not a God who requireth sacrifice or meat offering burnt upon his altars. The declaration is equally true, without doubt, whether the meat offering be burnt or frozen. It seemed to me a departure too from the principles of the Church itself: They held it necessary to adhere rigidly in every particular to apostolic practice. But we have no instance in apostolic practice of the ice being broken in baptism to get at the water of the river or of assistants standing by with hooks to protect the minister from the floats in fragments. No such events were ever witnessed — in Jordan. They are departures as far as they go from the spiritual mode of baptism by immersion. The Baptist who immerses in ice disregards the apostolic precedent. He has no "thus sayeth the Lord" to sanction it — the sanction which the Church always demands.

In the year following my induction into the office of pedagogue I was elected by the influence of my friend Richard Habersham of Savannah principal teacher of the Academy in that city.[2] Judge Law of Georgia was my assistant.[3] We occupied a room in the Academy, a large building of stone on what was the commons to the West of the city burying ground. Judge Law was newly married like myself and we were pursuing our pedagogical labours under similar obligations. It was dreary work — the work of Sisyphus when "up the high hill he rolled a huge round stone."[4] We drove out ignorance with a pitchfork or something of a similar nature and she returned pertinaciously. We strove to bend inflexible twigs. We solicited ideas to shoot that would never germinate. But there was something in the work even worse than these unfruitful labours and more annoying. It was to please the supercilious judgment of fathers and mothers, to satisfy their extravagant expectations of progress, to bear sensiless cavils, to be the mark of ignorant or malignant gossip. One lady sat, half a morning in the school room, while her household was wanting her attention at home, and was pleased at the end of the visit to express her approbation of what she saw and hears. On another occasion while dining with my friend Mr. Richard Habersham I met with an embarrassing and yet amusing adventure in the gossip class of pedagogue evils. Among the guests was the pastor of a church in the city — a flippant, conceited, newly arrived, son of the North, imported to instruct Southern barbarians in their Christian duties, in faith, hope and charity. We had never met in the bustle of a large company had not been introduced to each other. During dinner, the extent of Southern acquirements in Classical learning became the subject of conversation.

Our pastor treated every claim of the sort with derision. It was evident enough that his standard of excellence was not a high one. It reached no farther than the attainments of a graduate in a New England College or theological Seminary. But our City Academy teachers are Southern men our host remarked looking my way with some surprise. "Pooh, pooh," replied the pastor "what do they know about it." The host opened his eyes and looked astounded. The Divine saw there was something wrong, he did not know what. "Let me introduce you," said the host, "to one of our Academy teachers. He sits opposite to you." The Revd gentleman although coming of a race not easily embarassed, seemed utterly confounded. There was an awkward pause for a moment which our accomplished hostess broke by introducing a new subject of conversation. Our teacher of ethics took no part in it but applied himself with exemplary diligence to the discussion of his dinner. I met him some time after at Seymour's the city book store, and found him disposed to be amiable. But I did not encourage his advances. I had seen one phase of his Christian charity and distrusted the Greeks offering presents.[5] If I had been a better Christian myself I would have done otherwise. He was conceited only, not malignant.

While in Savannah I had frequent opportunities of hearing the celebrated Doctor Kollock of the Presbyterian Church.[6] He was popular beyond measure with his church and in the City. Later in his ministry a shade came over his reputation which only served to show how greatly beloved he was in the community. It distressed everybody and all rejoiced when the shadow past away. He was one of the two most eloquent men I have ever heard in the pulpit. His style was clear and forcible, his voice musical, his appearance preposessing, his whole manner the perfection of good taste. The only action he used was to raise his right hand with the forefinger alone extended. The great charm of his delivery consisted in the full pronunciation of every word and the perfect adaptation of his tone of voice and expression of countenance to every thought and sentiment. He was the Tillotson of his day, far more fortunate however than the great English divine in commanding or winning the good will of his contemporaries.[7] Yet even Dr. Kollock did not please everybody. Mr. Foster, the Unitarian minister, the predecessor of the accomplished and excellent Dr. Gilman and a somewhat remarkable man in his day,[8] told me Dr. Kollock was a bed bug compared with Dr. Gallagher of the Catholic Church in Charleston.[9] I never heard or saw Dr. Gallagher and am unable to judge now far the comparison may have been just. But I thought there was something rather unsavoury in the simile. A man who could perpetrate such a figure might rob a church. Mr. Foster never did this; he only divided one by revolting from the Presbyterian to the Unitarian faith.

The air of Savannah was not favourable to us. There was much sickness. It seemed to me to be general in the city; although my friends assured me it was a very healthy season. My whole household, myself, wife and two children, were seized with fever. I became apprehensive of what a sickly manner might do if a healthy one dealt so hardly with us, and resigned my post at the end of the year. In January, 1817, I was able to resume my place as assistant teacher in the Beaufort College. We began the year with favourable auspices. The principal occupied one wing of the College edifice and I the other. We had ample space, a dozen large rooms for each with spacious closets and three wide halls or entries. We indulged in the hope of a great success in this temple of the Muses as my friend Mr. Findlay had called it. We proposed to make it a great resort with the country about for all ingenuous youth ambitious of learning and its honours. But alas! for the vanity of human expectations. Savannah had been a salubrious spot compared with our new residence. It was a year of pestilence; such a season as had never before been heard of in the town's annals. Of six hundred white inhabitants in Beaufort, one hundred and twenty died.[10] Among the survivors more than half were sick. The whole village was a hospital. The College suffered with the town. The boys were dispersed. The College building was abandoned. A small school house was erected in the town in what was judged to be a more healthy quarter and trustees and teachers gave up their hopes and expectations of future greatness. The site of the large College building proved permanently sickly. The part of Beaufort adjoining the college underwent a similar condemnation. It was subject to fever. In that as in many similar cases on the Southern Coast the distance of a mile or less made the difference between a healthy and unhealthy situation. Many houses at the best end of the town next to the jungle or to cultivated fields were abandoned or removed. The College building was pulled down. The name only of the institution, the name of the corporate body, remains, although as applied to the present humble establishment, the term, Beaufort College, is a palpable misnomer and will probably continue so.

The year 1817 was remarkable for great mortality throughout the Southern States. The summer was excessively rainy. From early in May to the first week in September heavy showers were of daily recurrence. The river in front of Beaufort, always salt before, assumed the dark hue of brackish waters. The oysters, it was said, died in many places. The floods of rain ceased in September. The weather became beautiful. But beneath the bluest sky, in the most agreable and apparently salubrious air, the pestilence which began in the last of June raged on till frost without abatement. The last case, as late as November, was that of Dr. Potter, a learned and eminent divine from England. The sickness seized on its victims without a moment's notice and prostrated their strength at a blow. In common years it is customary to go from the Country to the City for health. In 1817, the practice was reversed. The field were safer than the streets. The intermittents of the Country were trifles compared with the terrible malady of the town. There were some singular examples of exemption from disease. One of the most remarkable was that of the Revd Delavaux afterwards pastor of St. Bartholomew's parish. He was a stranger lately come from England. He devoted himself to the sick; was the ready nurse of all who needed nursing; went about during the heavy dews of night and the daily rains, and in spite of fatigue and exposure was not sick for a moment. Never was greater benevolence seen nor has devotion to duty been protected by the hand of Providence more manifestly on any similar occasion.

My family were all assailed by the fever. We lost our youngest child, a girl of eighteen months old. I remember, as though it were of yesterday, the poor little sufferer's plaintive call for water a few hours before her death and the pale, sweet, wasted, face when her spirit had gone to him who gave it. The death of a grandchild forty years afterwards seemed a repetition of the scene. Nature compels us to mourn over the loss of these little ones and will not be cheated out of her claims by any plausibility of consolation. And yet how manifold are the reasons that should check and stay our grief. The parent that has hung over the couch of the apparently dying child, that has grieved and murmured and importuned Providence to spare the treasure so much cherished, has lived after the repining prayer is granted to mourn over the sufferings or sorrows, the vices or crimes of the little one's subsequent years and to see that prolonged life was a curse, that death in the days of innocency would have been a blessing, that submission, not rebellion is the part of short sighted humanity to the will of God.

I made one of a party of convalescents on a visit to Pinckney Island, in October. The island was the property of General Charles C. Pinckney of Revolutionary fame. His house was always open to the sick. The site on which it stood has since then been overwhelmed by the waters of Port Royal sound. It is now a haunt for sea monsters. In a great gale not many years after the year of pestilence, the spacious house and gardens were swept away. The small island on which they stood and which had been connected with the larger one by an ornamental bridge has disappeared entirely.

These encroachments of the sea on the land are observable on all the island of the coast. Wherever the shore bluffs on the rivers or creeks it is eaten away gradually but constantly by high tides and violent winds. A storm accelerates the process but it never ceases. If the land is in wood the trees are uprooted in succession and carried into the stream. There they are soon covered with oysters and barnacles and become a fishing ground for sheephead. If the bank has been cleared and cultivated the destruction is more rapid. I have known more than a hundred yards in depth carried away within a few years of my remembrance. The grave yards of plantations have been undermined and the remains of coffins exposed to view. The sites of roads have become the channels of creeks giving rise to perplexing law suits. The result is not surprising. The soil of the islands is a fine sand without a rock or pebble. There is nothing to resist the action of the water. The stream is not always increased in width. The abrasion of one bank is frequently productive of an equivalent enlargement on the other. The other is generally of marsh corresponding with the swamp lands of the large rivers in the interior of the Country. As the high land recedes the marsh and swamp advance and the breadth of the creek or river is preserved unchanged.

Chapter Six

Northern Travelling

The sickness of 1817 made a change of air and scene desirable and in the spring of the following year we sailed in the Ship Wade Hampton, Capt. Baker from Charleston for Philadelphia. The close of the voyage, the sail up the Delaware river, was very charming, delicious. We entered the capes of the bay the evening before reached its head the next morning and were all day sailing from the head of the bay to the city. It was the first week in June. The day was brilliant; the wind fair and moderate; the orchards as we glided past them were in full bloom; the shores freshly green and exceedingly beautiful. It was one of those days when to live is a joy and to look on the flowers and fields, the valleys and hills, abundant happiness. The scene was lovely in itself. To us just arrived from the dreariness of a sea voyage it was inexpressably pleasing.

We arrived late in the evening. It was night before we left the ship. On our way in a carriage to the hotel we encountered a tumultuous uproar such as I had never heard till then. There was an alarm of fire. We fell in with the fire companies rushing in rivalry with their engines to the scene of action. Nothing out of the infernal regions could exceed the din and clatter. But our horses were city hacks and unable to run away, our coachman was master of the occasion and we reached the hotel in Chestnut Street with no damage after a little delay. The hotel was crowded and we could get no rooms. The master transferred us to a private boarding house in the next street kept by a widow and her maiden daughter of mature age. The exchange was a happy one. We were more quiet and comfortable. There were but two boarders besides ourselves. One was the celebrated Abbe, Correa De Serra. The Abbe was a famous scholar and philosopher, very amiable and pleasant as far as we saw of him.[1] But he lived in his room among his books; I am not expert at extemporising an acquaintance; the time was short and I missed the opportunity of reaping any advantage from his wisdom and learning, or rather I failed to improve the opportunity that fortune had given me. The other boarder in the house was a young lawyer, with excellent endowments of mind and temper, but belonging nevertheless to the class unsuited by nature for success in the battle of life. He was an idler, with somewhat loose habits and a wonderful talent for borrowing small sums of money which he never thought of returning. We cannot judge such men severely. How should we? Their defects are the gifts of nature. We may as reasonably quarrel with the colour of a man's eyes or the shape of his nose as with his lack of energy or application. No effort can obtain what nature has not imparted, either in the mental or physical formation. She makes drones as well as working bees. Let us not fancy that we are wiser than she is. If the world held none but men of intense natures, it would be unfit to live in. It would be unendurable even to the energetic themselves.

We found the quaker city an agreable place. My wife had friends residing in it who received us kindly. We admired the clean streets unceasingly washed by housemaids with red feet and arms, enjoyed the shady squares, saw the abundant market with its unequalled butter, and trimly dressed quaker ladies; visited the remarkable places, the hall of the confederation, the tomb of Franklin, and all other objects of historical note; spent a night on the banks of the Delaware under the auspices of our hostess a friend of the family at the Country seat of a retired merchant who seemed to be repeating the old experiment with the usual success of retiring from business to green fields in pursuit of happiness, and turned our faces Northward after a fortnight very agreably spent in the city of brotherly love and rectangular streets.

I found New York grown out of memory. The city was larger, the crowd more dense, the bustle greater, many times, in every quarter. The ships had grown to greater size. Steam began to be seen and heard. It was still in its infancy however. On the river its exploits as yet were very moderate. Our passage from New York to Albany occupied from ten o'clock one day to twelve the next. It was thought to be a very creditable performance. Now, it would disgrace any craft to take half the time.

During our stay in New York I was anxious to revisit the scene of my school days at New Utrecht. I hired a carriage at Brooklyn and in company with my wife rode across the Country with high anticipations of pleasure. I told her extravagant stories drawn from youthful memory of the beauty of Long Island and the attractions of the Dutch village. We found the Country without a charm. It was very dry; the dust covered the trees by the road side; the fields were no longer green; the village looked coarse, commonplace and stupid. My wife laughed at my Dutch paradise and I could say nothing in its defence. We dined at Bath, a sort of watering place on the bay side.[2] The house there had been burnt down while I was at school in the village. It was now rebuilt on a larger scale with higher pretensions. On returning to Brooklyn I missed my way, drove by mistake into the yard of a farmer who appeared to think us suspicious characters and got back to the City thoroughly cured of all my juvenile delusions on the subject of Dutch villages and Long Island scenery. It was one of life's illusions dissipated by time and experience, such illusions as attend us from boyhood to old age unable any of them to stand the test of time and experience. The result was so discouraging that I refrained from visiting my New Jersey home. The picture of fancy or memory has not been displaced there by a rude reality. Even in the other case, the old impression has resumed its place and I think of the scene rather as I formerly knew it at fourteen, than as I found it at thirty. The colours in the picture of boyish fancy are indestructible; those in manhood's have already faded.

We went through a month at Saratoga as summer idlers commonly do; inhaled the dust of the streets; drank the Congress water, rushed with the crowd to dinner and supper; occupied a room ten feet square; slept on a hard mattress of straw and corn shucks, and paid for all these enjoyments the long bill that Northern watering places inflict on Southern simpletons. At this time the Northern Contributions to Society at Saratoga and other places of Summer resort were of moderate proportions. The North had not yet reached the riotous period of enormous wealth and the presumption that comes of it. The glare and glitter of the newly made rich were rare. The glories of the soap boiler and tallow chandler, the shoe maker and hat manufacturer grown into millionaires, were as yet in the Chrysalis State. They had not began to illustrate the refinement of American manners on the continent of Europe or even to lead the fashions at Saratoga and New Port. We were too early to enjoy the advantages society has since derived from this brilliant quarter. The manners of the day were tame and rude, those of old families of moderate fortune. Forty years have made immense changes. Now the American rich from the Northern States encumber and perplex the gentlemen ushers in every court of Europe and flutter like moths over every watering place in their own Country.

From Saratoga we rode across the Country through Lebanon, Pittsfield, Northhampton, Wooster [*sic*], to Boston. The journey was very pleasant; the Country in its summer garb; the weather fine; the crops luxuriant and maturing. We stopt a few days at Lebanon to visit the singular sect established in the neighbourhood. They are certainly a pattern of industry and neatness. Their tenets and practices are somewhat absurd but that is not a new thing among religious sects. The Shakers are quiet and useful citizens at least which is more than all can say. I caught their song and shuffle and could go through their Sunday dance for the worship of God with something of the grace exhibited in the original performance.

Of all the cities in the North we found Boston the most agreable. The police were more like our own. The matters of Charleston and of Boston were thought to approximate more nearly than those of any other places in the Country. They were more acceptable perhaps on that account. In Philadelphia, but above all in New York, there was more gilding than solid gold, more surface and less solidity, more pretension and less cordiality of nature. There was always some assumption peeping through the garb of their civilities.

Nahant had begun to be a place of summer resort for Boston on a modest and moderate scale. We spent a day or two there with comfort and pleasure. The peninsula ends in rocks torn and shivered into every fantastic form by the full swell of the Atlantic. In quiet nooks where the water was smooth and still the ladies angled for small fish. I went with a party a mile from the shore, in a small sloop and caught cod and haddock in deep water. It was good sport enough but not comparable to our Port Royal drum fishing. The haul on the fish was a dead pull from a great depth. The fish were unresisting. They made no play. It was little better than dragging up a dozen pounds of lead from the bottom of the sea.

In our lodgings we became acquainted with Mr. Shaw a genial, simple, warm hearted, man with nothing of the sharpness and hardness usually imputed to his Countrymen. He had been the private secretary of ex-president Adams and was the nephew of Mrs. Adams who seemed greatly attached to him.[3] Through Mr. Shaw we obtained an introduction to the venerable master and mistress of Quincy and spent an afternoon at their farm. It was the fashion of the Country or the house to take tea before sun down. The hour perhaps was hastened for the convenience of the visitors. The tea was handed round to the company as it formerly was in South Carolina. The nerves of the old man were so tremulous from age that it was necessary to place a small table before him. On this he rested both arms to steady his hands in raising his cup to his lips. But however feeble his frame his mind was clear and strong. His conversation abounded with anecdotes of Revolutionary times and men. They were told with simplicity and ease and we listened to them with delight. They were all new to me whatever they may have been to Mr. Shaw or Mrs. Adams. Many of them related to the celebrated D. Warren of whose character and abilities the old President seemed to entertain a high opinion.[4] The master of Quincy lived unostentatiously. His house and furniture were those of a country gentleman of moderate fortune; his orchards and outbuildings the appurtenances of a prosperous farmer. We left Quincy before sunset and at parting, the old gentleman bestowed a kiss and a blessing on our little girl of four years old who made one of the visitors. She had become a pet and playmate of Mr. Shaw and he would not permit her to be left in the city and deprived of the Country ride. There are few incidents in my life to which I look back with more pleasure than my visit to Quincy and its venerable inmates. A year or two more went by and the Successor of Washington passed away to his final account. Another illustrious citizen who had toiled with him through his Revolutionary career accompanied him on his last journey. They died within a few hours of each other on the 4th of July, 1826, one at Quincy, the other at Monticello.[5]

We passed a few days at New Port. At that time no huge hotels were filled with fashionable multitudes. Opulent citizens of distant towns and States had not yet erected villas in the neighbourhood. It had long been a favourite resort in hot weather but its appliances were yet simple and modest. Its advantages were those of nature chiefly abundant and choice fish, fine sea bathing and a climate both pleasant and healthy. There were no steamers as yet. A sailing packet sloop carried us from Providence to New Port. A similar vessel took us on to New Haven. We left New Port one day and arrived at New Haven the next. With favourable weather the voyage made in this way was more pleasant than the steamer's if not so expeditious.

At New Haven everybody was in a state of bustle and excitement. It was the season of commencement when all Connecticut rejoices over the doings of Yale College; when grave old men and pretty young women and parents and legislators and solemn divines assemble to do honour to the occasion. The country was emptied into the city. It was difficult to get a bed, and we found accommodations with some trouble in a small private boarding house kept by Mrs. Benham whose daughter had married a native of the old North State. He had been a student of Yale. The college seemed thus to serve a useful purpose in many more ways than one. It supplied money to Professors, teachers, booksellers, tradesmen, and furnished husbands to the young ladies of the town and its vicinity. We joined the crowd in the church, listened to the speeches and addresses, and added our mite to glorify what was, at that time, a favourite place of education with Southern men.

In all our journey through the North and East during a week's stay in one place and a month's in another, we had with us, as child's nurse, a thorough specimen of the South Carolina low country slave. Her talk, her dress, her manners, made it impossible to mistake her condition. It was with difficulty we could induce her to wear a hat; she preferred to tie up her head as at home in a party coloured handkerchief. She refused to occupy the bed provided for her at the hotel; it was fit, she thought, for white folks only and she preferred a blanket on the floor. A bedspread and white sheets were luxuries that she left for her betters. Yet neither in the city of Penn, nor in that of Webb and Greely [sic] nor in all New England, was one word whispered to us on the subject of Slavery. No one molested our servant, the plainest type of her class. She and I were regarded as occupying our natural relations as master and slave. No man's or women's sensibilities were roused, nor was any pious divine's conscience outraged although Dr. Channing was then preaching in Boston.[6] The North was not yet as proficient in the higher law which abrogates all law. The feeling of the Revolutionary period with many of its Statesmen and soldiers yet survived. We heard no word of the contumely and denunciation of Southern customs now so common, but were treated everywhere with kindness and respectful attention. If a prophet had risen up among the people of Boston, in 1815, and said to them—in forty years when a Southern man comes among you with his slave, you will seize upon his property and subject him to mob violence, you will pass laws to destroy his rights, you will raise by a conspiracy of the governors of States, in contempt of the constitution, large armies to invade Southern territory and plunder

Southern property — if anyone had told them the half of this he would have been adjudged a fit inmate of the lunatic asylum and his prediction would have been laughed at as absurd. And yet all these things and more and worse have come to pass while the whole North clap their hands and approve and consider it an evidence of progress in philanthropy and Christian charity.

From New York we returned home in a large schooner commanded by Captain Tombs an active and ambitious skipper. The wind was fair and strong and the passage speedy. There was another packet in company all the way, often so near as to be within speaking distance. From our eagerness to get first into port we overshot the light house, in the clear moon shiny night, and found ourselves the next morning opposite to the houses on Edisto Bay. Our Captain was mortified and his passengers were greatly disappointed when told they were twenty miles to leeward of Charleston bar. The North East wind hitherto favourable was now ahead. Our Chief swore that he would beat his craft to Charleston light house if he beat the masts out of her. But the assurance with the contingency brought little consolation to his company. The exploit was performed and the masts remained unhurt but the process in a head sea was any else than a pleasant one. We arrived the next day, twenty four hours after the rival ship that we had exultingly past on the way, showing that our speed had not been equal to our haste.

Among the passengers was Daniel E. Huger a leading man at the time in the Councils of South Carolina.[7] Judge Huger, as he afterwards became, was an admirable marine traveller. He was never sick. The segar that occupied his lips "from morn till noon from noon till dewy eve" seemed to charm away all the discomforts of the sea. His mind was unembarrassed by the inconveniences of the voyage. His conversation gave it life. He talked freely on the topics of the day. One of these was the subject of slavery. It occupied the attention of the Country generally. In Virginia particularly it excited and agitated the mind of the people. The opinions then prevailing everywhere were different from those now entertained, almost universally, in the Southern States. Judge Huger had spent a part of the summer in Virginia. He said that many men of distinction in the State were disposed to get rid of their Slaves. They thought that Slavery had done its work; it had cleared and opened the Country and prepared it for other and better hands. The building was finished; it was time to take down the scaffolding. A short time after Slavery became a question of fierce discussion in the Virginia Councils. Western Virginia was vehemently opposed to it. They continued to be opposed although defeated in attempting to destroy it.[8] The most violent denouncer of Slavery I ever met was a Western Virginian, Mr. Allen, a member of Congress in 1834 and afterwards a judge of the Supreme Court of Virginia.[9] The position of Western Virginia in 1861 ought not to be surprising to anyone who knows its former opinions.

There was another subject that engaged the thoughts and conversation of the judge during our voyage. It was a time when democracy was running riot in the land and candidates for office were labouring to surpass each other in those arts of cajolery and solicitation which in monarchies are imputed to the servility of Courtiers. The judge was indignant at the base arts that he despised. He thought it would become impossible for a man of any self respect to enter the arena of political strife. Its contentions would be intolerable. I suggested that, no matter how odious the task, it would be the duty of gentlemen to contend for the leadership. The people must have guides and rulers. If the virtuous, well educated and honourable withdrew, the place would be filled by unprincipled demagogues. For the good man to step aside from the contention, however disagreable the contest was to abandon his post and neglect his duty to the community, his friends and himself. He must rule or be ruled by the base. There was no such thing practicable in a democracy or in any government as the educated and influential property holder rightfully or safely standing apart and contenting himself with looking on at the conflict of parties. Such retirement is not pemissible in human affairs. Those who regard law must make and execute the laws or government must fell into the hands of such as have no respect for justice or right. It is a battle of life and death and the true and upright must gird up their loins and meet the contest come in what shape it may. They must meet it or be ruined, and the Country with them.

I subsequently found this view of the subject illustrated strikingly in De Toqueville's history of the causes and conduct of the French Revolution.[10] It is remarkable how little part or influence the aristocracy of France had in swaying the course of events. They knew no sympathies with the people and therefore held no control over them. They were strangers to each other. For the nobility, Paris and the court were France. The provinces were only sources of supplies for courtly expenditure. Over the minds of the people the nobles could exercise no modifying or moderating power. The guideance of the masses fell into the hands of unprincipled demogogues as brutal as the mobs they headed. There was one exception to the conduct of the nobles and to its consequences. In La Vendee, the gentry lived on their estates, and in La Vendee, the peasantry sustained the monarchy and the church with a courage and fortitude never surpassed, The noble families of England would be swept away in a day, if they should pursue the modes of life adopted by those of France in the eighteenth century. The gentry of Great Britain live among the people and exercise over them the influence that education and kindly intercourse will always command. This constitutes their security and strength.

In 1818 on my return home I betook myself to a new employment. I studied law, was admitted to the bar and commenced practice on the Beaufort District Court at Coosawhatchie. But there was something lacking. I was too sensitive, too fearful of failure to make a bold effort for success. My preparation had been hasty and superficial and not suited to impart confidence. I had not the faculty of ready talk where I had nothing to say. I was destitute of the modest assurance or rather of the face of bronze and tongue of iron so indispensible at the bar. The idea of damaging a client's case by want of skill filled me with terror. An insurmountable weakness disabled us from making large charges and exacting heavy fees. My difficulties were all of a personal kind. They grew out of no scruples as to the nature of the profession itself. And yet there is cause for many. The indiscriminate defense of right and wrong cannot serve to cultivate a nice sense of their difference. The lawyer is mixed up with the bad passions of the community and becomes their agent and supporter. He helps the unjust; he sustains the vindictive; he protects the knave. He is of some use, it is true. He does for the community as Counsellor Pleydell of Edinburg says in "Guy Mannering," what chimnies do for a house when they carry off the smoke which would otherwise put out the eyes of the inmates.[11] It is not surprising, the Counsellor adds, if the vent becomes somewhat foul in performing its duty. Some vents get very foul indeed and endanger the household and neighborhood. There are noble exceptions. There are layweres who are not carried away by the evil influences of the profession. But they are rare as snow at midsummer. They are found about the lofty eminences only in the moral and physical world. Before I had time or opportunity to see much of the practice of law

I was carried away to the pursuit of politics. On the little I saw of the profession I look back with no kindness or respect. The life is not to be coveted which ministers to the evil passions of a neighbourhood; which serves as a tool for its contentions; as a sewer for the passions of the community to gather in and be carried off. I know nothing more disgusting in civilized life than a Court of law with its lawyers defending right or wrong with equal ability and zeal; its judges supporting falsehood as often as truth; its consequential servitors noisy in keeping silence and its idle, heartless audience that find amusement in the calamities of unhappy criminals and anxious clients. The contentions of the bar supply for the people the same kind of recreation as the Spanish bull fight or the old Roman show of gladiators. These indeed are much the more manly amusements. They exhibit courage and endurance. In the Courts what is there but trickery and fraud or the subtlety and dexterity that resemble them? And yet they are necessary to society, necessary like the jail and gibbet, manacles and chains. I know it is said that the lawyer merely states the merits of his case and puts them in their best light for the furtherance of justice only; that he does for the client what the client is unable to do for himself; that he is a minister of equity and law and nothing more. This is the theory. The practice is that the fee not justice is his object. His purpose is to win his case. Right, equity, truth, are secondary considerations or rather no considerations at all. He as often overthrows as he supports them and with equal readiness and ardour.

Chapter Seven

Public Life, Nullification, Party Leaders

I was fairly afloat in politics and public life. For some years the murmur of that contention between North and South had been swelling and deepening which has now reached its natural issue, a war of sections. Up to the embargo system of Mr. Jefferson the most absurd act of State policy that mortal man ever executed or conceived, the South had been uniformly prosperous.[1] The introduction of the cotton culture had given an immense impulse to her fortunes. The embargo, the war, the protective tariff, stopped or retarded their progress. For all these disastrous measures the South is indebted to Southern politicians. They have always been more vigilant in looking after Federal honours and offices than the welfare of their own people. They ruled in the government by the ready sacrifice of Southern to Northern interests. Their last performance in this way was to fasten the protective tariff system on the Southern States. The protective tariff made the Southern States dependent provinces. It is one of those laws that under the cover of general provisions have a particular and partial application. It proposed to protect American industry, it meant the industry of New England and Pennsylvania. There as no manufacturing in the South to be protected. To establish it the South would require a protecting system against the North as much as the North against England. For all such industrial pursuits North and South are different communities. If it be an evil to America to be manufactured for by Europe, it is as great an evil to the South that her manufacturing should be done in the Northern States. If it would impoverish New England to import her manufactures from Old England, it would equally impoverish South Carolina to obtain her manufactures from Massachusetts. It can make little difference to the South, if she is placed in a ruinous position, whether it be for the benefit of an old or a new master.

The politicians of the South who had supported the first, feeble, steps of the Protective Monopoly perceived their error when it was too late. Mr. Calhoun and Mr. McDuffie had sustained it in Congress with speeches and at home with pamphlets; they now denounced it in resolutions and barbacue harangues.[2] The tariff men who had come to Congress at the end of the War of 1812 with humble petitions soon came with importunate demands. They contended for a great prize and won it. They made the Southern people their commercial vassals their growers of raw material and consumers of second and third rate American goods. The South was no longer permitted to enjoy the benefits of that free trade on which the Federal government was founded, for which the war of 1812 had been fought, and under which the Southern people had prospered during the early period of the Government. They were obliged by a system of laws to turn their trade into Northern Channels, to pay freights to Northern ships, to employ Northern agents and buy goods from Northern manufacturers. The prosperity of the North advanced with immense strides; the South fell into comparative decay.

The evil of this system of legislative plunder became so great and intolerable that Southern men were indignant and prepared to assert their rights against a one sided policy which was injuring one section of the Country for the benefit of another. The State of So Carolina resolved to submit to this abuse of power no longer. She affirmed that the Federal government had no power over So Carolina which So Carolina had not conferred. She had conferred no power on the Federal government for the promotion of New England interests at the expense of her own. The protective tariff was a sacrifice of Southern to Northern industry. The constitution had been violated. The law violating it was null and void and should not be enforced within her limits.

The doctrine thus proclaimed by So Carolina is the doctrine of nullification.[3] It led to debates among politicians as interminable as the deliberations of Milton's fallen angels in which "they found no end in wandering mazes lost."[4] The doctrine was deemed a heresy by all at the North and by many at the South. It was warmly supported by its adherents. Mr. Webster assailed it. Mr. Calhoun defended it. The more the disputants wrangled the more hopeless grew the dispute. They set out with their faces in different directions and the farther they went the wider they stood apart. They based their arguments on opposite premises, how could they hope to reach the same conclusions?

It is admitted, the South said, that every State has reserved rights, rights with held from the Federal Government. It is so stated by the Constitution in express terms. If a State has reserved rights, she has some adequate mode to protect them. A mode to be adequate must be within her own controul. If not, if the mode be subject to the will or discretion of another it is no redress at all and the tenure of her rights is worthless. The rights would not exist. But is admitted that the rights do exist. The adequate mode to maintain them must therefore exist with them. If a State has this power to the rights she has necessarily the right to decide on the manner in which to exert it. The State determined that when a law of Congress violates her reserved rights the most effective manner to redress the wrong is to arrest the execution of the law within her limits. In doing this she does the least possible damage to her sister States consistent with justice to herself. If in doing justice to herself some injury arises to others, it is an evil inseparable from a Confederate form of government. A confederacy of States must be a government of consent not of force. To deny that a State may vindicate its reserved rights in its own mode is to make a confederacy a government of force and not of consent. To apply force to a State is to make the States, provinces, to turn the confederacy into a consolidated government, to affirm that a confederacy of States is an impossible form of polity.

The Southern politicians appealed to the resolutions and report of Virginia and Kentucky in '98 and '99, as sustaining their opinions.[5] Mr. Madison, the author, in part of the report and resolutions repudiated the sense imputed to them. It was replied that, if they did not mean Nullification substantially, they were sounding platitudes only, specimens merely of wordy no meaning, puzzles of the kind that politicians habitually use to perplex the people and delude them. If the resolutions do not mean Nullification they mean nothing.

In the North, on the other hand, it was denied that the States have reserved rights independent of the Federal Government. The States, it was said, are in effect counties or provinces only, with certain local regulations and powers subject to the supreme rule of the United States. The Federal government is a national government, not a confederacy. It would be as absurb for Cornwall to refuse obedience to the government at London or the city of Marseilles to the authorities at Paris, as for South Carolina to withhold submissions to an act of Congress no matter what that act may be. It might abolish her State government and her duty would be obedience. When the constitution says "We the people of the United States" it recognises the people of the whole Country as one people determines that the will of the majority expressed in certain forms is the supreme law of the land. The Federal government are antiquated forms maintained for convenience only. It is plain that from promises so various no conclusion could be reached except that in which the soldier undertakes to solve the question and settle the dispute.

Surely nothing can be more uncandid than to confound a State with a county. They are evidently different things substantially and essentially. All reasoning from this or that theory or construction of the constitution to prove a State and a county the same or a similar community is useless and idle. We cannot by dint of logic change a fact. The unchangeable fact is that a State of the United States is a substantive power, a distant people with legislature, judiciary, chief magistrate, treasury, army of militia armed equipped and officered by the State and under her controul. The States in the exercise of certain rights and powers are as independent of each other as they are of the nations of Europe. These rights and powers ae among those most important to the well being of a people, the power to regulate by law the relations of marriage and descent, the transfer of property, the punishment of capital offences. In the exercise of these great social and civil rights, the States are Supreme each within its own boundaries. To say that a State so constituted is a county, or like a county, is to trample on truth and common sense in pursuit of party dogmas. It is to assert what was disclaimed expressly and repeated by the Federalists who formed the Government. I have heard a friend speak enthusiastically of the sentiment of nationality. He knew no Country but the United States. His sympathies were too large for State limits. It is all a delusion I think. There can be no foundation for any such exclusive sentiment of nationality where there is in truth no nation. The "United States" is only a number of States united by voluntary agreement. The argument of the North is founded on loose expressions like that in the preamble of the Am[erican] "We the people." The argument of the South on facts like the existence of separate and independent States independent as to nineteen twentieths of the civil rights. To make a nation of them these States must cease to exist as States. So long as they continue what they are every man's first attachment will be to the State of his nativity or adoption. It meets him at every turn. It masters and subdues the more diffusive and feebler sentiment of regard for the Union. His relation to the State meets him at every turn. This truth is thoroughly established by late events. If there be a class of men in the Country who might forget the State in the General Government, it is the army and navy officers. Their relation to the States seems merged in that to the Federal Government. They are educated by the Government, are in its exclusive service, and represent it abroad and at home. Yet what have the Southern officers done in the present conflict between the Federal Government and their States? They have taken sides with their States. They have renounced their commissions, abandoned their old associations and assumed arms for their own people against the government they were accustomed to serve. Those who neglect to do this are accounted infamous. And what have the Northern officers of the Federal army and navy done? The same thing substantially. They adhere to their States. Their States sustain the government at Washington and so consequently do they. Suppose the case reversed and that Pennsylvania or New York should abandon the Federal authorities at Washington. Where would then be the people of New York or Pennsylvania? Very few would remain in the Federal service. The great majority would be where the people of Georgia and Alabama now are, on the side of their States. Can any man doubt it? The results would be as certain North and South. It is dictated by nature. The human heart proceeds from individuals to the whole not from the whole to its parts. It is more at home with particulars than with abstractions, the smaller than larger associations.

> "God loves from whole to parts the human soul
> Must rise from individuals to the whole.
> Self love but serves the virtuous mind to wake
> As the small pebble stirs the peaceful lake
> A circle formed another straight succeeds
> Another still and still another spreads
> Home, children, kindred, friends, the first embrace
> Our country next and next all human race."[6]

A few men of comprehensive sensibilities may place the human race before their country, as Howard's philanthropy is said to have overshadowed his domestic affections.[7] And so imaginative gentlemen may prefer the Union to the State. But so long as the States exist they will continue to be the first object of affection with the great mass of people who refuse to reverse the order of nature. With them the State government will stand between their firesides and the govenment more distant and less familiar.

In view of the irrepressible fact that the States are States not Counties; that they are people independent to a certain extent of all the world; and in consideration of the inference that inevitably comes from this fact that states so organized and armed will assert their rights, forcibly if necessary, with the certain support of their citizens if they do, it seems to me that our government must of necessity be a government of consent so far as States are concerned and not of force; that force is incompatible with its essential conditions. It would have been fortunate for the stability of the Federal government therefore if the constitution had formally recognized the right of a State to suspend under certain solemn forms the execution within her limits of what she might judge to be an unconstitutional or oppressive law. It would be a partial veto by the State not on the making of laws but on the execution of them—a sort of protest more weighty and efficient than one of words only. It may be safely affirmed that such a power could be used in extreme cases only; that if resorted to factitiously, it would fail immediately or ultimately. The right clearly admitted would have furnished to an aggrieved State a remedy for wrong within the union. It would have been a safety valve for popular discontent giving it time to wear out, if groundless and, if well founded, to be removed by the action of the government immediately or by a general convention. The very knowledge that such a provision exists in the constitution would prevent any such exercise of power by the Federal Government as might endanger its existence. It would render cupidity cautious and the greediness of sectional legislation more timid and moderate. The belief that a majority in Congress is supreme removed all restraint from its course and the tyranny of a faction is the unavoidable consequence. The result of attempting to substitute force for consent as the principle of the Government has been the dissolution of the Union.

In the absence of some such formal, expressed recognition in the constitution of the right of a State to suspend within her limits the operation of a law deemed unconstitutional, the mass of Southern politicians and people refused their adhesion to the nullifying creed. They held that so long as a State was a member of the co-partnership of States she is bound to observe the rules of the co-partnership; that to decide whether a law was constitutional or not, is the province

of the Courts—in the United States, of the Supreme Court, in the
States, of the State Courts; that a convention has no authority to
make or abrogate laws, it has no political power, its proper purpose
is to construct or remodel governments; that in the exercise of its
functions in changing the government of a State, a State Convention
may resume all the powers it has before imparted, those intrusted
to the Federal Government as well as those placed in the government
of the State; that to do more would be to go beyond its just powers.
It is for legislatures to make or repeal laws; for courts to decide
whether laws were constitutional or otherwise; for conventions to
form or modify governments. To permit a convention to exercise the
powers of legislatures and courts was to establish an oligarchy, a
tyranny of the worst kind. A convention would usurp this power if
it undertook to nullify a law whether of the United States or the
State. In a word a convention of South Carolina might withdraw the
State from the union but could not set aside a law of the United
States while the State continued to be one of their number. The
country acquiesced in this opinion and the next effort of South
Carolina was, not to nullify, but to secede.

Whatever may be thought of Nullification as a theory existing
in the nature of the government or possible in itself it was not
without its effect in practice.[8] It broke down the protective policy
for a time. If good faith had been observed, it would have destroyed
the high tariff system for ever and prolonged the life of the Republic.
There was an immense amount of bluster at Washington on this
occasion. The democratic administration was sustained by a coalition
of parties. Mr. Webster and President Jackson were hand and glove.
A proclamation was issued which the advocates of a Consolidated
government delighted to see and which the whig party zealously
supported. A bill giving the President extraordinary powers was
passed by Congress. It was called the force bill and was in substance
an act to make war on South Carolina.

The general at the head of the government was not a man to
sleep over his opportunities. He began in Tennessee to prepare his
battalions for war. He talked of hanging certain Carolina politicians
as high as Haman. Moderate and thinking men became alarmed. An
autocracy seemed to be rearing its crest among them. They consulted
to find a mode for diverting the threatened calamity and Mr. Clay
proposed his compromise. It was accepted by a majority of the two
houses and the evil day passed by. The compromise proposed to

concede so far to the anti-tariff interests of the Country as to repeal the protective tariff and to abandon the protective policy. The repeal however was to be very gradual. It was to spread over ten years in biennial instalments. The biennial reduction was to be ten percent only of the excess of duty over twenty percent. It was only when the tenth year approached that the reduction was to be large. On the tenth year the duties were to be lowered to twenty percent. This was to continue the permanently settled rate. Everything went on smoothly while the reductions were small. It was an inconvenience to trade and embarrassed importers. It was complained of but submitted to. But when the tenth year approached and duties under the compromise were to be reduced to twenty percent as a fixed rate, the tariff men demanded a new tariff. The compromise was trampled under foot by the very men who had formerly offered it, and a new protective tariff was established not less objectionable than the old.

The worst consequence of Nullification was that it produced great divisions and animosities in South Carolina, the more seriously felt because the society affected was a small one. In some parts of the State parties were nearly equal. The convention separated old friends and dissevered families. It arrayed on opposite sides the most intelligent of her public men. And yet amid all the heat and acrimony of the controversy, it must be said in honour of the people of South Carolina that they fell into no broils and that the discussions in her public journals were decorous compared with those of other States on occasion much less exciting.

Of the conspicuous men marshaled by Nullification in adverse parties on the one hand, were Hayne, Hamilton, Calhoun, McDuffie, Preston, Turnbull, Rose, Barnwell, Hampton, Hammond and many more;[9] on the other stood, in a list as long, Daniel E. Huger and Drayton and Poinsett and Petigru and Alfred Huger and Yeadon and Elliott and Manning, a man too warm hearted, amiable and excellent, to be a politician at all.[10] Many of the opposed leaders were personal friends. The controversy estranged them. This was subject of great concern to those of generous and ardent tempers. Manning and Alfred Huger grieved without ceasing and refused to be comforted. Although the conflict cut apart many ties, yet many survived the feud and were cherished during its continuance. It was this which served in a great measure to preserve the peace of the State when civil dissention threatened to destroy it.

During the most momentous period of the controversy, when Jackson sent out his war edict from Washington, Robert Y. Hayne occupied the chair of the chief magistracy in South Carolina. Governor Hayne was the grandson of Col. Hayne, the victim of Balfour's brutality in the war of the Revolution. The grandson was distinguished by a happy combination of the qualities that suited the occasion of difficulty and danger in which the state was involved. He had boldness and moderation, firmness and discretion, courtesy and decision of character. His mind was solid and practical, suited by nature for State affairs; equal to them and not above them — not liable to be carried away from the sound and useful by pursuits more brilliant but less important. With these qualifications for office he united integrity, frankness, cordial manners, and ardent zeal for the honour and safety of his native State. He had been a not unworthy opponent of Mr. Webster in the Senate of the United States. If not the equal of the New England Senator at the bar and forum, he was superior to his antagonist in the conduct and courage that are essential for a leader in public affairs.

The Executive of So Carolina had able supporters. Of Turnbull I knew nothing personally. He acquired great reputation by a series of Essays on the nullification controversy under the signature of Brutus. He was among the most determined, vehement and uncompromising of the men who advocated extreme measures. Like all men ardent in asserting their own opinions, he was impatient of argument or remark on the part of others. His essays were replied to by a writer of the Union party. There was some pungency about the reply. I don't know that it exceeded the just limits of discussion. But Brutus was not satisfied with the phrases of the enemy and invited a resort to a more pointed and summary logic. The friends of Brutus imputed the offence he had taken to the personalities of his opponent; his enemies to the force of the argument. The writer at any rate was silenced and the controversy closed.

Hampton was a brave, frank, courteous gentleman, of hospitality as open as it was cordial, to whom all the unfortunate of every party looked for aid and who never disappointed an applicant.[11] He was always moderate in his views, forbearing to his adversaries in politics and intolerant only of meaness and dishonour. He had a tinge of the Old School about him not in urbanity of manners only but in rapping out, occasionally, an expressive form of words more emphatic than evangelical. It seemed to be the natural outbreak of a warm, generous nature and only served to give a certain racy originality to his conversation.

The manners of Mr. McDuffie were cold and austere. He was always grave and apparently absorbed in his own thoughts. He could not unbend. He was not what Dr. Johnson called a clubbable man. His temper was not social. He was impatient of the visits and interruptions which his public station and high character continually imposed upon him. It was amusing to witness the small regard he paid to those deputations from the great cities which in the times of Biddle and the bank visited Washington and waited on the South Carolina orator to warm his sympathies in their cause. He received them with cold civility and gave little heed to their hints or information, their books, or Statements. He was master of his subject and disdained their aid. He was contending for great principles and cared nothing for the men who were watching their interests only in all their proceedings. It was not for them or their cause that he spoke. I never saw Mr. McDuffie engaged in careless chat during the session of the house. It is common for members to go from desk to desk, to take a chair wherever one happened to be vacant and talk with their brother members freely and indiscriminately. Mr. McDuffie was always in his place, or he would take a seat near the speaker's elevated post and survey the house, by the hour, in quiet rumination. Though not inaccessible to skillful flattery he was rather a proud than a vain man. His temperament was more Roman than Grecian in its character.

The merits of leaders were not confined to one party. It is hard to say on which side they preponderated. There was not in all the South a more complete example of the finished gentleman than Daniel E. Huger. He was for many years a distinguished member of the State legislature. It was only during the time when he was in the House of Representatives that it could be said of the house that it had an acknowledged leader. This was indisputably true while he served in it. He was a keen, vigorous, debater, fluent, energetic in delivery, nicely observant of all the courtesies of debate and prompt but never captious in exacting them. He was the guide of the house, a watchful guardian over the legislation of the State to protect it from any departure from justice and elevated principle. Nothing escaped his vigilant attention that could tend never so remotely to stain the State's reputation for honesty and honour. His personal advantages were remarkable. He had the graceful carriage of a fine person, tall, erect, and active. His manners were perfect. He possessed the art which belongs to the thoroughly well bred gentleman only of putting the young and the Stranger at ease in his company. He practiced no devices of popularity, yet his influence was unbounded. He was anything in the State that he wished—Judge, military chief, member of the United States Senate. It would not convey a correct idea of his position before the people to say that he was a popular man. He was something more. Every young man in the State of Spirit, honour, and ability, as proud of his friendship or favourable consideration and he was always ready to give it. He was a model and example which all desired to imitate and which few or none could equal.

Of the Union party Poinsett and Petigru were the acknowledged leaders. On the other side, Hamilton and Hayne were the most active, energetic and influential chiefs. Under the able guidance of these men supported by others both parties were carried through the various drills that attend all popular excitements. They went to great meetings, eat immense dinners and barbacues, heard speeches without number, gave toasts of pungent meaning and passed endless resolutions. The speeches were eloquent beyond measure. If we may judge from the eulogies on them in the public journals; they were hardly inferior to those that the great Athenian "fulmined over Greece" against the Macedonian tyrant.[12] The toasts were pointed and polished, witty and humourous, fiery and scornful. They made immeasurable pledges. Life, fortune and sacred honour were devoted to the cause. The pledgers filled with good cheer were ready for any extremity of suffering, prepared to spend the last dollar and to die in the last ditch. The resolutions were summaries of Constitutional law, the most exact, profound and luminous. Not a village meeting was held which was not at home in all the depths and shallows of the organic law of 1788, its history and provisions, extent and limits. Marshall never gave his opinions with half their confidence. The State became for a time a great talking and eating machine. The appetites and lungs of the conflicting parties never failed, nor faltered until the compromise adjusted by the joint efforts of Clay and Calhoun settled the controversy, composed the minds and relieved the stomachs of the people. It was like the handful of dust thrown on contending swarms of bees, as Virgil describes it. The tumult ceased in a moment. The combatants went back to their ordinary pursuits. The luckless seekers after State offices who had stumbled into the minority resumed their calculations resolving never again to be found on the wrong or less numerous side, while the victors quietly divided the spoils.

It was just after the adjustment of the Nullification controversy by Mr. Clay's fallacious compromise that I was sent to Congress from the election district of Beaufort and Colleton, the district of Lowndes, Hamilton and Barnwell. I had been a member of the State legislature frequently of the Senate once, of the house of Representatives many times. In no election have I ever asked for a vote, or distributed liquor, or expended money to secure a voter. I mention this not as a claim to any personal merit, but as an evidence of the purity that prevails in our State elections. I have heard that those of the city are exceptions; that they are degraded by corruption; that the elective franchises are marketable articles; that mayors and senators and members of Congress have paid heavily for their Successes. But it is not so in the Country, if it be true of the city. I can say, at least, from some personal experience, that a candidate has no need to employ corrupting influences to obtain success.

Chapter Eight

Congress—Jackson &
Calhoun—Calhoun & Clay

I left Charleston on my way to Washington, the last day of November 1833. During the month [31st October 1833] my eldest daughter, the young child who had been honoured with the kiss and blessing of the elder President Adams, was married to Dr. Thos. L. Ogier of Charleston and prepared to assume her share in the serious duties and adventurers of life.[1] The rest of my little family joined me at the North during the ensuing Spring. I crossed the river to Mount Pleasant in a canoe of six oars, the ferry boat of the day. It was night before we set out in a stage coach of two horses. We eat a late supper at the fifteen mile house, breakfasted in Georgetown the next morning, and proceeded on through Marion, Fayetteville, Raleigh, Petersburg, Richmond, to Acquaia Creek. At Acquaia Creek we took the steam boat for Washington. From Georgetown to Petersburg the Stage carried but two passengers, myself and a merchant of Richmond. Occasionally we took up a way passenger for a few miles. Now hundreds travel the route daily. The rapidity and comfort of the Steam car have induced multitudes to travel who would never have been tempted to try the horrors of a Stage coach at four miles an hour over deep ruts and heavy sand.

It was a beautiful day when we passed Mount Vernon and saluted Washington's home and tomb with uncovered heads and a ringing of the Steamer's bell. I saw for the first time the lofty dome of the Capitol admirably set off by the surrounding scenery of hills and forests. I felt proud of the progress of the Country exhibited in objects of so much grandeur and beauty, the Stately public offices that caught the eye in Succession as we approached the city dedicated to the memory of Washington. I little thought how soon the madness of knaves and fools, of political black legs and puritans more selfish than their mates would prostrate the incipient fortunes of its people and blast all their hopes of future greatness. I little dreamed that before my few remaining years should pass away armed men from Washington's city would be marching to invade Virginia; that Section could be arrayed against Section and State against State; that we could be imitating the mad follies of Mexico and South America; that the right of Self government, the burthen of every fourth of July oration during seventy years would be absolutely denied or forgotten. I heard fierce denunciations, uttered around me in Congress by the men of Philadelphia and Boston against Andrew Jackson for removing the public money from one bank to another, from the custody of Biddle to that of Smith or Brown.[2] The Conqueror who had defended New Orleans was painted as a tyrant blacker than Stuart or Bourbon, as trampling on the constitution and liberties of the Country and now an obscure Attorney from Illinois wipes out, at a Stroke of his pen, Habeas Corpus,[3] the authority of the Supreme court, the whole constitution, while the Binneys and Ingersolls stand by and approve and Mr. Everett supports the outrage in laboured speeches.[4] It is almost as strange as a story in the Arabian nights, though not quite as pleasant.

My friend and colleague General Griffin of Newberry had secured for me very comfortable lodgings with Mrs Peyton at the corner of four and a half street and Pennsylvania avenue. It was a house of Southern resort. Among our inmates were McDuffie, Felder, and Griffin of So Carolina and Allen and Robertson of Virginia.[5] The house was large and commodious; our landlady, a model landlady, not omitting among her other excellent gifts a small spice of fun and mischief.

I looked with the eye of a countryman in wonder and admiration at the fine buildings of Washington, the President's house, the Post Office, the Treasury, the Capitol. Mr. Randolph, it is said, criticised the Capitol in his usual caustic manner, but to my inexperienced eye accustomed to the old wooden State house of Carolina, the Capitol at Washington was a noble and beautiful building.[6] The Hall of Representatives with its lofty columns, its spacious galleries and amphitheatre of desks and seats, surpassed all my expectations. But imposing as it was in appearance it was nevertheless a failure so far as the main purpose of such a hall is concerned. It was badly contrived for speaking. You might be very near the speaker and not be able to hear a word he uttered; another in some remote corner would hear distinctly everything that was said. The evil was not confined to the orator engaged in debate. Gentlemen in the gallery whispering soft phrases in the ears of ladies had their expressions accurately conveyed a long way off to ears for which they were little intended. The tumult and disorder of the house were indescribable. One man would be calling out for a page to do an errand, another would be shooting off from finger and thumb red wafers or bits of paper, others, in groups, would be talking about indifferent topics, while a member was declaiming with loud voice and violent gesticulation on the question under discussion. If the members cared to hear a speech, if it was of a personal nature, or from a new member, or on an interesting subject, they assembled in crowds immediately in front of the orator. When the house was particularly attentive, when the galleries were unusually crowded, especially with ladies, it was to hear a personal explanation which commonly meant a personal dispute. It was difficult to understand how the business of the house could be conducted amid the continued noise and confusion. Yet it managed to go on.

The session of 1833 was one of great importance and excitement. Party Spirit was excessively exasperated. General Jackson had placed the heel of his military boot on the necks of enemies. During the preceding summer he had trampled under foot Nicholas Biddle and the bank. The removal of the Public Deposits of money from the United States bank by the President's order roused the rage of the Whig party almost to frenzy. The intensity of the Nullification quarrel was abated, it is true, but the angry passions excited by the controversy were still alive. Jackson and Calhoun from being friends and allies were irreconcilable foes.[7] So Carolina made the cause of her great Statesman her own. No member of the Carolina delegation visited at the White House with the exception of Blair from Sumter, a Union district. Personal animosity increased political strife. It brought about a curious combination of parties. The democratic State of So Carolina was in fellowship with the Whigs of New York and Pennsylvania, free trade with protective tariffs. Calhoun and McDuffie fought in the same ranks as Webster and Clay. They rivalled each other in their fierce invectives against the great Tennessee embodiment of the Country's democracy. He was compared to every tyrant that had ever disgraced humanity. Caesar was a model of patriotic self controul compared with Jackson and Marius and Scylla were men of moderation and public virtue.

The quarrel between Calhoun and Jackson with all these new party combinations and their consequences grew out of a cunning political intrigue. The intrigue brought to light a secret of Monroe's cabinet. The exploded secret like a grenado blew up the entente cordiale between Carolina and Tennessee "like a grenado shot into a magazine."

The secret related to the Seminole war. General Jackson had judged it necessary in the war to carry his arms into Florida and seize the Spanish posts. The act was a violation of neutral rights and of national law. It sorely perplexed the government of Mr. Monroe. To censure the commanding General in the hour of victory and boundless popularity was not to be thought of. On the other hand to incur a foreign war would be a costly adventure. The President compromised between the two difficulties. His Government defended the general abroad and at home, but gave up the posts to Spain and so disavowed the act of their officer. Although this was the decision to which the cabinet came, it was not without some difference of opinion. It was suggested by a member that the commanding general had transcended his orders in conducting the campaign and that in all such cases a Court of Inquiry was indispensible to preserve the discipline of the army and maintain the dignity of government. The proposal was not sustained. A rumour of the cabinet proceedings got abroad. It reached Jackson's ear. He ascribed the "hostile movement" to Crawford. There had been some dissention between them before. Crawford had interfered with an Indian treaty negotiated by Jackson at a previous time.[8] To thwart the general in a public measure was to be involved with him in a private quarrel. The supposed additional offence in the cabinet increased the feud, and Jackson, after his custom, devoted his enemy to the infernal gods. But this disagreement between Tennessee and Georgia stood in the way of certain political schemes. The schemers, friends of the belligerent parties, consulted together. They set about to adjust the dispute, and reconcile the two chiefs. Hamilton of New York spoke to Mr. Forsyth. Forsyth spoke to Crawford. Crawford declared he had no ill will to General Jackson. He had given Jackson he said no cause of offence in Monroe's cabinet. It was not he who had suggested a Court of Inquiry on the General's conduct in the Seminole Campaign; it was Mr. Calhoun. The declaration of Crawford was communicated by Forsyth to Hamilton. General Jackson was told of Crawford's statement and requested to see it, was furnished with a copy and enclosed it to Mr. Calhoun requesting to be informed whether the Statement was true. It was admitted by Mr. Calhoun to be true as to the fact relating to the Court of Inquiry and the old chief became at once and forever the vindictive foe of the man whom he had toasted at a public dinner not long before as the "noblest work of God."

General Jackson maintained that he had been unfairly treated in the cabinet, because, as he professed to believe, he had acted in conformity with the wishes of the Government if not with the orders of the war Department. On taking command of the army he had written to the President respecting the proper mode of carrying on the war. In a letter of January 8th 1818 he had asked for authority to push his army if necessary into the Spanish territory. He had not required formal orders. A hint would do. He was ready to relieve the President of all responsibility. A wish, or consent, expressed through a third party would be enough. He received, he said, a letter from Mr. Rhea, a Senator of Tennessee, the common friend of himself and the President, giving him the desired authority to conduct the war at his discretion. He proceeded on this authority in seizing the Spanish posts. When he asserted, as he had done, that he acted in conformity with orders, he construed his orders in connection with Rhea's letter. He had been invited since, by the President to open a correspondence with the war Department in reference to the Conduct of the war. He could not open such a correspondence without appealing to Rhea's letter as modifying the orders of the Department. Such an appeal would be a violation of confidence. He preferred to be silent. The Country, he was confident, would sustain him without compelling him to resort to a confidential letter for protection. He would rely on the people and the people sustained him accordingly.

Mr. Monroe, on the other hand, always denied any knowledge of the Rhea letter. He was sick when Jackson's letter of January was received. He laid it aside without reading it. He had never authorized an answer by Rhea or by any other person. Mr. Calhoun was with the President when the letter came and read it at the time, but knew nothing of the pretended answer. The answer was not a cabinet measure; it professed to be the confidential act of the President alone. The knowledge of it was confined to the President, Mr. Rhea and General Jackson.

In the Cabinet Council on the seizure of the Spanish posts, Mr. Calhoun rested his suggestion for a Court of Inquiry into the conduct of the commanding officer on the orders issued from the war department. If Mr. Calhoun remembered Jackson's letter of January, as he could not fail to do, and knew there had been no official reply, as he must have know, he certainly regarded Jackson's letter as the most conclusive evidence that the writer had exceeded the orders of the government in taking possession of the Spanish forts. The letter asked for secret authority; why ask it, if the orders from the department of war were sufficient? The request proved that the orders were not sufficient. The general had violated his orders. He had disregarded the law of Nations as well as the orders of his own government. The act demanded investigation. Mr. Calhoun as Secretary of War was the proper person to propose it. He had proposed it, with no ill will to General Jackson but as an act of duty to the Country.

No candid mind can censure Mr. Calhoun for suggesting a court of inquiry on an officer in his own department who had violated its orders and invaded the territories of a neutral nation; who had sacrificed to expediency the character of the Country for good faith and lessened the stability and dignity of international law. The act of the Secretary in demanding an inquiry was a duty and furnished additional evidence of his fitness for the place he was filling. But this was not General Jackson's mode of judging in any case in which he had a personal concern. He conducted public affairs as he managed his own. He assumed the responsibility to do whatever he thought most conducive to the interests of himself, his friends, or his party. If he was opposed, he divided the world into two classes, those who sustained him in the quarrel, public or private, and those who did not. The first were friends, good men and patriots; like Benton and Blair.[9] The last were bad citizens; like Clay and Calhoun. His reasoning in such cases was concise and conclusive. Could any man doubt the patriotism of Andrew Jackson? Had he not always acted with a view solely to the general welfare? Did not every man who opposed him oppose the public good? Were not such men enemies of the Country to be put down, like Nick Biddle, by all possible means? Has sounder logic ever been chopped in the schools? The people thought it unanswerable and supported the logician with unlimited zeal.

But although Mr. Calhoun was right in proposing a court of inquiry and in doing so gave no just cause of offence to General Jackson, yet there remains another question respecting the relations between the two parties which is not so easily settled. Whether rightly or wrongly it was Mr. Calhoun who moved the resolution concerning a Court of Inquiry on Jackson's conduct in the Seminole war. Jackson believed the mover to be Crawford. He was at feud with the Georgian before, he hated his supposed assailant now still more intensely. He supposed that Calhoun had sustained him in the Cabinet. He was therefore the warm admirer of Mr. Calhoun. Did Calhoun know anything of the additional feud with Crawford and the cause of that feud? Was he informed of the favourable opinion respecting himself entertained by General Jackson and the reason for that favourable opinion. Had he done nothing and said nothing, had his friends done and said nothing, to keep alive his double misapprehension? If he was entirely blameless in this respect, as no doubt he was, and only knew that such misapprehensions existed without promoting them was it proper for him as an upright man to allow the mistake to continue? Could a man of nice sensibility permit another to be hated and himself to be held in honour with the knowledge that the disclosure of a single fact would reverse their positions?

It may be said the Mr. Calhoun could not reveal the counsels of the Cabinet, however anxious to undeceive Jackson and do justice to Crawford. But this would be claiming a degree of sanctity for Cabinet deliberations to which they are not entitled. A Cabinet is a public body of a Constitutional government. It is not an Aulic Council nor a social meeting of friends. Many things may require disclosures. In any case the motive would characterize the act. No revelations should be made for idle or sinister ends. But where the purpose is to do justice, to redress a wrong without injury to any public interest, will it be said that the member's lips shall be sealed even when his colleagues consent to his speaking? Who can doubt that Mr. Calhoun could have so spoken on the present occasion? Mr. Adams and the other members of Monroe's cabinet made no scruple to give their Statements, at Mr. Calhoun's request, of what passed in the counsels of the cabinet. Why should Mr. Calhoun have scrupled to do the same thing at another time, from a similar or higher motive?

If it be suggested that Mr. Calhoun was ignorant of the feelings of Jackson towards Crawford and himself and of the causes of those feelings; the suggestion is by no means probable. Living as Calhoun lived in the world of politics and kept aware by a hundred friends of all its movements, how could he miss the knowledge of what others knew? Other persons were informed of Jackson's sentiments and opinions. Intimations had been made to the General from time to time that he was mistaken in his judgment of the two Secretaries. Can we suppose that Mr. Calhoun was kept in the dark as to what was passing? General Jackson made no secret of his likes and dislikes or of their causes, Mr. Calhoun could not fail to be informed of them and to know therefore that he was holding a false position in his relations with General Jackson.

It is evident that this was Jackson's view of the subject. When he heard of the Statement made by Crawford of what had passed in the Cabinet of Monroe he demanded to see it. He enclosed it when received in a note to Mr. Calhoun and requested to be informed whether the Statement was true. Mr. Calhoun replied at great length. He animadverts severely on the conduct of Crawford and on the motives of the men secretly engaged in reviving the memory of events passed twelve years before for the manifest purpose of sowing dissention between himself and General Jackson "making an instrument of one and a victim of the other." But the truth of the statement as to the Court of Inquiry he substantially admits. General Jackson answered briefly that he had no concern about the conduct of Crawford or the motives of Crawford's friends; that from everything what had passed between him and Mr. Calhoun he had supposed Calhoun his friend and supporter in Monroe's cabinet; that when it was intimated many years since that it was Calhoun who had been hostile to him, he repulsed the intimation indignantly; that he never expected to be obliged to say to Calhoun "et tu Brute"; That he had met the suggestion of Mr. Calhoun's having made "injurious movements" against him in the cabinet with a flat denial as an unjust charge on Mr. Calhoun's honour; that until he saw the written statement of Crawford he had given the charge no attention; that he had sent the Statement to Mr. Calhoun as a duty due to a friend expecting a prompt and positive denial; that on the contrary he had received an admission of its truth to his "poignant mortification." This was the single fact, he added, about which he felt any concern. He had received Mr. Calhoun's admission that the fact was true and he would close the correspondence and have nothing to do with any further altercation. He supposed Mr. Calhoun had been his friend and Mr. Calhoun was his enemy. He had given his friendship under the supposition stated and his friendship was betrayed. He expected a frankness which he had not found and his confidence was gone forever.

If the disclosure of the cabinet proceeding to Jackson at an early period by Mr. Calhoun was due to candour and justice, it must be admitted on the other hand that ordinary State policy led very much the other way. It was deeply to the interest of Mr. Calhoun as a politician that the deliberations of the Cabinet on the Seminole war should not be revealed. It was obvious to any one knowing the temper of Jackson that the disclosure would excite his anger, make him Calhoun's enemy and destroy the prospects of the Carolina Statesman for the great office which had been the object of his life. Jackson's support would be decisive into whatever scale it might be thrown. To expect Mr. Calhoun to be insensible to all this and to volunteer a revelation of facts which would make his foes triumphant and himself "a victim" would be to expect a degree of self sacrificing virtue quite beyond the limits of public life. No ambitious man could reach it and no ambition of the day was so intense and absorbing as that of Mr. Calhoun. Clay's ambition was tempered by a taste for social pleasures and Webster's by a feeble will. Mr. Calhoun was pure of all vices but the vice of ambition which grew stronger by the virtues that restrained him from other indulgencies.

Whatever may have been the reason for the long concealment of Monroe's cabinet secrets, whether it was Mr. Calhoun's misfortune or his fault, the delay and forced disclosure placed him in a disadvantageous position. It enabled his enemies to represent his conduct as wanting in frankness and fair dealing. It took away from his explanations, when they were drawn from him, all grace and force. The irascible autocrat was enraged at what he considered, or was enabled to call, the long hidden treachery of a supposed friend. He would not have been able under any circumstances, to remain neutral between the two sections into which his followers were divided under Van Buren and Calhoun. He would be disposed to side with the supple and subservient, with Van Buren and Blair.[10] These men were enabled to secure his favour by the statement of Crawford and to arouse his implacable hatred against Calhoun and his supporters. The highest office in the Government was the reward of a political intrigue. Whether Mr. Calhoun might not have played his game better, whether a franker course with Jackson at the beginning would not have been the sounder policy may perhaps admit of a question.

About the Rhea letter of which I have spoken there is still a mystery. There is no doubt that such a letter written to Jackson by Rhea respecting the mode of conducting the Seminole war; that the letter was burnt some time after by General Jackson at Rhea's request that Rhea asserted he had written the letter and made the request to destroy it at the President's desire. Mr. Monroe denied all knowledge of Rhea's letter. Except the assertion of Rhea there is nothing to connect the President with the transaction. The question is one of veracity between Rhea and Monroe. We must choose between the Senator and the President. Perhaps we may solve the difficulty partially by conjecturing that Rhea, a good humoured man, informed of Jackson's wishes, had some conversation with the President and anxious to promote Jackson's plans construed vague expressions into assent and made such a report to the general as would enable him to act at discretion in conducting the war. But this solution would not extend to the pretended request that the letter should be destroyed. That may have been Rhea's device to get out of the dilemma in which his good nature had involved him with his two friends.

During the time of the unlucky quarrel between Jackson and Calhoun the South Carolina delegation, as I have said, refrained from visiting at the White House. They refused to pay their personal respects to a man who had threatened their chief city by sending a sloop of war into her harbour and who had shaken a halter over the heads of her most distinguished statesmen. The delegation abstained from a visit even on the great occasion when a cheese, six feet in diameter and nearly a ton's weight, gave evidence on a table in the East room of the devotion felt by Northern dairy men for the President's virtues; when all who wished, attended, admired, eat and carried away in their pockets a fragment of the feast. In consequence of this self exclusion from the President's mansion I had no opportunity of getting a good look at his features. The best I enjoyed was at Church. He attended the preaching of the Rev. Dr. Post and sat in a pew on the right hand side of the pulpit half facing the larger part of the congregation.[11] There was great firmness but no ferocity in the long, thin, solemn, face and white bristling hair of the old soldier. He might have taken the Preacher's place in the pulpit, so far as appearances go, with decided advantage to the Sunday services. The pastor's face was rather sour and querulous than grave or impressive. The President's aspect gave one a fair notion of a Cameronian in the days of Dundee. It was calm, resolute, ready, it would seem, at a moment's warning, for fight or exhortation. He was devoutly attentive to the services, shook hands at their close with the few who were near him and went his way thinking perhaps of the deceased wife whom he tenderly loved, who had been his good angel and to whom the church had always been a place of joy, or, possibly, he may have departed pondering on the evil machinations of Nick Biddle and the Bank. There was some resemblance between the two men, the President and the great South Carolina Senator, once friends, now implacable foes. They were of the same Scotch Irish stock and exhibited its characteristic traits. In both were seen the long face, the hollow jaws, the thick bustling hair, the tall gaunt erect figure, which belong to the race, each of them had great strength of will and force of character. There was one feature of their common ancestry in which General Jackson was probably superior to his opponent—he was the best hater. But even here the resemblance is not lost. It is said of Mr. Calhoun that he tolerated no political heresies and broke down in his own State and never forgave the politician who opposed his opinions. He made many enemies in doing so. One of these was Judge William Smith for some time a member of the Senate at Washington from South Carolina.[12]

Judge Smith had lost his seat in the Senate through the hostility of the Calhoun party. His district, York, sent him to the Senate of the State where he carried on the war by a series of resolutions in opposition to others offered by Judge Prioleau and passed by the legislature previously under the influences of Mr. Calhoun and his friends.[13] Smith was not a man to submit tamely. His temper was irascible and his will as strong as that of his enemy. During the Session a print was shown to the Judge exhibiting Calhoun as a fiery young racer, eager for the course, and kicking down all who came near him, Judge Smith among the rest. "Yes!" said the old man after grimly examining the picture. "Yes! but damn him if he had been bridle wise, he would not have done it." It is not surprising that Judge Smith was indignant at being kicked out from the Senate of the United States. It was the choicest place in the gift of the people. Nor is it at all improbable that the too free use of his heels on those that stood in his way has much to do in preventing the young charger's success on the course. It increased the weight that he carried in the race and was probably the cause of his losing it at last.

If the impatient ambition of Mr. Calhoun was unfavourable to his own fortunes, the autocratic spirit of his antagonist was disastrous to those of the Republic. Jackson revolutionized the government. He established the pernicious system which Marcy concisely described when he said "to the victors belong the spoils."[14] The maxim before had been "office to the most meritorious." The practice of Washington in distributing places was in accordance with this maxim. Is he able, is he honest, were the questions asked in reference to persons appointed. The principle was respected if not strictly followed by all succeeding Presidents until Jackson came. He changed everything. The spoils must now go to the victors. Is the applicant a thorough party man, is he a staunch adherent of the President, has he been an active supporter of the dominant faction—these are the questions that have displaced the old fashioned inquiries of the early Republic. The change demoralized the Country. Offices are now the rewards of party tools. At the end of every four years there is a fight of factions. In every pot house there is a scramble for office. Hordes of mercenaries, carpet bag in hand, swarm in the streets of Washington. They gather after every election like ravenous wolves. They beseige the departments. They invade the White House. They harass the President. The Chief Executive Officer of the Government is a great office broker for four years. The final cause of a Presidential election is to distribute place anew, to arrange jobs, to reward partizans of every grade from Secretary of State to the door keeper. Is it surprising that speedy ruin to the Country has been the consequence? If fit men had held the great offices of the government the measures which have destroyed the Republic would never have been known.

The alliance between Mr. Calhoun and the Whigs proved to be a hollow truce. It terminated as such truces are apt to do in a more violent quarrel between the parties. They had united to hunt the old lion of the Hermitage. He had now disappeared from the field. The New York "Fox" was in his place. In the extra session of 1837 called by Jackson's successor, the Carolina Statesman changed his position and went over to the democratic side; or rather, as he was accustomed to say, they came over to him. He saw and said that any victory resulting from a league with the Whigs would conduce to their benefit only. He found that the counsels of the "Fox" who was presiding were sounder than the doctrine or practice of the abdicated lion. He supported the more astute animal accordingly. The invectives of 1834 were no longer remembered in 1837. After a few months of decent delay Mr. Calhoun visited Mr. Van Buren. They buried the hatchet and smoked the calumet of friendship in the parlour of the White House. Carolina sustained her Statesman as she always did. She had repudiated the New York politician as a trickster in 1838; she voted for his reelection in 1840. A few refused to perform the somersault and were driven, like Preston, from the councils of the Country, contrary to the usual and more manly practice of the State.[15]

The sneerers in Washington were addicted to saying that if Mr. Calhoun took snuff, the State of South Carolina sneezed incontinently.

The action of the State in reference to Van Buren was regarded as a confirmation of the scandalous assertion. There was one exception among the people of South Carolina. The election district in which Mr. Calhoun resided and which General Waddy Thompson represented in Congress refused to sneeze and disappointed the scoffers.[16] Thompson was triumphant against the attempt to drive him from his seat for not appreciating the newly discovered virtues of Mr. Van Buren.

It is not to be supposed that so important a change could pass without notice. In the nicely balanced State of parties the support of Mr. Calhoun was enough to turn the scale to give victory to the democrats and defeat the Whigs. Mr. Clay was not a man to see his party defeated with quiet acquiescence. He launched against his late ally all the lightnings of his vehement and sarcastic eloquence. He upbraided the "deserted." He assailed the whole political course of the South Carolina Senator as a series of desertions. He charged the Senator with having abandoned every principle that they were once united in supporting the bank, the protective tariff, the internal improvement system. The Senator, he said, now denounces all; he once maintained them all.

Mr. Calhoun replied in a vigorous speech. He denied that he had deserted a party or abandoned a principle. He belonged to no party. He stood still only and if he acted sometimes with one party, sometimes with another, it was because they sought his company, not he theirs. He had supported the bank, the tariff, internal improvement, it was true, but there had been at the time some special reason why they sould be supported. He had always seen and sustained the measures most conducive to the public welfare. His judgement had not been at fault; his motives were always pure. It had not been so with his opponent. He taunted Mr. Clay with the bargain that had made Adams, President, and Clay, Secretary of State. He represented the Kentucky Senator as a rider of hobbies all his life and as riding them always to death. He charged the Senator with abandoning principle habitually for Compromise, truth for expediency.

Mr. Clay replied at once with great vehemence. He scorned the stale slander set afloat by George Kremer of Pennsylvania respecting a corrupt bargain in the election of Mr. Adams.[17] He had voted for Mr. Adams as the better Statesman and the better man. That Adams was the better Statesman Mr. Calhoun himself thought at the time of the election. He retorted on the Senator from South Carolina. The Senator not long since had denounced Mr. Van Buren as everything pitiful and contemptible, as a crouching, creeping, crafty, fox, and had lately kissed hands at the White House and taken service under the Van Buren flag with the hope of future advancement. The Senator had charged him with riding hobbies and riding them to death; his accuser was like a courier on a journey and rode relays of expedients changing them as necessity or convenience suggested. He and the Carolina Senator began political life together as advocates of a protective tariff, of a system of internal improvement. He continued to advocate them; the Senator now opposed them all. The special reasons assigned for opposing today what was supported yesterday are subterfuges only, the ready resort of every deserter and trimmer. He was a friend of compromise, he admitted; all legislation implies compromise; government itself is a compromise. He had proposed the compromise between nullification and the force bill. He had interposed to save the gallant State of South Carolina from the peril and disgrace into which the counsels of her Senator were about to plunge her. But for his interposition and compromise then, he doubted whether he would have the honour now of meeting the Senator face to face in the Senate. Mr. Calhoun, he said, had been glad to escape from the military chieftain at the head of affairs and from his summary proceedings. To escape, the Senator had submitted to every provision required in the compromise however averse to them—the long time, the ultimate rate of duty, the home valuation, the most hateful provision to the Senator of them all. The author of Nullification fled from the consequences of his own schemes and was glad to get away at any sacrifice.

Mr. Calhoun affirmed, in answer that the compromise bill of 1833 was a measure arranged by the Senator of Kentucky for nobody's benefit but his own. General Jackson with Mr. Webster was about to draw away Clay's party from his side, to turn him out of his own house, to leave him floundering like a whale in shallow water. To escape this fate the Kentucky Senator fled to compromise. It was Mr. Calhoun who ruled the occasion, who had been Mr. Clay's master, who had the Senator flat on his back, who had assisted the compromiser to retain his post and party.

Mr. Clay replied with unmeasured disdain. "He my master," the indignant orator exclaimed, "I would not own him as a slave! He my master! I submit to his dictation! I gloried, at the time, in my strength. I carried the bill through Congress in spite of Jackson, in spite of the Senator from Massachusetts, in spite of the unavailing efforts to modify it of the gentleman himself. He was compelled reluctantly to take what I was willing to give."

And thus these two distinguished men, hour after hour, bandied words and hurled at each other crimination and recrimination to the mortification or amusement of their brother Senators and the intense delight of the mob that filled the galleries. Each claimed for himself perfect consistency in his political career, infallible judgment and unwavering integrity pure from all mixed motives of personal advancement. Each imputed to the other the basest designs of a vulgar amibition. To the impartial observer, the contention was the conflict of two angry and aspiring rivals pursuing the same objects with equal eagerness. If they believed what each said of the other, it should have taught them a juster judgment of themselves.

It is amusing to see the readiness with which a party leader will arrogate for himself an entire exemption from interested motives. He may have erred, he will modestly say, in the choice of his measures; who is not liable to err? or he may have been feeble in supporting the measures chosen; though he had given his best ability to the Country's service. But as to the purity of his motives and his disinterested devotion to the people's welfare and nothing else—that, he assumes boldly, is above all suspicion. If a lawyer should assert that he manages his cases, cajoles the jury and bullies the judge, from sheer love of justice and his clients, or a physician declare that he prescribes and administers his drugs daily and nightly, with a view only to promote the art of healing and help the people's health, he could not be a more impudent imposter. It is but justice to the lawyer and physician to say that they never attempt to cheat themselves or any others with such pretences. The small annual bills presented to their friends are too regular to permit such delusions to be possible. But the politician lives on the general fund at Washington or Richmond. He takes no fees directly from his supporters and sends in no bills at the end of the year. He rather confers benefits than receives them while in office. He is able to play the part therefore of a disinterested patriot serving his Country for his Country's good, never for his own. He identifies himself with the Country. I am the State, has been said perhaps by the French monarch alone; but it is thought by every aspiring politician who makes public employment the object of his life. He and his party are the State. While they are in office, the Country prospers. When they are quoted by their opponents, the Country is ruined. It is the practice for the patient's health only; lawyers labouring all their lives for the love of right with no thought of fees. And with this impudent imposture the good people are perpetually duped. The hook is always in Leviathan's jaws and the fisherman never fails to persuade the gullible beast that the process is one intended for his welfare or amusement solely.

Chapter Nine

Senate of 1833

The Session of 1833 was about the time when the Senate of the United States reached the highest point of elevation in dignity and talent. In addition to the three eminent Statesman, Clay, Webster and Calhoun, to whom the first place was universally conceded, many others little inferior to them in reputation or ability occupied seats in the Senate chamber. Among them were Clayton, Southard, Preston, Rives, Berrien, Benton, Poindexter, Wright, Frelinghuysen, Bibb and others.[1] It was an August body hardly equalled, certainly not surpassed, by any English house of Lords that ever sat in Parliament. Yet it was before this body of remarkable men that the most ridiculous farce was played, month after month and year after year beginning in 1834 and ending in 1837. On one side it was proposed to censure the President for removing the public money from one bank to another.[2] The removal was represented as a violation of the laws and dangerous to the liberties of the people. It was replied on the other hand that the public money was unsafe in its former place of deposit and it was the duty of the President to transfer it to more honest hands. The debate was carried on with unparalleled acrimony and violence. It was difficult to say who was most vehement, Clay, Calhoun, or Webster. If the President had attempted to usurp all the powers of the government their denunciation could not have been fiercer. They succeeded in their purpose after four months labour. The resolution was passed.[3] The censure was imposed. Forthwith, on the other side, Mr. Benton brandished his expunging resolution, a resolution to wipe out the censure from the Senate records. This again was debated month after month with increasing fury. At the end of three years the resolution was adopted. Jackson's lieutenant was triumphant and the great triumvirate were prostrate in the dust. There is not perhaps in the language a more amusing specimen of the mock heroic than Benton's account of what he calls "the last scene." The supporters of the measure held a council and decided that on a certain day the vote should be taken in the Senate. The

day came. Ample supplies for supporting the strength and courage
of the Jackson party were provided in a committee room. The Senate
chamber was crowded. The people filled the galleries. In vain, Clay,
Calhoun, Webster and their followers strove to wear out the energies
of their opponents by much talk. They were allowed to make their
dying speeches without a reply. At midnight the question was demanded. The Ayes and Nos were called. The resolution to expunge
was adopted. The journals were produced. At the sight of them the
galleries hissed and yelled The great Expunger in a roar of fury
demanded the arrest of the bank ruffians. It was done and order
was restored. The great work went on. The hateful resolution of
censure passed in 1834, was enclosed within black lines, crossed and
recrossed, and on its face was written "expunged by resolution of
the Senate, March 9th, 1837." Clay, Webster and Calhoun were made
to eat dirt before the people. Their enemies were feasted at the
White House. A great dinner was given to the victorious expungers
and their wives. The President was sick and Benton presided. They
were jovial and happy as Homer's gods in having vindicated the
insulted honour of their illustrious ruler.

The coolest, shrewdest and most successful in the political game
which all were playing on this occasion was the presiding officer of
the Senate, the vice president, Mr. Van Buren. He has been painted
very black by his opponents but he was no worse than his neighbours.
The chances turned in his favour and he used them as they would
have done if it had been in their power. If not a good natured man
Mr. Van Buren was an excellent actor of good nature. He was never
ruffled, but always calm under attack and steady in the hottest fire.
When our Senator launched at him terms and phrases more forcible
than decorous he received them all with a smile. He was always
ready to preserve friendly social relations with his opponents and
was too accomplished a hand in the game which all were playing to
get angry at defeats and losses. In the grand debate of 1834 on the
removal of the deposits when Mr. Clay solemnly turned to the chair
and addressed its occupant not as presiding officer of the Senate
but as the confidential friend and adviser of the President, when he
adjured the Vice President to deliver a message, to represent to the
Chief Executive the ruin which the policy of the Government in
reference to the bank was fast bringing on the whole Country, Mr.
Van Buren listened with a gravity and attention at least equal to
the solemnity of the speaker. When the speech was ended, the Vice

President left the chair, walked over to the Senator's seat, intimated to his brother politician that he understood the game in which they were engaged and was willing to play it with proper decorum. They were like two Roman augurs recently come from inspecting the entrails of an offering to their gods, both aware of the farce they were acting, but both thoroughly trained to keep a grace countenance and to refrain from laughing in each other's face. None of the priests attendant in the temple of Demos at that time behaved so well as Mr. Van Buren in this part of their duty. Mr. Clay was too irascible. Mr. Webster too indifferent and Mr. Calhoun too earnest and abrupt.

It is fortunate for the world's peace that the people are subject to strong illusions as to the motives and character of their rulers, as to the singleness of their ends and the purity of their patriotic purposes. Government otherwise would be an impossible thing. If it were commonly understood that legislation is a mere scramble of private interests; that long discussions turn not on questions of public good but of personal advantage; that the advancement of a party not of the Country directs the politician; that the orator is really thinking of himself and not of the people; how could laws and law-givers command obedience or respect? Mr. Clay says in a letter to Judge Brooke "it is inexpressibly disgusting to find that consider-ations affecting in election four years distant influence the fate of great questions more than all the reason and argument that can be used."[4] If so disgusting to an old politician, a veteran member of the corporation, what would it be to the simple honest people if they happened to know it. But they do not know it. They have the same faith in their prophets that Joe Smith's followers had in him and with no better reason. And so in either case government goes on. Remove the faith, expose the reality and anarchy would follow. Some-times the reality is exposed and revolution ensues to be replaced in turn by renewed faith, fresh delusions, and other revolts.

There is great variety of character in an American Congress in the house of Representatives especially. They come from a wide extent of Country and represent every diversity of manners from the refinement of the great city to the rudeness of border life. Among those most remarkable in 1835, David Crockett was not the least famous. He was a dull, heavy, almost stupid man in appearance.[5] I never heard him utter a word that savoured of wit or sense. To judge from his features one would have supposed such an event impossible. Yet by some freak of fortune he became the reputed author of innumerable queer sayings and stories, a man of infinite joke, an incarnation of frontier oddity, a sort of Western Joe Miller. He was a good natured, kind hearted man and a general favourite in the house. He was a brave soldier too and had seen service in the Texan war with Mexico, but he was the last man in the house that a stranger would have pitched upon as a wit and humourist.

At a desk not far from Crockett, Wilde of Georgia presented a thorough contrast to the Western member. One was stout and clumsy in person with a blotchy fair complexion and light eyes, ungainly in address and manners; the other dark, of good figure with black eyes, easy, sprightly, engaging in conversation, a good speaker and still more a poet. He was the writer of the song beginning "My life is as a summer rose" the authorship of which was challenged in various quarters and gave rise to some literary controversy.[6] The song is from a poem which I believe was never published or completed. The poem tells the story of a luckless Spaniard from De Soto's expedition who has been captured by the Indians and remained a prisoner in Florida during many years. When now an old man he paces the beach of Tampa bay and while the visions of his youth rise up in his memory he casts a longing look on the ocean that separates him from his native land. He gives voice to his grief in the song to which I have alluded.

I sat near Col. Richard M. Johnson of Kentucky, "the man who killed Tecumseh."[7] He was a favourite with the people of Kentucky from his services in the Indian wars of the North West and from his frank popular manners, though some sneers were current respecting certain of the old soldier's domestic relations. I was greatly obliged on one occasion by his friendly interposition. The incident may serve to illustrate the mode in which public business was transacted during the partizan administration of General Jackson. A constituent, a mill contractor, had sent to me from home a claim for ten thousand dollars on the Post Office Department. The claim was undoubted. I called at the department again and again but could get no money. I was not an adherent of General Jackson. Worse than that, I was from the pestilent State of South Carolina, a compatriot of John Cataline Calhoun as Francis P. Blair, the disinterested patriot, was accustomed to call the South Carolina Senator. On one of these fruitless visits, I was descending the steps of the Post Office, in very bad humour, at the ill success of my efforts when I met Col. Johnson. "What is the matter?" he asked. I told my story. "Give me your papers," he replied, "and let me see what I can do to assist you." I gave him the papers and received a draft for the money on the day following to the great joy of my correspondent at home who had been waiting for a year or two almost in despair. The explanation is easy. Col. Johnson lived, while at Washington, in the family of the Revd. Obadiah Brown, chief clerk of the post office department and reputed author of the celebrated report on Sunday mails presented to Congress by a committee of which Col. Johnson was chairman.[8] Brown was virtually head of the department. Post Master general Barry was incapable of business and was soon after sent on some foreign mission which he filled with success as there was nothing to do. Johnson's influence with the acting head of the Post Office and with the ruling party secured payment for me without delay.

The great battle between Jackson and Nicholas Biddle backed by the Bank, the Whig party, and South Carolina, produced an unusual display of elaborate oratory. Clay, Webster and Calhoun strove to surpass each other in their efforts. Philadelphia sent her great lawyer, Horace Binney to take a part in the fray. He went reluctantly from the bar to add his voice to the storm of argument and invective that assailed the administration. Crowds of people from all parts of the Union drawn by interest or curiosity assembled at the capital. For months the removal of the public money from the safe keeping of Mr. Biddle was the standing topic with both houses of Congress. Both parties appealed to the passions of the people. The great cities were in constant agitation. They sent deputations with monster petitions to Washington. The deputations found Jackson inflexible and invincible. They complained of impending commercial ruin. He charged them with overtrading on fictitious capital. They bewailed the universal scarcity of money; he referred them to Nick Biddle. It was Biddle who caused the distress for sinister purposes. Biddle has millions locked up in the bank vaults; let him put them in circulation. The deputations transferred their griefs from the President to their delegations in Congress and gave fresh impulse to the excitement. Jackson was denounced, day after day, as something worse than Nero or Caligula. He, on the other hand accused his adversaries, Poindexter particularly, with designs to assassinate him. The attempt of a lunatic to fire a pistol at him, in the Rotunda, while attending the funeral of Warren R. Davis furnished a pretext for the accusation.[9] There was indeed in the act of the madman no very remote connection with the proceedings in Congress. Day after day violent denunciations were uttered against Jackson as the sole cause of the derangement in business and of the suffering that pervaded the Country. It was his act that removed the public deposits from Biddle's bank. It was the removal of the deposits that produced the general distress. A man with a mind heated and unhinged by personal losses hearing all this from the highest authorities might easily bring himself to repeat the scene witnessed by England in the death of Percival when he was killed by Bellingham as the author of the commercial calamities of which Bellingham and his friends were victims.[10]

Among all the celebrated speakers assembled on this remarkable occasion, W. C. Preston,[11] I thought, had most of the genuine spirit of the orator—the gift which Nature imparts and which no art or labour can produce—the power possessed by Chatham and Patrick Henry, that enabled Whitefield while preaching in behalf of a charity to empty the pockets of Franklin, first of their copper, then of their silver, and at last of their gold, in spite of the resolution to give nothing with which the Doctor had gone to the meeting. It is the fate of many good stories to be apochryphal. This may belong to the number. It is certainly not in keeping with "Poor Richard's" reputation for frugality and self controul. But the anecdote true or false illustrates strikingly the power of great natural eloquence. Mr. Preston's oratory wrought no such wonders. It was not without its triumphs nevertheless. An imputation was one day made in the Senate on the factious proceedings of South Carolina. Mr. Preston replied at once in a speech of a half hour which Mr. Everett declared was the most eloquent he had ever heard. This was high praise especially from Mr. Everett because Preston's manner must have been the reverse of his own; one was fire, the other ice.

Mr. Clay was an orator, long and carefully trained and of imposing manner and appearance. His declamation was magnificent, his figure tall and commanding, his voice powerful, flexible, musical, and under perfect command. He had more action with one exception perhaps than any speaker in the Senate. He moved from his desk. He walked up and down between the rows of seats. He took snuff. He used his hands freely. He varied his voice; was sometimes rapid, sometimes slow; sometimes solemn, sometimes playful. He mingled wit with reasoning and invective with argument. But with all his success in the arts of rhetoric he never seemed to me to reach the highest art. His art was not concealed. He had the air of an accomplished actor playing a part with great skill but with an eye always on the audience and their applauses. Mr. Clay was the great "compromiser." Long before Macauley announced to the world that "the essence of politics is compromise," Mr. Clay had acted on the maxim. Unfortunately for the reputation of the Kentucky statesman as to sagacity or consistency he abandoned his role when a steady adherence to it would have increased his fame and prolonged the life of the American Republic. He opposed the proposition to extend the Missouri line of compromise to the Pacific ocean. He destroyed in 1842 the compromise tariff act of his own making ten years before. These were fatal mistakes on two vital points.[12] The ruin of the commonwealth has been the consequence. Mr. Clay in his compromises seems to have acted more the part of a dextrous arbiter between contending parties than of a far sighted Statesman provident of the Country's welfare.

The distinguished Statesman of South Carolina was not a pleasing speaker. He was exceedingly angular in phrase as he was in figure. His manner was abrupt. His sentences were often left incomplete. He cut them short in the heat and hurry of his utterance. His ideas appeared to outrun his words and to leave them limping in the rear. His delivery was stiff and without grace, but it was impressive from its intense and eager earnestness. There was a glare, a fire, in his eye, the fire of a soul that seemed to burn within him. It fascinated the beholder and rivetted his gaze. Mr. Calhoun's argument was always vigorous, subtle and clear. In all his refinements you understood him perfectly and with ease. He was never muddy or confused. He was a powerful and skillful debater, not a declaimer or rhetorician. The arts of the rhetorician, he seemed to despise. His mode of speaking suited important subjects only. On small occasions, in reply to a complimentary toast at a dinner for example he was the lest felicitious of politicians or men. Yet his conversation was attractive in the highest degree. But his conversation was always a disquisition. He appeared to talk his best, as Dr. Johnson advises everybody to do, at all times, and his conversation had about it the earnestness and attraction of a set speech from an able speaker on interesting topics. He appeared to be always thoroughly convinced of the truth of what he said whether in the parlour or the Senate and to believe ourselves is the only efficacious art to make others believe.

The speaking of Mr. Webster, on common occasion, was heavy and uninteresting. But when roused by a subject worthy of his great intellect, he poured forth magnificent sentences of perfect English, so round, clear, vigorous and musical as none could equal or imitate. There was great dignity in his figure and face. His manner and appearance were Senatorial. His voice deep and sonorous. His action Stately and composed. He was a great power, a steam engine in pantaloons, as Sydney Smith describes him.[13] Yet he left on the hearer's mind the impression that he was a mighty partizan fighting a battle with vast skill and power but without caring very greatly about the cause which he was defending, ready if interest required him, to carry his arms to the opposite camp. He was a staunch advocate of commerce against manufactures. In a short time, he was a vehement promoter of manufactures against commerce. He took up a cause as a lawyer takes a case. He talked all his powers to defend it and left the issue to fortune without anxious inquiry or care. On one occasion only he seemed to be deeply in earnest when he urged the democratic Autocrat to make war on South Carolina.

The speech of Mr. Binney was listened to with unbroken attention.[14] It is the only speech I ever heard in the house of Representatives of which this could be said except the speech of Mr. McDuffie on the same occasion. To every other on whatever topic a partial attention only was ever paid. Mr. Binney had the air rather of counsel speaking from his brief than of a Statesman or a politician discussing a party or political measure. His speech was a purely constitutional or legal argument and nothing more. It was not imbued with any portion of the ardour or vehemence that marked all others in the discussion. He seemed to me to be and to feel that he was out of his place. He laboured under the disadvantage too of being regarded or represented by his opponents as an advocate sent to Congress by the bank interest to make a plea in its behalf. The charge was false, but it was none the less believed and circulated on that account.

Mr. McDuffie's speech was the great speech of the House. He was always a favourite speaker. He was now the idol of the bank party. Its adherents overwhelmed him with attentions. He was not only the champion of the bank but had wrongs of his State to avenge on the President. He exhausted all his stores of invective on the man who had dared to threaten South Carolina. He ransacked history to find a parallel for the tyranny of Andrew Jackson and searched all history in vain. His delivery was as fervid as his language. He raged over the subject like an angry lion. His heart, soul, and whole

James L. Petigru. *South Caroliniana Library, University of South Carolina.*

South Carolina College. Scene from the 1830s. *South Caroliniana Library, University of South Carolina.*

Customs House, Charleston, S.C., during the 1850s. *South Caroliniana Library, University of South Carolina.*

Sarah Matilda Grayson, artist unknown 1830(?) *Collection of Henrietta Barnes Parker.*

strength seemed consumed by the fierce desire to annihilate the enemy of the Country's prosperity and the foe of his native State.

Among the men who took a prominent part in the Session of 1833 Mr. Benton may be mentioned not for any superiority in intellect or knowledge but for preeminence in violence, insolence, audacity and assumption. He had been many years before at feud with Jackson and had inflicted on his antagonist a wound that was never thoroughly cured.[15] He was now the greatest admirer and most devoted adherent of the President. Never was there military chieftain in civil authority better suited with lieutenant. They were alike furious against opponents and unscrupulous in reaching their ends. It was Benton chiefly who carried on the war for four months in defense of Jackson against the coalition of Clay, Webster and Calhoun. It was Benton who devised the expunging resolution and urged it for three years with the pertinacity of a blood hound. His mode of speaking was in keeping with his character. He was loud, boisterous, arrogant, contemptuous and insulting. He roared and paced to and fro as he spoke, like a caged tiger. He discussed a question before the Senate as he would have conducted a street fight. His single purpose seemed to be to knock down, and trample on his opponent. His book bears ample evidence of his character. He sees nothing in his adversaries but sinister motives and never views the success of a measure except as a party victory. His volumes of reminiscences betray inordinate vanity on every page. Yet the vanity is refreshing. It is the least repulsive feature in his character. There is something redeeming in it. It serves to vindicate his claim to be of kin with ordinary mortals. Mr. Benton was accustomed to boast that he never sought official station, that he had been offered cabinet appointments and rejected them all. Yet he certainly made every effort in his power to be placed over Taylor and Scott as commander in chief in the Mexican War. It is not easy to say what his visions of the future may have been had he succeeded in his wish. He believed that it was not military men like Caesar or Napoleon, who were the destroyers of a Nation's liberties. They find freedom already prostrated by the acts of politicians. They only reconstruct in a new form the order overturned by demagogues. Mr. Benton regarded the liberties of all the American people as strangled by the intrigues of Presidential Conventions controuled by corrupt party leaders. The right of the people to elect a president was gone. The American Republic was in the condition of Rome in the time of Caesar. The forms only remained. Mr. Benton asked to be placed in Caesar's position; might he not have dreamed dreams of playing Caesar's part? He could not have imitated the Roman in generosity or magnanimity, in genius as a warrior or Statesman, but in many things he may have surpassed his model in insolence, vindictiveness and a gross vulgar ambition.

These fierce debates were sometimes interrupted by solemn event. One of these was the sudden death of Judge Boulden of Virginia.[16] It became the duty of Boulden as successor of John Randolph in the Roanoke district to announce the death of the distinguished orator with the customary eulogies. The announcement had been delayed. The delay produced censure. The Virginians murmured. Boulden was mortified and excited. At last the day came when he was preparing for his task. The floor was conceded to him. The galleries were crowded. Mrs. Boulden was present with many of their friends. The successor of Randolph began a sentence of apology, hesitated, bent over the desk behind which he was speaking, lower and lower, fell on it at last with his arms extended and was dead in a moment. Business was suspended. The Houses adjourned. The next day Mr. Rives of the Senate did for Judge Boulden what the Judge had been about to do for John Randolph. The Senator announced the death of his friend with great feeling. He quoted a pathetic pasage from Burke saying "What shadows we are and what shadows we pursue." His hearers listened with emotion, attended the funeral with solemn heart and faces and the next day carried on the renewed din of wordy war as if nothing had happened to interrupt it.

Another death yet more lamentable in some respects startled the members of Congress not long afterward, on the first of April 1834 General Blair, a representative from South Carolina shot himself through the head and died immediately.[17] He was in a bedroom with Murphy of Alabama, opened a bureau suddenly, took a pistol from a drawer and discharged it before his companion sitting near him was aware of his intention. He was a man of great size, strength and courage, a match, it was said, in a fray for seven ordinary men. He enabled one to realize the possibility of those exploits which we read of when one man completely armed was able to put to flight troops of half armed and disorderly soldiers, when even the sight and shout of a hero could stop and turn the tide of battle.

The South Carolina delegation lost another of its members in a short time. Warren R. Davis was a man of society, of accomplished

manners, ready wit and pleasant humour. He was a general favorite
at home and abroad.[18] His wit never wounded. It was like that which
is ascribed to Sydney Smith. Davis' friends might have said to him
as was said to the canon of St. Paul's—you have been laughing at
us for years and yet nothing you have said has ever wounded or
offended us. His mind had a turn for poetry and might have excelled
in that kind of composition which is called verses of society if he
could have found time to cultivate the talent. But this he was rarely
able to do. One song of his writing was popular for a time in
Washington. The subject was the wife of Mr. Johnson of Louisiana,
a lady of great beauty and attractive manners. The song was an
imitation of "Roy's wife." I give the song as it will be new and may
be acceptable to many of my readers:

> Her voice was softer sweeter far
> Than winds o'er beds of violets blowing
> And bright her eye as Evening's Star
> In winter skies at twilight glowing;

The life of a member of Congress is not without attractions.
He goes to Washington with his country experiences and is amazed
to find how important a man he has become. Great is the deference
shown him in various quarters. Pages and door keepers bow down
before him and do his errands. He is a power in the city. He is the
dispenser of the public money not only to shops and boarding houses,
but to the body corporate. It depends on his vote whether the city
debts are paid, its streets and avenues improved, its public ground
enclosed and planted. His power commands respect. Society is open
to him. He is no longer the man he was in his native village. There
he played Sycophant to his people; here he is small divinity with
his altars and offers of incense. Yet there are some troubles. His
masters at home exact his services sometimes without much reason.
He is required to do many things each of which is impossible. Fifty
constituents want an office. There is but one to give. The successful
applicant never falls into the weakness of supposing that he has
received a favour; you have done your duty only and given the office
to the most deserving in giving it to him. The disappointed forty of
them become grumblers, perhaps enemies. Everyone of them can
demonstrate that his claim to the appointment is better than the
man's who received it. The disappointed has been treated unjustly

and the next election gives him the opportunity for revenge. The ministers of crowned heads are not alone in their experience of the difficulties of distributing office. The servants of king Demos are as severely tried as those of other princes. Then too there are accounts to be settled for constituents at the various departments and claims to be established, and patent rights to be secured, and wearisome speeches to be heard, day after day, and month after month and exhibitions to be witnessed of selfishness, petty vanity, vulgar ambition and mean sub-serviency to party. With all its attractions the member's seat becomes at times a seat of thorns. He is sometimes disgusted and sometimes annoyed with his honour. Yet he adheres to them with tenacity. I was one day assembling the long flight of steps on the west side of the capitol with a Southern member. We paused for a moment to take a breath. As we moved on again he remarked—this being a member of Congress is not so great a thing as it is commonly thought to be. Yet my good friend went home and at the end of his term moved heaven and earth to be sent back to his seat again. The passion for public life like the taste for narcotics is not easily subdued when once acquired. The feeder from the public crib is a lotos eater not to be weaned from his dainties without difficulty.

Independent of its attractions for a public man Washington is a pleasant place of residence. It is common to condemn its climate, but its climate is not worse than that of Baltimore or Philadelphia. It is not hotter in summer and not so cold in winter. The situation is fine. The scenery of the Potomac is beautiful, the public grounds are pleasant, the general Society is agreable and various. You see everybody. Travellers from abroad find their way there. The city is visited by all the distinguished men of the Country. The local society is refined and easy of access. There is less conventional form than any where else. The city has the advantage of an extensive library and good market furnishing supplies amply for mind and body. Its streets are spacious. The sneers on its magnificant distances have little weight with those who are not disposed to admire the closely packed blocks of houses in commercial cities with their narrow streets and filthy lanes. I would prefer Washington as a residence to the best of them.

But I speak of it as it was in 1835. The transient society at the time of which I speak was unusually brilliant. Miss Martineau was perhaps the most celebrated foreign contribution and Miss Walton, now Madame Le Vert, the brightest of our home productions.[19] Miss Martineau's charms were intellectual only. She was plain in figure and face and so deaf as to require an ear trumpet in conversing. It was a serious undertaking to talk with her in a room full of company. You took a seat at her side. She placed in your hand the trumpet formed end of a long flexible tube worn round her neck in the form of a boa. You spoke into one end of the tube and she applied the other to her ear with an expression of attentive expectation. It was a solemn sort of proceeding. Many of the company looked on in silence, curious to know what you would say to the female philosopher and prepared to criticise your attempts at entertaining her. There was this comfort in the adventure, the critics were exposed to criticism in their turn.

The other celebrity of the season, Miss Walton, was not known then as she has been since by her literary works. Her attractions were grace, beauty and fascinating manners. She was universally popular. I called with General Campbell of South Carolina to offer my homage with the rest of the world to the reigning divinity of the season. Her rooms were crowded with visitors. It was like the levee of a president's lady or the salon of a Parisian queen of Society. The visiter was introduced, exchanged a word or two with the lady and made way for others. A week or more afterwards I met Miss Walton and she immediately addressed me by name. I expressed my surprise that in the multitude introduced to her, day after day, she could be so prompt in remembering. She replied that she never forgot a name or face. It is said of an ancient king that he never failed to remember anyone of his numerous soldiers. The politicians of Rome cultivated the art of recalling the names and faces of the people and employed expert trainers to improve their skill and prompt their memory. Miss Walton's dexterity may have been the result of similar care. If the faculty of recollecting readily is important to the General and politician it is not less so to the belle. It contributes as much to social as to military or civil victories. One feels it to be a delicate flattery to be remembered at once. Our subtle self love imputes it to some merit of our own. Even when made aware that we are no more fortunate than the rest of the world, we find that the charm is not entirely lost. I have been the lady's admirer for life although I have never since had the honour of seeing her.

But time sweeps on and neither ladies nor members of Congress are exempt from its changes. Miss Martineau, her books and her boa are almost forgotten. Miss Walton ranks among elderly married ladies with children, I hope, as pretty and attractive as she was herself. I have long since been a stranger to Congressional life. It ended with me in March 3rd 1837. I saw Mr. Van Buren inaugurated on the 4th of March, a bright, beautiful but very cold day. We looked on with no congratulations at the success of the New York magician. Jackson went out of power with undiminished popularity. He had trampled upon all his enemies. He had transfered the purple to his favourite adherent. On his last day of rule, in a laboured farewell address in imitation of Washington, he congratulated the Country on its boundless prosperity and above all on its flourishing finances. It had all been the work of his hands. He had saved the people from the machinations of Biddle and the bank. He had placed their money in other and more honest keeping. The state banks were faithful and secure. Before the end of the year the boasted financial system was a wreck. The State banks stopt payment. Commercial ruin pervaded the Country and the Spring of unexampled promise ended in an autumn of universal disaster. I don't know how the veteran of the Hermitage explained the catastrophe. "Nick Biddle" without doubt was in some way the cause of the ruin. The wand of the "little Magician" had not been potent enough to controul the enemy. The result would have been different if the master spirit had continued to preside over the fortunes of the Republic.

The change of administration brought about many other changes. Mr. Calhoun and Mr. Clay, after fighting in the same ranks were foes again as I have said already. Mr. Van Buren from being a object of scorn and ridicule to South Carolina became her favourite candidate for the presidency. He had been painted as an unprincipled and crafty politician with no faculty but a fox's cunning and in four years he received the vote of the State for the chief magistracy. Was this the result of the New Yorker's astuteness? He perceived that the scheme of the independent treasury would divide his enemies; he suggested the scheme and divided them accordingly. The coalition was broken up and new combinations followed. But with all the changes and party alliances, the open enmity and hollow truces, with all their toils, schemes and speeches, no one of the great triumvirate in talent came any nearer to the coveted prize. The White House was tabood to Clay, Webster and Calhoun. It was open to Polk, Pierce, and Taylor.

According to the theory of Republics, the highest places in the commonwealth are the rewards of the most distinguishing virtue and ability. It was so at first in our practice. But now the most exalted station is the prize of the man who is most plastic in the hands of political managers and demagogues. How could the government go on when its forms only were left, when cupidity took the place of public spirit, when greediness for office and emolument became the sole principle of action with politicians of all parties, when members of Congress hungered after petty appointments, consulships in obscure places, clerkships in Washington, the merest old clothes of executive patronage. The rabble had come to rule. The Republic was at an end. This has been the substantial cause of the Country's ruin. The reasons usually assigned were themselves effects not causes. If the right men had continued to govern there could have been no tariffs to promote monopolies and no improper interference with the institutions of the States.

Chapter Ten

Collectorship Secession
Poinsett Hamilton Cheves

I left one field of public life to enter another. My friends procured for me the office of Collector for the port of Charleston, South Carolina. I went into office in August 1841. In a few months the time arrived when, according to the compromise act of 1832 the tariff would be reduced to the rate of 20 percent ad valorem and the protective principle abandoned. Four tenths of the excess of the old duty over twenty percent had been taken off under the provisions of the law; six tenths yet remained and were soon to be struck off at a blow. The change would be very great. The whole system had been a bad one. The biennial reduction for a succession of years served to embarrass importers of foreign goods and derange commerce. Their goods encountered the later importations at the lower duty. The whole scheme was odious to the manufacturers. They became alarmed at the near approach of something like freedom of trade. They combined as usual. They petitioned Congress. The Country, they said, was on the eve of ruin. By the Country they meant nobody but themselves. Their friends in Congress repeated the old arguments in favour of protecting American industry. Mr. Clay disregarded the obligations of his own compromise and the agriculture of the Southern States was again saddled with enormous taxes for the benefit of Northern manufacturers.

To reach their ends the manufacturers associated themselves with other parties. The advocates of high duties and the adversaries of negro slavery combined their forces. From small beginnings, the abolition party had become strong enough to hold the balance of power. In 1833 they began permanently to threaten the peace of the Country. An anti-slavery feeling pervaded the North. It was the spirit of liberty, equality, fraternity, modified to suit the occasion. It derived its existence from the false French philosophy of the eighteenth century. Mr. Jefferson a disciple of the French school arrayed its creed in trim phrases in 1776 and introduced it into the Declaration of Independence. In 1785 he engrafted it on the ordinance for the government of the North Western territory prepared by a Committee of which he was the chairman. The ordinance with some change limiting its application to the Country North of the Ohio was adopted in 1787 during the last moments of the old confederation.[1] The anti-slavery spirit of the ordinance found its way into the Senate of the United States in one of its earliest sessions. It came in the shape of a petition from the Quakers of Pennsylvania. The petition was received, referred, and put to rest by an adverse report. The spirit of intermeddling slept for a season. The time for success was not yet come. Adverse interest in the North stood in the way. The Northern people no longer sold Indians as slaves to the West India planter. They had excluded slavery by law from within their limits. But they still carried on a lucrative trade in negros bought in Africa for trifles and sold to Southern planters at high prices. This traffic tied their hands. But, in 1808, the traffic ceases. The North had no longer any interest in Slavery. They were free to begin a crusade against the Southern people for retaining the slaves bought from Northern ships. The abolition spirit became formidable enough twelve years afterwards to endanger the Union and to enable Mr. Jefferson to taste, in his retreat, the first fruits of his own speculations. The effect was not pleasant; it shook his nerves like a fire bell at midnight. The Missouri Compromise allayed the controversy however without any apparent injury to the Country present or prospective. But the spirit of Jacobinism, of liberty, equality, fraternity, grew on in secret strengthened, year after year, by the influx of myriads from the wildest broods of democracy in the old world.

At last in 1834 the abolition party reached the degree of boldness and strength that enabled it to take the last steps and bring the two sections of the Country to arms and a final separation. It began the war with a host of petitions for the abolition of slavery. The reception of them was objected to. The petitioners construed this into a denial of the right to petition. An outcry was raised throughout the Northern States. Its chief promoter was John Quincy Adams. He raved over the right of petitioning to do what he admitted the petitioners had no right of doing.[2] He presented petitions without number from men, women and children. Mischievous persons sent him petitions professing to come from Slaves. He presented them with the rest. It was throwing a firebrand into the house but to throw firebrands suited his tastes. A storm of indignation from Southern members followed. They demanded his expulsion. Furious debates ensued, but the old man kept his seat. He became the most enraged of abolitionists and waged unrelenting war on the South for the rest of his life. He was no friend of the Southern people before. They had defeated his reelection to the presidency. He was tenacious of public office. When driven from the chair of State he refused to observe the graceful custom established by Washington and followed by every other president. He was too much attached to the honours, or emoluments, or contentions of office to betake himself to retirement. He subsided from the White House to the House of Representatives but not to play the part of the man conspicuous for virtue and venerable from age and wisdom, ready and vigilant to disarm the violence of party and calm the tempest of factious strife, by the interposition of temperate councils. His part was to add bitterness and virulence to every dispute. No man was more acrimonious, extreme, or uncompromising. With much learning and long experience, he had acquired neither taste nor tact. His famous toast "Ebony and Topaz" illustrates his lack of both. The toast was given at a public dinner. No one present could conceive what it meant. Mr. Adams explained. The explanation was an apologue inculcating sound morals not unsuitable to his former office of professor at Cambridge, but for a dinner table before a large and mixed company as little fitted as a homily from an English prayer book.

At the time that I knew Mr. Adams in Congress he was over seventy years old. His head was singularly bald even for a man of his age. It was smooth, white and shining. When he rose to speak we who sat behind him could always tell, without seeing his face or hearing his words, when the passions of the speaker were thoroughly roused. His head afforded a certain index to his temper. The polished whiteness disappeared and a slight tinge of crimson suffused itself over the surface continuing while he spoke and fading away slowly after he had taken his seat.

It was said by Mr. Adams or by his friends for him, that if his petitions had been referred to a special committee at his suggestion he would have made a report adverse to their prayer in the strongest terms that the language could supply. It may be so. But such a report if made could have had no influence in permanently arresting the anti-slavery agitation The petitions were disposed of by a sort of compromise. They were received and laid on the table without being read. But the nuisance was no sooner abated in one form than it assumed another. It became a hobby on which politicians rode in to power. By its help men like Mr. Wilmot became notorieties who would not have been known otherwise beyond the limits of their States or counties.[3] The affiliated factions succeeded in gettting up a sectional anti-slavery, tariff party. All efforts to compromise and conciliate failed. Party platforms took the place of the constitution and of the Supreme Court. The demonstration was complete that Northern and Southern interests, sentiment and character were incompatible and their union no longer possible.

Again throughout the South the voice of indignant complaint was heard. The Southern people were resolved not to be the unresisting victims of Northern cupidity and Jacobinical misrule. The spirit of resistance grew stronger every year with the spread of abolition opinions. In 1850, the people of South Carolina appeared to be ready to oppose in arms if necessary what they held to be a violation of the constitution and an outrage on their rights. They no longer talked of Nullification, or a remedy consistent with the form of government, of a desire to preserve the Union. But they differed as to the mode of proceeding. Some were ready at once and alone to "cut loose" from the United States. Others equally convinced of the necessity of seceding deemed it due to the adjoining States to wait for their approval of the measure. The Southern States they said were equally interested, let the whole South act together. The State was divided into what were called Secession and Cooperation parties. The vote of the people was taken and it was decided by a great majority to wait untill the Southern States were ready to act in conjunction with South Carolina.[4] Of the nine election districts into which the State was divided one only, the district of Beaufort, Barnwell, and Colleton voted for the Separate Secession of the State.

I was opposed like many others to the dissolution of the Union and ventured to say so in a letter to Gov. Seabrook.[5] Who could tell what unknown and unmeasured calamaties might befall the whole Country if the Republic were broken to pieces? Many we could easily foresee, fortified frontiers between North and South, standing armies, immense expenditures, enormous taxes. A thousand evils besides, such evils as follow the dissolution of existing governments may lie in wait for us, lawless violence, pillage, the insecurity of life and property for years. We might fall into the disjointed condition of the Mexican provinces, always wrangling like ill conditioned curs, the tools and prey of military rulers, wretched at home and contemptible abroad. As to the single Secession of the State it seemed a folly too egregious for even boys of ordinary reflection to adopt seriously. Some of the most prominent leaders of the old nullification party advised the State to delay. Among these was General James Hamilton.

No man in Carolina had been more active or influential promoter of Nullification than James Hamilton.[6] Nature had fitted him in many respects to be a popular leader. He was brave, frank, of captivating address, with a happy combination of the courteous in manner and the resolute in action. His person was well formed, his face handsome, his voice pleasing, his smile singularly conciliating. He was restless and enterprising in disposition and thoroughly at home in the turmoil of political excitement. He had been the right arm of the Nullifiers; yet he advised delay. He addressed a letter to the people of Carolina counselling them to wait for the adhesion of their neighbours.

Another of the conspicuous men who advised the same course, in a public address, was Langdon Cheves, a Carolinian but then living in Georgia.[7] The opinion which he gave in favour of making the action of the State attendant on the action of the Southern States, he had always maintained. Twenty years before he had said that the wrongs done by the North to the South were enough to justify the Southern States in abandoning the Union. But the wrongs were common to them all and their action to resist the evil should be united. On returning to the South in 1831 from a long residence in Pennsylvania he was received in Columbia with distinguished honours. It was during the meeting of the legislature. The members and citizens of the town gave him a public dinner. The period was critical and intense anxiety was felt to know his opinions. He expressed them in a speech delivered on the occasion without reserve. He had no confidence in the creed of the dominant party. He regarded Nullification as revolution. He was in favour of revolution but of revolution by the South united and not by a single state. The views of so eminent a man were received with marked respect, although they satisfied neither party. He could not go with the Nullifiers because he differed from them as to "the mode and measure of redress." Still less could he side with the Union party since his principles and theirs were irreconcilable. The opinions expressed by Mr. Cheves in 1837, he again announced in 1850. They remained unchanged. As he had opposed Nullification so he opposed secession. They were equally revolution by a single State. His redress for the wrong complained of was revolution by all the South.

Mr. Cheves, as I have said before, was one of the heroes of Weems, the preacher, historian and travelling book seller, of fifty years since. Washington himself was hardly a more cherished topic than Langdon Cheves with the veteran hero worshipper.[8] He described his favourite as a little boy, a fair, flaxen headed lad, attending in the shop of a Country merchant on Edisto Island. The old preacher dwelt with delight on the youth's intelligence, resolute industry and gradual rise to the bar, to the legislature, to Congress, to the Speaker's chair, to unsurpassed popularity and reputation. And all this he would do in a sermon delivered with great unction from the text "God is love." Mr. Cheves himself was accustomed to talk with easy unreservedness of his boyish experiences on Edisto Island whenever he met an Edisto man in his steam boat trips from Savannah to Charleston. There was a wide interval between his first and last position, between the friendless boy and the wealthy citizen distinguished for honourable services in eminent public stations. The reminiscences of his early life appeared to give him pleasure and his auditors listened to them with great enjoyment. Mr. Cheves was surpassed by no man of his times, distinguished as they were for ability, in vigour and reach of thought. There was something of a marble solidity about him both in body and mind. His person was square, massive and strong, his intellect compact and equal to any demand in the affairs of life public or private. There was no surplus age about it, no inequalities. It was full, round and complete, totus teres atque rotundus. No man occupied a higher place in public estimation for practical ability, force of thought and soundness of judgement in public or private affairs.

Many others expressed opinions in some public form similar to those of Hamilton and Cheves. Among them were Bishop Capers and Mr. Poinsett. I was a fellow student with Bishop Capers in College.[9] He was "the merriest man within the limits of becoming mirth" that any College has ever known. He left his studies after a year's residence and began in early youth the life of a Methodist preacher. In his lively way he had been accustomed to imitate for us, in extempory addresses, the peculiar preaching of the Church which he was so soon to embrace and of which he became the ornament by the purity of his life and his singular eloquence.

Of Mr. Poinsett I had no personal knowledge. He had been the reputed leader of the Union party and was not ill suited for the place.[10] He was subtle and fertile in expedients, well acquainted with men and adroit in enlisting their interests to accomplish his ends. He was the father, I believe, of our State scheme of internal improvement. On his return from travelling in Europe he contrasted what he had seen abroad with what he witnessed at home. In Carolina there was not a road fit to travel. They were almost impassible in winter from mud, in summer from deep sand. The streams were encumbered with logs. Boats were snagged in the rivers, waggons by scores stuck fast in the roads. Mr. Poinsett set out to reform and improve, to make turnpikes, dig canals, open swamps and deepen rivers. He addressed a professedly private letter to Judge Johnson of the Supreme Court. Judge Johnson made the letter public as was intended. It was too important to be kept from the people. The diplomacy was not profound but none the less fitted to take with the State. The letter proposed a comprehensive scheme of road and river improvement. The scheme took like wild fire. Every District and Parish had its pet plan. One wanted a road constructed, another a swamp or river cleared of logs, another a canal dug, another a mountain gap converted into a highway. One scheme supported another. Mr. A voted for Mr. B's canal and B voted for A's road or swamp. Everybody got what he wanted. A gigantic system was constructed reaching from the swamps of the low Country to the Saluda gap. Mr. Poinsett took fortune at the flood and floated into official station and the State gradually recovered its senses after enormous losses.

Of all the grand projects which cost millions of money one or two only served any practical ends. The road over the Saluda mountain is still useful to travellers, and Wall's cut affords facilities to the Yankee gun boats for assailing Savannah, a purpose of which the projectors never dreamed. With the exception of these two, all the schemes were blunders. They failed in the execution or were found worthless after being finished. One may serve as a specimen of the rest. It was proposed to dig a canal through James Island to avoid the crooked and narrow parts of Wappoo creek and facilitate the passage of Steam boats by the inland route from Charleston to Savannah. The work cut off seventy acres from the tract through which it ran. The fee simple value of the land was about forty dollars an acre. The owner received one hundred and retained the land. He obtained seven thousand dollars as a compensation for the inconvenience of passing over the ditch in going from one field to another. The work cost many thousands beside. The cut was made wide enough for a steam boat, but it encountered a quicksand. All efforts to make it deep enough were fruitless. It now enables a planter's boat or a countryman's raft, at high water, to save a mile in their passage to Charleston. Many of the once popular projects are unable to do as much.

It was with this scheme as with all similar projects; it was difficult to get rid of the system when once established. Individuals of influence and communities became interested. A thousand plausible reasons were ready to prove that it is better to go on with what is begun than to throw away the money already expended. The result was to throw away, not the first only but the subsequent expenditures also. It was the public money that was voted away not the money of those who voted it and so to the thousands lost other thousands were annually added. The State has been building a new State house recently on somewhat the same principle.

To the exhortations of bishops and the addresses of retired diplomatists and Statesmen the bench added its words of counsel. Certainly no man in the State was better fitted to give advice in emergencies, than Judge O'Neall.[11] No man was his superior in purity of motive, quickness of perception and solidity of judgment. He was every way entitled to speak authoritatively on a question affecting the peace of the Country and the honour of the State. His life and character gave weight to his opinions with all temperate and rational men. He advised delay.

The vote of the State condemning as it did immediate and unsupported Secession allayed the popular ferment for the time. The peace of the Country was preserved. The election of "Poor Pierce" as the "Herald" was accustomed to call him, raised hopes of a sounder policy in the National councils, but his measures were unfortunate. The repeal of the Missouri Compromise was a specious but mischievous measure.[12] It gave a field to the abolition faction which they have not failed to cultivate. Pierce meant to do no harm. He wished only to stand well with what were called the Fire Eaters of the South. He took to them on the same principle or instinct that induces women to fall in love with their opposites. He hastened to conciliate the Secession Nullifiers by removing in their behalf all who had expressed any desire to preserve the Union sentiment in South Carolina. They had been unsuccessful in the effort and Pierce treated them as the English treated Admiral Byng after he had fought, without success in behalf of his flag. They shot him, executing one Admiral as the French said, to encourage the others.[13] I went out of Office with the rest of the Federal Officers in the State who had opposed Secession and were now obliged to make way for thorough going advocates of the opposite creed.

Chapter Eleven

Poetry and Poets

It was not unnatural that, becoming an idle man, I should betake myself to what Pope calls the "idle trade."[1] I resorted to writing verses. I was able to claim a resemblance to the translator of Homer, at least in one particular. I could say, as he did, "I left no calling for the idle trade, no duty broke, no parent disobeyed." I could say even more. I not only left no calling but my calling had left me and this desertion was with no consent certainly or approbation on my part. I could indulge in pen and ink therefore with a clear conscience so far at least as this class of moral obligations is concerned. I broke no duty, "disobeyed no parent," and abandoned no employment.

The primary difficulty in such cases is the choice of a fit subject. To select one constitutes the first step which, it is said, makes half the battle. The question of negro Slavery in the United States had been discussed for many years. It had assumed all garbs except the garb of verse. I thought the subject possessed aspects both of argument and description which admitted a poetical dress. In a broad view of the transfer of the African to America it may be regarded not merely as an act of commercial enterprise or avarice but as an emigration of the Black to a new Country. It was an emigration hardly more forced than that of the starving Irish peasantry and not attended perhaps with greater suffering. The negro was brought to a Country where he could be trained to those habits of industry which alone constitute the foundation of civilization and make it possible for a people to improve. The advancement of the Black in all relations, civil, social, or religious, must come from the White race. The negro has never been able to originate a civilization. The White man cannot live in the negro's country. The negro must therefore be brought to the home of the White. This has been accomplished by Slavery only. The benefits bestowed on the negro are obvious. The Slaves of North America are the most civilized of the African race. In Africa there is no Black tribe comparable to the four millions of Slaves in the American States. They have reached this point of improvement under the master's care. No matter what the motive, such is the fact. Nor has the motive been merely selfish. Many slaveholders have devoted disinterested efforts to the improvement of the negro race. Instead of the libels lavished on the masters of North America, the eulogies of the Christian world are due to them as the only practical friends of the negro. In the various aspects too of the negro's life, in his church, his cabin, his field, his amusements and occupations, there is room for poetic description. If the peasant's life any where admits this, why not the slave's. Strip the subject of cant and the negro Slave is the peasant of the Southern States as comfortable, as joyous, as picturesque as any other. I wrote on this subject in 1855 the "Hireling and Slave." It was published in Charleston by John Russell, was well received by the community and went through two or three small editions. But the reading circle of the South is a small one. They rather receive book fashions than impart them. It was suggested to me by those expert in the art of publishing, to try an adventure on a large field. By this time I had prepared for the press another work in a different form of verse combining descriptions of Southern scenery with Indian legends.[2] I proposed to a Northern publishing house to undertake the publication of the two pieces in a small volume. There were passages in one not complimentary to certain politicians of New York. The publishers after getting the book ready for publication became uneasy and requested to be released from the engagement. Party Spirit ran high at the time between Democracy and Republicanism, Buchanan and Fremont. The publication might injure the interests of the house. It was a mistake no doubt. The politicians would not have cared for such trifles as a waspish couplet. It was no trifle however to put at risk however small the chances of profit with a commercial partnership in the sharp competition of New York trade. I consented to relieve the parties from their apprehensions and lost the opportunity therefore of circulating among the great democracy, which the tact and appliances of the publishers might have enabled me to enjoy. In 1856, Mr. Russell published for me "the Country," a poem intended not so much to celebrate the charms of woods and fields, so often celebrated before, as to sketch the changes through which our continent has passed from the rude hut and small clearing of the first settlers, to the fields, meadows and orchards, the farm houses and country seats of the present occupants.[3] In 1860, I had a few copies printed of "Marion" an attempt to do in verse what Weems and

Simms had already done in prose for the famous partizan warrior of South Carolina who more nearly than any other of her sons approaches the ideal of the heroic character in courage, gentleness and magnanimity.[4] These publications yielded no money to the writer. They made a slender substitute or no substitute at all for the thriving calling that the chances of political life had given and taken away. It may with reason be asked why I continued to write. It was to have something to do. It afforded employment however unprofitable. Besides to write verses, to build the rhyme whether lofty or humble is in itself agreable employment. It gives pleasure to the builder at least whatever enjoyment the edifice may furnish to others. In this sort of work too, as in other things it is the first step that costs the most labour. Begin and you must needs go on.

Everybody reads poetry and talks of poetry and has his likes and dislikes among the poets as he has among his other acquaintances. I have mine with the rest of the world. My select friends are not of the new schools. I adhere to the old masters and their followers. I believe in Dryden and Pope, the nonsense of Bowles and his coadjutors and of Wharton [sic] before him to the contrary notwithstanding.[5] I have faith in the ancient classical models, the masters directly or indirectly of all the great poets of modern times. My taste is too antiquated to fall into raptures over the metaphysical sentiment of Shelley, or the renovated pagan deities of Keats, or the Hindoo mythological monsters of Southey. It was the fashion, at one time, to look upon old ballads as comprising the truest poetry of a people. They were hunted up in antiquated books and sought eagerly and received orally from the ancient men and women of the Country. The more uncouth the rhyme and language of the poem the greater was its excellence. This love of old ballads is like the love for old china, relics, or autographs from great men real or supposed. It is commendable within moderate limits only. They excite interest rather by their associations than from any intrinsic value of any kind.

The Sin of modern poetry consists in exaggeration of sentiment, of passion, of description, of every thing. It wants simplicity and truth. It seeks to be sublime and becomes inflated. It strives to be deep and is obscure only. It strains after the new and the wonderful and sinks into the grotesque and unintelligible. The modern poet finds the field of thought occupied and is driven to shifts and expedients. Like the first colonists in a new Country, the old poets appropriated all the choicest spots of the poetic region. The after comers took what they could find. The first adventurers occupy the highest places, with few exceptions, in narrative, didactic, lyrical, pastoral and dramatic poetry. Their fancy is free; their painting of nature and expression of emotion are simple and truthful. They were not tempted, like later writers, to overdraw a picture or tear a passion to rags that they may seem to say something new or striking. With the older poets of every nation, the closest adherence to nature was the highest novelty and the readiest as well as surest way to success in their art.

It is for this cause, among others, that the old Greek poets are and will continue to be models for all subsequent writers. The advantages of priority in the field together with unsurpassed perhaps unequalled genius secures to them an enduring superiority. They are the founders of letters, in every department, among all nations. We repeat the lessons learned from the Greek masters in poetry, eloquence, history and philosophy. There is in all the world substantially but one literature—the literature of Greece, modified from age to age but essentially the same in all times and places. In Rome the most celebrated writers were little more than translators. There is hardly an incident or simile in Virgil that is not borrowed from Homer. Horace has transfused the spirit of the Greek lyrics into his mother tongue. Among modern nations, France, England, Italy, Germany, Spain, we may trace Greek forms of thought and expression in every page of their poetry or prose. The language of science and art is derived from Greek. Even the Gods and Goddesses of Athens are still denizens of modern song. A hundred years ago the whole Greek mythology was engrafted into English and French verse. Even now we meet with Venus and Cupid, Apollo and the Muses, in company with the poets. In every other department of fancy or thought, the creations of the Greek mind are equally discernible. The advice of Horace to the aspirant after poetical excellence, that he should devote days and nights to the Study of the Greek masters, is as sound now as in the days of Augustus. They who do not pursue it are none the less indebted to the old models. They are only imitators of imitators. They drink from the stream if not at the fountain head. They are not removed from the class of borrowers because they take from those who borrow.

I have the misfortune not to sympathise strongly with the admirers of Wordsworth. They are numerous and zealous. It may excite their indignation to question the superiority claimed for their favourite. But there is no disputing about taste. I might as reasonably be indignant at their admiration. Their poet's fate had been a singular one. At first unreasonably depreciated and criticised, he has been since unduly exalted. Some of his adherents place him in the foremost rank of English poets. He belongs I think to the same class with Cowper and is not superior to the poet of Olney, hardly his equal.[6]

Cowper, it seems to me, has not only more wit, humour and pathos, but also more truthfulness and fidelity to nature. He paints her various forms animate or inanimate and all the scenes of social and domestic life with a more delicate hand and truer sensibility. Wordsworth appears to wander over banks and braes, by woods and streams, in the Spirit somewhat of a school boy hunting after a bird's nest. They have the same purpose of plunder; the objects only are different. One seeks verses, the other eggs; one looks after winged words, the other after half fledged nestlings. The poet's enthusiasm is mechanical, a part of the stock in trade of one whose sole object in life was to make verses. I said so once and was nearly annihilated by an indignant admirer who overwhelmed me with quotations to prove how much I was in error.[7] The quotations did not change my opinion. I thought the passages from the "Excursion" declamatory and rhetorical. To say nothing of the immensity of the plan, I could see no particular appropriateness in selecting a pedlar to play the part of moral philosopher. There was the example, it is true, of Dryden who makes hinds and panthers discuss theological questions while they walk in the forest. But Wordsworth was a stickler for the true and the natural and Dryden belonged to another and an artificial school. In the passages adduced by my angry friend from the minor poems I thought I saw in the poet an affectation of love for nature rather than the genuine sentiment. I am afraid that Peter Bell's regard for the daisy was more natural in its simplicity than that of the poet. Peter never thought of viewing the flower in its verse suggesting capabilities. To him it was one of nature's beautiful things only and nothing more. For Wordsworth it was a different object and had important uses. I may be prejudiced against Wordsworth's poetry by his shabby attempts to depreciate the writings of other poets. He not only made hypercritical remarks on Pope and Gray but devised a new art of poetry to degrade their verses and exalt his own. He betrays in all this narrowness of heart and head that is not usually associated with great genius. It belongs to men in the class of Wharton [sic] and Bowles. See how differently Byron

speaks of Pope, with what indignant scorn he overturns the Soph-
istries of Pope's assailants. He places the poet of Twickenham in the
most exalted station. He prefers Pope not only to his critics but to
all other English poets.[8] Pope comes nearest to the forms of classical
excellence. What existed before him in English poetry was a Gothic
cathedral; what has come after him is an Indian pagoda, or a Ma-
hometan Mosque; Pope's poetry is the temple of Greek proportions.
If Byron errs on the opposite extreme to his opponents, he is at
least nearer the truth than they are.

There was no cause or occasion for any new theories of poetry
except the cause suggested. Wordsworth thought certain poets, Hay-
ley, for example — formal, spiritless imitators. They were ordinary
poets without force or vivacity. The critic was not content to say
this. He thought it necessary because there were bad poets in his
time to tell the world that the whole poetic system required to be
reformed. But bad poets were not peculiar to the age of Wordsworth.
They are found in all ages. The Euphuists flourished in the times
of Spenser and Shakespeare. Milton lived among the Metaphysical
poets. Horace denounced the bad taste of some among his contemporaries. Yet Spencer made no effort to reconstruct the system of
poetry. Milton with all his reforms attempted no new theory in the
essential principle of his art. Nor did Horace in his "Epistle to the
Pisos" pretend to make any late discoveries. He only enforced long
established principles and precepts. There was the less occasion for
Wordsworth's voyage of discovery on a sea familiarly known to every
body, because there were poets of his own time as true to Nature
in the practice of their art as he was himself. What did he claim for
poetry that Cowper and Burns and Crabbe were not accustomed to
exhibit in their verses? There was no need for a discoverer in the
poetic world. Poetry has not been a lost art to be acquired and
taught anew. All we know of it had never ceased to be known for
two thousand years, and the man who professes to teach any thing
concerning it not familiar to the world long since runs no small risk
of being deemed a quack or something worse.

Let us see what the discovery amounts to. It relates to the
language and the subjects of poetry. The language of poetry, Wordsworth thinks, should be the common language of life and fit subjects
are to be found in the lowest classes of society. If by the common
language of life, he means language simple, idiomatic and direct, the
opinion is as old as Homer; if he means any thing else, his theory

is erroneous. The doctrine, as Coleridge hints, is trite where it is true and false where it is novel. So far as his creed is new, Wordsworth abandons his own principles in his practice. His diction differs in no respect from that of other poets since Dryden, except in single lines introduced, as Coleridge says, here and there to maintain his creed at the expence of his poetry, or in poems written expressly to illustrate his theory and which nobody reads but as curious specimens of false taste or crotchety speculation. Even where the occasion invites him to exemplify his doctrine by his practice, he neglects the opportunity. The pedlar in the "Excursion" who plays the part of moral philsopher ought to have talked, according to the poet's precepts, in the language of a travelling hackman. On the contrary he talks like a rhetorician or professor of ethics.

Johnson, in his "Life of Dryden," has a few sentences on the subject of poetic language which cover the subject more fully than all that Wordsworth and his school have ever uttered. "Every language of a learned nation,"[9] the great critic says, "necessarily divides itself into diction scholastic and popular, grave and familiar, elegant and gross, and from a nice distinction of these different portions arises a great part of the beauty of style. Before the time of Dryden there was no poetical diction, no system of words at once refined from the grossness of domestic use and free from the harshness of terms appropriated to particular arts. Words too familiar or too remote defeat the purpose of the poet. From those sounds which we hear on small or coarse occasions we do not easily receive strong impressions or delightful images; and words to which we are nearly strangers whenever they occur draw that attention on themselves which they should transmit to things. The happy combinations of words which distinguish poetry from prose had no existence before Dryden except with a few favourites of Nature. Dryden established the poetical diction of the English language." It has been the diction of all subsequent poets Wordsworth included. The sentences quoted from Johnson comprehend the whole philosophy of the subject.

There is another point in which Wordsworth's practice differs from his precept. While he denounces the artificial and conventional in poetry he indulges in elaborate invocations to the Muse, the most conventional of poetic forms. He adheres to the old pagan ceremony of addressing the goddesses of song when the ceremony has no longer any sense or significancy. The Roman or Greek poet might very well invoke the Muses for the aid which he believed they could impart, but what meaning has any such invocation in the mouth of a Christian poet? Why should he cling to the Muse when he has abandoned Jupiter and Juno and the other branches of the Olympian family? Why above all men should Mr. Wordsworth be solemnly reciting the old poetic form while he is proclaiming his abhorrence of the false and artificial in poetry? Can anything be more artificial or conventional than an invocation to the Muse?

The other branch of Wordsworth's discoveries in poetry relates to its subjects. These he thinks may be drawn from the humblest walks of life. But who ever doubted it? Men of all classes are of like passions and characters and are subject to the same chances and changes, joys and sufferings. All the poetry of Burns is derived from humble life. A large portion of Crabbe's comes from the same source. The whole body of English poetry is full of its influences. The reformer has discovered nothing new unless we understand him as meaning that the babblings of idiocy, or the grossness of composition as they are exhibited in "Betty Foy's son" and "Peter Bell" and "Alice Fell" or in Coleridge's "Ancient Mariner." If this be so I neither subscribe to the theory nor admire the illustration. The theory is condemned by a precept of Horace. He cautions the poet against making his images resemble a sick man's dreams.[10] But the dreams of a sick man would be more tolerable than the ravings of a madman or the drivelling of an idiot unrelieved by other characters or emotions. The examples contributed by Wordsworth to illustrate his poetic theory are admitted to be failures. No one pretends to admire the "Idiot boy" whatever opinion he may entertain of other parts of Wordsworth's poetry. The "Ancient Mariner" of Coleridge deriving its images from a similar quarter has been more fortunate. It has been very greatly praised and demands particular notice. I have tried to like it but have not succeeded. It is called wild and weird. It seems to me grotesque, strained and unnatural. It has a savour of opium about its stanzas. If it be the purpose of poetry to impart pleasure should the poet go to the disjointed talk of insanity in pursuit of images or sentiments? Who finds enjoyment in a lunatic asylum? The scene is one of horror. We may bear it to satisfy curiousity but not to seek pleasure. The plan of the poem is bad. The auditor in the story is a wedding guest. He is arrested on his way to the wedding by a madman and in sight of the house with the music in his ears and the light in his eyes, he stands and listens all night to a tale of the crazy stranger about the shooting of an albatross and the ills that came of it. In the morning the guest goes home a wiser and better man. How he should have become so under such an unseasonable bore, except in being taught a lesson of patience and self-controul, it is not easy to understand. If the meeting had been in some more opportune time and place, there might have been some probability to support the story. As it is, it violates all the proprieties to time, place and character. It is one of those tales to which the "incredulous odi" of the poetical canon becomes applicable. It never happened and never will happen that a wedding guest has been similarly arrested and instructed in wisdom and virtue. The story disregards the logic or common sense which Coleridge himself says is indispensible to every work great or small of prose or poetry. A greater authority than Coleridge said the same thing long before him. Common sense Horace declares is the fountain of all good writing.

The defect in the plan of the "Mariner" is not concealed by the manner of its execution. If the one disregards truth and probability, the other is revolting to ordinary taste. We are nauseated with the endless detail of hideous images — bloated carcases, putrid seas, rotting ships, ghosts that whiz through the air like the bolts of a cross bow, slimy, crawling, abominable things resembling nothing but the horrible shapes of a drunkard's visions when he is suffering under mania a potu or a too long indulgence in opium. If the rules of art forbid that disgusting things should be exposed to the eyes of an audience by a dramatic poet, the rules must hold good to a certain extent of unseemly images offered to his reader's attention by any other writer. The "Ancient Mariner" may be regarded as an experiment to try what can be made of a madman's delirious fancies in poetry and is as successful as any such experiment could hope to be.

The "Mariner" and the "White Doe of Rylestone" of Wordsworth are poems written on a preconcerted system to illustrate a particular branch of thought. Such poems are rarely successful. They are like verses made to order for particular occasions, like birth day odes and celebrations of current victories or achievements. Even Tennyson could make nothing of Balaklava's celebrated charge of the six hundred. The whole scheme of writing to illustrate a principle, a single passion of local superstition is essentially erroneous. It necessarily cramps the genius of the writer. He moves in fetters. He is like a musician who plays on one string of his violin. We may wonder at the dexterity of the performer but with the conviction that he would give us better music from the whole instrument. It may be doubted whether the department of thought selected to be illustrated by the "Mariner," the "White Doe" and "Christabel" is fortunately chosen. There is nothing in a local superstition that comes home to the general business and bosoms of men. The most beautiful creation of Superstitions fancy is that of the Greeks. They peopled the air, the woods and waters, with graceful divinities. And yet the least attractive part of the ancient writers are those that are devoted to their gods. We turn from the deities of Homer to his men, from the fury of Mars or the wisdom of Minerva to the wrath of Achilles, or the craft of the much enduring man, from the assembly and feast of Olympus to the incidents of the camp, the truce and the voyage in which mortals only are engaged. Jove and Neptune, the thunderbolt and trident, excite but little interest. What shall we say then of an attempt to make a mere local superstition, like that of the "White Doe," the staple of a long poem. It can make no way to the heart. It is tiresome and dull. A song of Burns, or Gray's elegy, imbued as they are with the common feelings of humanity are worth more than all the "White Does" and "Mariners" that could be written or conceived. These things are fancy fabrics that glitter to the mind but never touch the heart. They are curiosities, like insects in amber. They have a sort of prettiness. We gaze at them for a moment but never return to them. The line most frequently quoted in the "Ancient Mariner," "He prayeth well who loveth well" lies outside of the subject and derives its interest not from the superstition illustrated, but from a widely different quarter.

The reputation of Coleridge seems to me in all respects greatly beyond his merits. He had fine faculties, but they were lost in vague disquisition as a broad river is lost in a desert of sand. In the Latin epitaph on Goldsmith, Johnson says of his friend that he touched nothing which he has not adorned, nullum tetigit quod non ornavit; it may be said of Coleridge that he discussed nothing which he did not mystify and obscure. He bewildered the world with dreamy and incomplete speculations on all subjects. His whole life was spent in transcendental, unintelligible, talk. His friends listened by the hour to his monologue and went away asking each other what it meant. The desire to say something deep or new led him into constant exaggeration and perplexity "Blest as he was with all the power of words" his long array of imposing terms enables him to dazzle loose thinkers who mistake the unknown for the magnificent. He imposes on us a shadow for something substantial. With his "Subjective, objective and aesthetic, his thesis, mesothesis, antithesis, esemplastic" and other similar terms he involves us in a mist which enlarges every thing to gigantic proportions. The low, sandy, shore looms up into a mountainous territory.

I have heard Hugh S. Legare talk half sneeringly of what he called lyrical orations — the sort of oration common in the United States on the fourth of July. There is also a lyrical or rhapsodical criticism where the critic's head is always in the clouds and he talks in a kind of ecstacy of art and its miracles where clear conceptions and precise rules are swallowed up in a mystical jargon of rapturous superlatives. "They talk of their Raphaels, Corregios and stuff." Their phrases are magnificent but never intelligible. They reduce all previously received systems to chaos. They turn every thing topsy turvey. They no longer talk of the art of poetry. They tell us of the poetry of art, the poetry of painting, the poetry of sculpture the poetry of architecture. They declaim on an abstract art independent of any particular art and an intangible unexpressed poetry which is something apart from the written poetry of a language. We have heard of the poetry of painting as we hear of the painting of poetry. We have taken them to be figurative expression, implied comparatives of the branches of all. But no, they are not figurative. They are to be taken literally. The common every day notion of the art of poetry is merged in a vague shoreless sea of the poetry of art.

To this transcendental oracular school of criticism Coleridge belongs. His opening remarks in the lectures on Shakespeare furnish an example of the manner in which he perplexes what is plain and makes the clear obscure and unintelligible. He is one of those commentators who see a thousand meanings in an author which the author himself never dreamed of seeing. He declares that you cannot change a word in Shakespeare without spoiling the passage and yet no two commentators agree as to the poet's text. In similar humour he defines or describes Poetry as the proper antithesis not of prose but of science. Another writer of the same school talks of the poetry of art as distinguished from prose writing. What more is this than to insist on using words contrary to their common acceptation? According to general usage is not art the proper antithesis of science? Poetry is one only among the branches or parts of art and there is no poetry except figuratively but written poetry. Sculpture, painting, architecture, music, stand in the same relation to art as poetry. Each is the part only of a whole and the whole alone constitutes the antithesis of science. Coleridge makes one of the parts equivalent to all. He might as properly have made any other. If poetry is the antithesis of science, why not painting or scultpure, or eloquence, or history? No one art any more than the rest can be all art. They are sisters and equals in parentage and purpose. Their origin is the same — the imagination. Their pursuit is the same — to imitate nature. They differ in dress only. In one garb or form, the imaginative faculty becomes poetry; in another, oratory; in another, painting; in another sculpture; in another, architecture. The form of poetry is words in a certain order; of oratory words of different selection and arrangement; of painting, colours; of sculpture, figures; of architecture, variously proportioned buildings. The form or dress constitutes the sole discriminating feature in the family of arts. Their origin and purpose being the same if one art more than another is the antithesis of science, the antithesis must exist in the form only. The form of poetry is verse. But how is verse any more the antithesis of science than coloured or chiseled figures, the forms of painting and sculpture?

The distinctive form of poetry, the property that discriminates it from other arts must necessarily constitute a part of its definition or description. Poetry resembles painting and sculpture, in imitating nature, in the description and expression of passions or emotion. Like them it is an imitative art. It differs from them in the mode of imitation and form of expression. Its essential form is, not colours or figure, but words; not words only, but words in rhythmical order or verse. Poetry can as little exist without verse as painting without colours, architecture without buildings, music without sounds, or a man without a body. To omit verse in a definition of poetry is to omit its distinctive property. I have heard lovers of paradox, the men who define poetry the antithesis of science, speak of a passage in a novel, or a speech, or a history, as poetry, not figuratively but literally. They might as properly describe such passages as painting or sculpture. They call "Ivanhoe" a poem. It might with as good reason be called a picture or a statue. A passage in prose can no more be poetry then it can be painting, because the essential form of poetry and of painting are alike wanting.

Dr. Johnson, accordingly, defines poetry to be rhythmical composition and a poet, one who composes in a measure. This is the definition that common usage assigns to the term and common usage in all such questions is conclusive. It is the norma loquendi. It is the part of the lexicographer to ascertain and express it. The critics who would give to the word a vague mystical meaning to support a favourite theory reject Johnson's definition as common place and insufficient. Let us see what they offer in its place. They present us with a hundred substitutes, no two agreeing, and not one intelligible. Coleridge, as we have seen, defines poetry to be the antithesis of Science. The definition is a metaphysical puzzle. It is as clear as an ancient oracle. It may mean any thing the interpreter pleases. Another says that poetry is "the recollection of the best and happiest hours of the best and happiest minds"[11] — like "Don Juan" for example, or "Beppo," or Moore's amatory lyrics, or Ovid's "Art of Love," or "Anacreon," or the looser odes of Horace. Another writer tells us that "poetry is emotion recollected in tranquility." He might say the same thing with as good reason of painting or sculpture. Another says, poetry is the expression of passion. So is the angry altercation of two porters or fishwomen. There is in their performance no lack of passion or expression. In a different passage of his writing, Coleridge affirms that "to ask what is poetry is very much the same thing as to ask what is a poet." It is no nearer the same thing than a barrel is the same with the cooper who made it. There is as little resemblance between the "lofty rhyme" and "the builder of the lofty rhyme" as there is between a house and a house carpenter.

We may trace in the definitions quoted the source of all the mystification and confusion of thought into which their authors have fallen. Two of the descriptions confound poetry with its subject matter. "The "remembrance of happy hours," the "recollection of emotion," may supply topics for poetry but are not poetry itself. They differ from poetry as the raw cotton differs from the web or chaos from the planetary worlds for which it furnished materials. The last notion of Coleridge confounding poetry with the poet identifies the art with the faculty which produces it. He tells us substantially that poetry and fancy or imagination are very much the same thing. But imagination is not to be identified with one art any more than with another. The imaginative faculty belongs equally to all the arts as their common source. It would be as satisfactory to tell us that painting is the same thing as the painter, or music as the master who produces it; that Mozart resembled a waltz, or Wilson an English landscape. Besides imagination without judgment and taste makes no good poetry. The great poets are as remarkable for one faculty as for the other. The artist is very often the very reverse of his art. The best comic actors have been melancholy men and the tragic player and writer, like Garrick and Shakespeare, are often cheerful and pleasant, companions. In no sense then either in reference to the faculties exercised or to the person exercising them can there be any reason in Coleridge's arbitrary dictum that poetry and the poet are the same thing.

The theory that seeks to make poetry something independent of verse, nobody knows what, is the result of converting rhetoric into logic. The practice is common enough in more important matters. It is the error, Selden asserts, of those who believe in transubstantiation.[12] The Savior says of the sacramental bread, this is my body. The transubstantialist takes the expression literally and transforms the metaphor into a theological creed. We say of a highly wrought passage in an essay or oration that it is poetry. We mean only that the passage is highly imaginative. We compare it mentally with poetry. The theorist overlooks the implied comparison and turns the simile into a poetical dogma. It is common by a similar figure to call dancing the poetry of motion and the aspirant after the profound in criticism at the expense of the intelligible may contrive from the expression to form a system showing that dancing and poetry are the same art and that a lyric and waltz, or an epic and a country dance, are similar things. The poetry of motion, of painting, or architecture, like the painting of poetry or word painting, are metaphorical expressions only. To take them literally and make them support a theory is as reasonable as to insist on feeding a man with thistles because we called him an ass.

In like manner, as we say of imaginative prose that it is poetry, we assert of bad poetry that it is prose. We are not to be understood literally in one case any more than in the other. If we affirm of an imbecile that he is not a man, we are not to be taken as denying his claim to humanity. Though he be maimed, paralytic or bedridden in person and morally more deformed than General Butler of N. Orleans notoriety,[13] we classify him in the animal world as though he were hale, active, vigorous and possessed of humanity and truth. It is a question of degree, not of kind. We are not to confound two distinct questions. Whether a work is poetry is one question; whether it is good poetry is another. We must not identify these diverse inquiries. If we do we produce confusion only. We shall make poetry depend not on the essential nature of the art but on the capricious taste of the critic. What is poetry to one will not be poetry to another.

Mr. Bowles' sonnets were poetry to Mr. Bowles and Pope's "Essay on Man" verse merely. To Lord Byron, the sonnets were verse and the Essay, poetry of the highest order. "Who shall decide when doctors disagree." Adopt Johnson's definition, consider poetry as metrical composition, the expression of thought or emotion in verse, and all difficulty is at an end. Both sonnets and Essay are alike poetry, whatever any one may think of their respective merits.

There is no end to the chimeras of those who depart from common sense and common usage in their fanciful speculations. The literature of every language is divided by this common usage into its prose and its poetry. There is no difficulty in distributing the writings of a people in conformity with this division. You classify this book or that at a glance. The fanciful theorist arranges them differently. He makes a threefold division into prose, verse and poetry. What prose and verse are, he can contrive to describe. What his poetry is, as I have shown, he is utterly at a loss to tell. It is a certain subtle, unknown, essence that admits of no description. It is sometimes found in verse, sometimes in prose. A work may be a poem but it is not on that account poetry. There is a difference but what it is nobody can say. In all long poems, the "Iliad," the "Aeneid," the "Paradise Lost," nine tenths of the poem are not poetry. They are verse only. But where the poetry ends and the verse begins, who can determine, except by an appeal to individual tastes about which it is proverbially said there is no disputing. If the expression of all thought in verse is not poetry what then is the particular thought the expression of which makes the poetic art? Who can tell? One says nothing is poetry but the expression of passion. But his would curtail the poetry of every people of ninety nine hundreths of its poetical wealth. It is an arbitrary dictum without reason or authority. It is like saying that nothing is music but the "Messiah" nothing painting but the "Crucifixion," nothing Sculpture but the dying gladiator; nothing architecture but St. Peter's or St. Paul's. But the arts embrace all modes and phases of nature in their various forms of expression, in sounds, in colours, in figures, in building, in rhythmical words. The figure of a placid philosopher is as much sculpture as the Laocoon; an English landscape as perfectly painting as the Mater Dolorosa; a private mansion as fully architecture as St. Paul's cathedral; and Cowper's description of the drawn curtains, the bubbling urn, the cup that cheers but not inebriates as thoroughly poetry as Satan's address to the sun or the speech of Othello over his wife's dead body. All poems are poetry whatever may be their merits just as all men are men whatever the degree in which they are wise or virtuous.

The speculations of Coleridge are to be taken with many grains of allowance. They were borrowed or struck out by his dreamy intellect to give the zest of seeming novelty to an occasional lecture. His theory of poetry has found favour with fanciful minds, with poets especially eager to exalt their calling to make it something praeternatural, "a vision and a faculty divine," an inspiration, a communing with what they call the Muse. There is not a word of reason whatever there may be of rhyme in all these extravagancies. The writer of verses, the composer of poetry, the inventory of rhymes is a very pains taking individual and works as hard at his trade as any other intellectual labourer, whether Essayist, historian, or novel writer. The ecstacies of the poet are for the most part conventional. He toils after thoughts, words, and images. Sometimes they come readily. Sometimes they refuse to come at all. His tools are pen and ink. His inspiration is the same as that of every other mental workman, the excitement of thought. It is nothing more. If there is any other imspiration it comes from homely sources. I am disposed to believe that the only water of Helicon Byron ever drank in writing "Don Juan" was the gin and water he used on the occasion. If the reader has any doubts as to the toils of the poetic tribe, he has only to refer to the recorded experience of every poet, to the manuscripts blotted, interlined, rewritten, like those of Pope a copy of which is given in Johnson's life of the poet. To many writers the labour is always irksome, taken up reluctantly and laid aside with alacrity. Johnson counted the lines as he went on to see how near he had got to the required number. A friend called on Goldsmith to invite him to a walk. Yes! he was ready. He had written two lines of the "Deserted Village" and was glad to run away and reward his diligence with a ramble. Sydney Smith says that Rogers, when he had been delivered of a couplet, went to bed, ordered the knocker tied up, and had it announced to inquiring friends that he was as well as could be expected. Byron with all his facility was continually annoying Murray the publisher with alterations in his verses. If the reader still doubts let him turn over the pages of the "Epistle to the Pisos" the Art of Poetry. Examine the precepts of the writer. He was himself a poet and in his odes magnifies his art with the usual conventional rhapsodies. But his precepts to the young poet tell a

different story. The master teaches the aspirant that he must work
diligently, discipline his mind with care, select his subject and prepare
his materials with judgment and assiduity. He must consult sound
sense, "sensus communis," and not deal too freely in horrors like a
sick man's dream or a lunatic's raving; the incredulous reader will
hate such disjointed images. He must choose the branch of his art
that suits his genius best; he must polish his verses with attention
and not spare the labour of revision. He must correct again and again
for seven years before he ventures to present himself to the people
or the booksellers. Not a word is said of the Muse's help, nor a hint
dropt of Apollo or the winged horse, nor of the advantages that
might be derived from the Pierian Spring a famous watering place
of old for Greek and Roman poets. The conventional ecstacies and
raptures of modern composers in verse are the dregs only of older
and different modes of thought and expression. These writers are
not yet quite emancipated from poetical paganism and certain intellectual fashions that existed two thousand years ago in Greece
and Rome. They will not realize the fact that the poet is not a high
priest of the nine nor a priest at all, but a framer of verses, a dealer
in pen and ink, a mental labourer with faculties that differ from
those of other men in degree only and with materials in the moral
and physical world familar to all mankind. If it were not so the poet
could command the sympathy of his readers by no device. He expresses to the multitude their thoughts and emotions. He furnishes
the winged words which the people cannot arrange as he does for
them in measured form. This is true of the whole range of poetry
from the epigram to the epic. There is no mystery about it. In all
its almost infinite forms, pastoral, dramatic, lyric, didactic or narrative, poetry expresses the thoughts, emotions, fancies, of the human
heart and mind in measured rhythmical lines and is most successful
when it comes most home to the common heart.

It may seem a waste of words to bestow so many on a fanciful
and false speculation. But the false is never insignificant. It is not
merely evil in itself, but begets evil consequences. It is so with vague
poetical theories. They lead to mischievous results. From the creed
that poetry is a mystical art, an inspiration, a communing with the
Muse, a vision and faculty divine, an indescribable something no one
can tell what, comes the tenet that poets are a mysterious race of
a particular moral nature different from the rest of mankind and
not amenable like other men to a just judgment for their offences.

If they are licentious or sensual, addicted, like Byron to gross amours, or like Coleridge to much opium, or like Burns to abundant whiskey, it is their stars, not they, that are to blame. When they go astray they are led by the light that burns within them and the light within them is light from Heaven. They are mortals of a peculiar temperament. A certain modification of character, a petulant, impulsive, sensitive, excitable turn of mind constitutes the poetic nature. We adopt the notion readily. It feeds our appetite for wonders. But there is not a word of truth in the notion any more than in the theory that produces it. The wounded vanity of the poet, his peevish complaints and outbreaks of resentment are open to the world's observation; that is all. He proclaims them. The anger or violence of other men may be greater and more frequent but passes unseen by the world, or without its notice. There is no peculiarity of temperament incidental to poets. There is as great diversity of character, temper, disposition, among a given number of the singing fraternity as can be found among the same number of persons in any pursuit of life. It is idle to reason theoretically on such a subject when we have facts in abundance from which we can draw certain conclusions by an easy induction. To do this with the greater exactness let us take the poets whose lives and characters we know best—the poets of our own language. The two first of great name, Chaucer and Spenser, like other able men of their times, were courtiers and men of affairs, not unskillful in conciliating the great and advancing their own fortunes. If they resembled each other it was not in petulance and irritability. They were as conspicuous for amiable temper and purity of character as from brilliant fancy and fertility of invention. Of those that follow there are no two alike. What resemblance is there between Ben Johnson and Shakespeare, or Milton and Dryden, or Pope and Thomson, or Prior and Young or Goldsmith and Gray, or Burns and Beattie, or Scott and Wordsworth, or Southey and Coleridge, or Byron and Cowper, or Moore and Crabbe, or Savage and his great Biographer?[14] Among the poets named, and the list may be extended indefinitely, there is found every diversity of manners, moral character, tastes and modes of living. They include the rude and the refined, the frank and the reserved, the bold and timid; the active and indolent, the austerely virtuous and the dissolute, the delicate and the sensual, the manly and the effeminate, the generous and the selfish, the careless and the provident, the social and the secluded. Is there any greater diversity between an equal number of lawyers, doctors, divines, farmers, merchants, mechanics, or gentlemen at large? Johnson and Shakespeare were alike in writing plays and in nothing else; one exhibited in his manners something of the campaigner's roughness and the pedant's arrogance, the other all the gentle and genial influences of a "Midsummer Night's Dream." Milton was almost an ascetic in life and his poems are as pure as his living; Dryden was loose in principle and prostituted his genius to the libertinism of his age. Pope was restless, querulous, exacting, captious and spiteful; Thomson a proverb of lazy self indulgence and easy good nature. Prior was an active man of the world of tact and skill in public business with lax morals and a loose muse; Young, a sombre recluse expounding in gloomy verse sin and sorrow and the judgments and punishments of another world. Goldsmith was the most careless, reckless, thoughtless and thriftless of human beings; Gray's whole life was one of perfect and somewhat prim propriety. Burns was bold, impassioned, jovial, sensual; Beattie, in all things the reverse, inculcated piety and ethics by diligent precept and exemplary practice. Scott and Wordsworth are antipodes; one frank, open, mingling with the world and actively sympathising in its pursuits or amusements; the other occupied all his life, with himself and his poetry. Southey's life was a model of exact conduct and incessant systematic labour; Coleridge sauntered through his whole existence and never by any accident performed a duty, talking eloquently of domestic love but leaving others to perform its offices to his wife and children. Byron's life was a tempest of passion and excitement; Cowper's a calm of quiet and unbroken seclusion; one was a reveller, the other, a hermit; one defied the world and made war on it; the other shrank timidly from its notice; one handled the dread topics of life and immortality with dauntless audacity, the other trembled as he reverently touched them. Moore was at home only in a drawing room; Crabbe only in a parsonage. The first lived to entertain the great and fashionable with music and song; the last to observe and describe misery in the streets of boroughs and villages. Savage was a profligate vagabond and spent his whole life in bullying his friends for money which he received without gratitude and spent in coarse indulgences; Johnson's sturdy manliness vindicated his independence even when dinnerless and spurned the patronage of a Lord when indelicately offered after it had been carelessly withheld. These men had no taste, pursuit or property in common except the faculty of writing verse. It is said that poets are vain; there is more self conceit among the coxcombs of a single drawing room than among the whole clan of rhymers. They are charged with being petulant and quarrelsome. They are not more irritable than other writers. Who will pretend that poets have as much irascibility as theological disputants, political pamphleteers? or Newspaper editors? Scott never answered a criticism on his writings; what son of Calvin, or Caxton can say as much?

Moore in his life of Byron rests an apology for the vices of his friend on this received theory of the poetical character. He thinks there is something in the poet's temperament that tends to make him a profligate. The poet's vices, he says, are shadows cast from the eminencies of his genius and great in proportion to the heights from which they come. His own Fedladeen never talked more solemn nonsense. Are we to believe that Chaucer, Milton, Spenser, and Shakespeare were the four greatest rascals of their tribe? They are among the purest as they are the brightest of their craft. Are Savage and Churchill the most lofty in genius? The height, Moore tells us, is great in proportion to length of the shadow that falls from it and S & C were certainly among the greatest blackguards of the poetical brotherhood.

Whatever vices may beset a poet they have no more to do with his ability to writer verses than the length of his nose or the colour of his eyes. It would be as rational, perhaps more so, to ascribe Byron's licentiousness to his deformed foot than to his genius for poetry. He was a profligate with few scruples; but hundreds of Byron's time who never wrote a stanza were greater profligates than he. Shelley played the fool or madman in assailing the religious faith of the civilized world and illustrating his ethical substitute for Christianity by the abandonment of his young wife to insanity and suicide, but he was not sillier or madder than Tom Paine who was equally an infidel without forming a rhyme and whose practice was a long course of vulgar licentiousness. Burns drank whisky inordinately but not more inordinately than the Campbells or McGregors of the land of Cakes who joined him in his tavern revels but never invented a couplet. These poets had vices and follies, not in common with poets, but with other immoral men. In a word the genius for poetry has no necessary connection with any peculiarity of temper or modification of moral character. It is found united with every variety of virtue and vice from the coarsest sensuality to the greatest purity. The loftest genius is generally the best man. The four greatest names of English verse, Chaucer, Spenser, Shakespeare and Milton, were men of morals. Spenser, the most imaginative of poets was of simple, gentle nature and stainless reputation. It is worse than idle to tell us that when the poet indulges in wine or whiskey or profligate amours he is led astray by light from Heaven. The light comes from another region. The writer of verses is entitled to no immunities for cultivating sensuality. There is nothing in his verses whatever they may be than can authorise or excuse his violation of the great laws on which the welfare of society depends. The best songs are the crackling of thorns under a pot compared with the interests of truth and virtue. If it were true that poetic talent is necessarily connected with licentious living or has even a natural leaning towards it, then Plato certainly had good reason for banishing the whole clan of singers from his Republic. But it is not true in spite of Tom Moore and his elaborate speculation to prove that men of genius are unable to behave with the decorum of ordinary men. Was not Scott living before his eyes to give the lie to his theory? Was there a dunce in the kingdom superior to the author of "Marmion" in any relation of life, as son, husband, father, friend, neighbor, or citizen?[15] Even Moore himself, notwithstanding his peccadilloes, behaved for the most part as decently as if he had been dull enough to be an alderman or a Lord Mayor. He had grace sufficient to be ashamed of the lyrics of Little and Moore. His loves were only imaginary and his greatest temptations a fashionable drawing room and its flatteries for which he was always too willing, it is said, to leave his wife, poor Bessie, at home. Byron would have scorned the cant of Moore's apology. He had no nonsense in him. He knew that his excesses were the results of ill governed childhood and unrestrained passions, and had nothing to do with his genius except to weaken even when they served to prompt and direct it. He would have despised and ridiculed Moore's ethical creed as he despised the false poetical theories of his day and the pitiful attempts of Bowles and his clan to disparage the poetry and character of Pope.

Chapter Twelve

I have now reached the great event of the age—the dissolution of the North American Republic. The convention of South Carolina met in Charleston and ordained on the 20th of December 1860, that the State was no longer a constituent part of the United States. Other States, Mississippi, Alabama, Florida, Georgia, Louisiana followed the example in January, and Texas in February. The Southern Confederacy became at once an accomplished fact. A convention composed of Florida, Georgia, Alabama, Mississippi, Louisiana, Texas and South Carolina, assembled at Montgomery, on the 11th day of February, 1861.[1] They formed a constitution, established a provisional government and invited the cooperation of the remaining Southern States. Virginia, North Carolina and Tennessee soon gave in their adhesion, the first in April, the two last in May. Missouri and Kentucky followed but with more doubtful councils and a divided people. I witnessed the death of the great Republic with sorrow. I was born with it and I survive it. It seemed to me an unnatural event for an individual to be longer lived than a powerful State. The causes of discontent were grave and numerous. The policy of the Federal government had been adverse for years to the interest and rights of the Southern people. Their agriculture had been sacrificed to Northern manufactureres; their social condition had been made a target for the persistent, scurrilous attacks of the Northern press and pulpit; the comity common among unassociated communities was refused by one confederated State to another. Less insult has often produced war between nations. But something is to be borne under every conceivable policy. We found evils in the Federal government but there are evils in all governments. Selfish and unprincipled rogues had obtained possession of the halls of Congress and the Executive mansion but one does not burn his barn because it is infested with rats. We have suffered wrongs but a great Country, etc. We have a right to withdraw from the Confederacy but it is not always necessary or expedient to exercise a right although it may be a certain one.

We were defamed and libeled by Northern sentiment but nothing is so mutable as popular opinion. Fifty five years ago the Southern planter traveled through the North with as many of his servants as he wished without a whisper of objection or remark, fifty five years hence he may do the same thing. Opinionum: A government is not established for a generation or two only. It is not as Mr. Burke tells us like a temporary partnership for the sale of calico spices or tobacco to be formed or destroyed by the capricious will of the partners. It is to be treated with other reverences.[2] Time brings many changes in public sentiment. False opinions are not enduring opinions. Our Southern people were less patient. They had a feebler faith in time and truth. They spurned the cold caution and had no sympathy with the procrastinating scruples of age. It is easy to persuade men to fly to revolution even when they have no good cause for complaint; how much more easy when they have. To be better governed the South resolved to abandon the Union and to govern themselves. Up to the time of decision it was the privilege of every citizen without reserve and I used the privilege to express his opinions; after the decision it was equally his duty to adhere to his State. He owed no allegiance to the Federal government. He owes allegiance to the Sovereign power, to the State alone to which he belongs. This Sovereign power has the right to change its government. The maxim has been universally received in the American Republic and never denied except where interest or passion required the denial. It matters not what the act may be called, Secession, Revolution, Rebellion, the name in no wise alters the thing — the principle that every people has the right to govern itself; a principle which constitutes the foundation of all American governments since 1776; a right which, whether wisely or unwisely exerted, belongs to every free, sovereign, independent State and to which every citizen is bound to submit.

Could the revolution have been avoided in 1860? Perhaps it might have been if the government had been in able hands. Macaulay says "we know of no great revolution which might not have been prevented by compromise early and graciously made."[3] "No wise ruler," he adds, "will treat the deeply seated discontents of a great party as he treats the fury of a mob which destroys mill or power looms." The wise ruler conciliates. But rulers are rarely wise, the Republican party rulers least of all. They equalled Lord North in arrogance if in nothing else. They stood upon their dignity. They refused to listen. They scorned conciliation; they disdained compromise; they ridiculed the discontents of great States; they resolved on force and were met with defiance and revolution. You cant make a piece of timber out of a bundle of sticks. But admitting the right to change their government, was the change expedient? We say it was for her [the South]. What unprincipled writers we find them to be, setting all principle aside, trampling on the rules of civilized war, on humanity. But we have put it in their power, we have armed them for evil. We look to the future prosperity of the Country. It was already prosperous.

It rarely happens in any quarrel between states or individuals that one party only is in fault. The present quarrel is hardly an exception. There are men, South as well as North, who used Slavery as a trumpet to excite sedition, who desired a dissolution of the Union and seized on slavery as the readiest means to bring it about, who sought a cement for party union and found the negro the strongest within their reach. In both sections of the Union were short sighted men striving to avoid slight or imaginery evils by rushing into others of incalculable magnitude. In both were heated shallow partizans scoffing at dangers because their limited faculties were unable to perceive them. The carnage, the desolation, the destruction of property, the enormous public debt, the insupportable taxes, the standing army, the fortified frontier, the ruin that awaits all parties, were beyond the reach of their feeble vision. They were eager to sever the Union because they saw nothing more in the act than their own personal advantage. Are these men without blame on the South side any more than on the North side of the Potomac? The verdict of impartial history will be that of guilty for both.

But although conciliation "graciously and early made," or wiser and more moderate political leaders may have enabled the Republic to escape the dangers of 1860, no conciliation perhaps or effort of human wisdom could have prevented the ultimate separation of the States. Division must have come sooner or later. To suppose that a continent already divided into thirty four States, with a perpetually increasing number, each State with its separately organized government complete in all its parts with its independent treasury and army of militia — to suppose that a continent of States so constituted could remain forever united and at peace within itself would be to believe in a North American millenium, in a miracle not vouchsafed heretofore to any portion of the human race. The successful building of a tower of Babel would not be a more wonderful event. There is nothing in our own short history, to say nothing any other that would justify such idle expectations. It had been difficult to unite the thirteen States in 1787. The signs of future dissention may be seen in the debates of the convention that formed the Union. They naturally led in time to discord, disputes and mutual abuse. The way for separation grew broader every day. The partnership became hateful. It had served its purpose apparently and lost its value. The animosity grew so strong between its parties that even a peaceful separation was no longer practicable. War has ensued, a war sought by the abolition party for sinister purposes, approved by Northern capitalists to preserve commercial advantages and pursued by contractors, speculators and politicians for their several selfish ends.

It has thus become the lot of our Country from whatever cause to exhibit to the world another example of human folly and madness and to prove by our conduct that the religion which enjoins on its disciples to love their neighbours as themselves has but little influence on its professed disciples. We still show our love, like the veriest heathen by cutting our neighbour's throat and setting fire to his homestead. Christian pastors preach crusades of hatred and carnage to their flocks. It is common to talk of the laws of civilized war, but it is not easy to show any substantial abatement of its horrors. We no longer eat our prisoners, it is true, nor take their scalps, nor build pyramids of their skulls, but war is none the less a combination of robbery, arson, rape and homicide. Every year invents some new weapon to tear, crush and destroy, that would do honour to the ingenuity of the devil. I suppose indeed he is fully entitled to the honour. The inventions are no doubt of his suggestion. I have heard plausible discourses on the advantages of war public and private but have never been able to see them. If I am told that men are so prone to brutal violence that wars and duels will never cease I can understand the proposition and assent to it. If it is said that Providence brings good out of the evil I can believe that also. But to assert that there is something beneficent in public or private war to society more than in robbery or murder is to insult common sense with idle words. War is the greatest curse and crime of nations. A great victory, an English Field Marshal says, is the greatest of national calamities except a great defeat.[4] Few I suppose think otherwise who have gone over a field of battle after the conflict is ended or seen the sorrowful faces produced by it throughout a Country. For this great calamity, this crime of War between North and South,

Northern people are chiefly chargable. The cupidity and intermeddling spirit of New England were the main causes of dissention. Her greedy tariff exaction, her perpetual irritating interference with negro Slavery in the Southern States, her avaricious monopolists & political priests sowed the seed of which we are reaping the natural harvest. If ever a people wantonly destroyed their own prosperity it is this people of New England. They are accustomed to call the brain of New England the brain of the Union—it is the brain of a lunatic who cuts his own throat. No chain of cause and effect in all history is more clearly traceable than the destruction of the Federal Union by Northern folly and madness.

But is the North alone culpable? Is the South altogether blameless? We say we are but I doubt it. It was the moral vanity only of R[ousseau] and B[oswell] that arrayed revelation of their vice and meaness to the world. They see the relevancy of vice and meaness by R & B from nothing but moral vanity and they feel for the violators no sentiment but contempt.

Wars are the results of ambition, the caprice, the real or supposed interests of rulers. It [war] is hideous in all its aspects. It demoralizes as it destroys. Our fancies dwell on war in its pomp and circumstance, its parade and pageantry, its gorgeous displays and triumphal processions. We view it as Louis 14th viewed it when he visited his camp with his courtiers and left it for Paris before the brilliant array has been deformed by the havoc of battle. We never think of the inhuman ferocity, the field strewed with dead and wounded, the mutilated bodies and garments rotted in blood, the putrid carcases and sights too hideous for human eyes to look upon. We pass over unregarded the ravaged fields, the burning houses and the wretched women and children driven from their homes to starvation and despair. Nor do we remember that it is not the ferocious passions only that war engenders and nourishes; it nurses into rank profusion all the meaner propensities and appetites, servility, sensuality, treachery and greediness for gain. It gives opportunity to the base, to extortioners, thieves, and speculators. The rage for office is increased. The scramble never ceases. All parties, high and low engage in it. The noisy and clamorous always the least fit to hold office are commonly the most likely to obtain it. The man of merit stands aloof. He has a proper self respect. The impudent pretender shoulders his way through the crowd and succeeds in proportion to his impudence. The maxim of which we sometimes read in books that office should be given to the honest and able only is never heard of in practice. The man who courts authority by petty arts is the applicant who obtains place for himself, his sons, his kin and dependents. Patriotism means an eager devotion to the cause of the loaves and fishes. The patriot is one who ardently desires and solicits emoluments and honours. Disinterested service to the State is almost a myth. To suggest another of superior merit for office, to promote the public good by aiding to put the right man in an important place, to distrust one's own ability for any employment that can be got, never enters into any man's imagination. The sarcasm of Sydney Smith on Lord John Russel [sic], that his lordship would undertake at a moment's warning to do anything—to command the channel fleet, to operate for the Stone, to solve a difficult problem in the higher mathematics, to write an epic poem—with no distrust of his ability to do either, is a sarcasm equally applicable to multitudes of applicants for office in all times of ordinary war. Every office seeker is a Lord John Russel. This is the sort of man which war engenders abundantly and to which it gives opportunity and success.

Our present experiences in the nature of war have not changed our opinion of its evils, of its greater crimes or meaner vices. Its terrible destruction of life and property meets us every where; its baser arts and acts are not less obvious. The sycophancy, the impudent pretension of men without merit on the one hand, the want of judgment, impartiality and caution in bestowing office on the other, have been open, glaring and disgusting. Why has this man obtained an appointment, it is asked. The reply is that he is the son, or brother, or nephew of some one high in office, or he went to school with the President, or he is recommended by some popular politician of a certain State, or any other reason is assigned except the one that ought alone to govern—the fitness of the party appointed. One class of applicants for office were especial favourites. The officers who resigned commissions in the Federal service, civil or military, were sure of easy access to the Executive ear. The resigning sufferers were like the disciples when they said to our Lord—Behold we have left all to follow thee, what reward shall we have therefore? Like the disciples, the modern inquirers received much more than they abandoned. The Captain became a Major; the Major a Colonel; the Colonel a Brigadier or Major General. The graduates of the West Point Academy were also a favourite class. The man who had been to the Federal school forty years before, though he may have learned little while there and had forgotten every thing he learned, was assumed to be a skillful engineer and able commander. Forts were built by such men in improper places; defence was attempted at points not defensible, cannon were put in position only to be withdrawn, or, still worse, to be spiked and abandoned with a loss of the troops who manned them. West Point had made President Davis a great military chief and he was injudicious enough to infer that the school had been equally efficacious with all its graduates. These are the inevitable evils attendant on all wars in various forms.

But if such are the evils of all wars, still worse are the mischiefs of revolutionary wars. If the ordinary warfare between nations is a crime and curse, civil wars are doubly crimes and curses. They are not crimes only, they are mistakes, pernicious blunders that do nothing but destroy. If they fail, they damage the cause they pretend to sustain and if they succeed they acquire nothing which time and advancing civilization would not more surely impart. This is true of all revolutions when they are carefully examined. We declaim on the revolution of the Netherlands and the virtues of William and what is the result? Seven provinces succeeded in the attempt; the rest failed. What is the difference now between Holland & Belgium – the States that succeeded and the States that did not succeed. They are both petty monarchies, one quite as prosperous as the other. To what is the prosperity of one or the other due – not to the success of the revolution or its failure but to the gradual advance of civilization in Europe. The success of Protestant States in vindicating their religious opinion by army added nothing to the freedom of religious opinion – the government changed and Catholic and Protestant were bigoted alike. Religious freedom is the fruit of subsequent general progress. The ambition of the Duke of Maganza [Braganza?] made Portugal from a province of Spain to a petty monarchy. What has she gained by the change? She ceased to be a great province of a great kindgom to become the dependency of a foreign power. Can we see any thing in the movement but the ambition of an aspiring noble or any permanent effect favourable to the people of Portugal? But the field is so wide. Let us circumscribe our view. Let us confine it to our own Continent its recent experience. The evils to the States resulting from their revolution would have been vastly greater but for the fortunate adoption of the Federal Constitution. What do we learn from our history and that of our neighbours? Has revolution bestowed any benefit on North or South America? It has delivered up the

Northern United States to the evils, present and to come, of unmixed democracy. Their prosperity is factitious, the result for the most part of accidental causes, of the French government on the other. After all what does it amount to? Is New England better governed than Canada? Is life, liberty or property, more secure in the colony that rebelled than in the colony which has not rebelled?

And what has the revolution done for the Southern States? It has involved them in long and fierce disputes with treacherous friends and in war finally with unscrupulous enemies. The Southern people revolted at a small tax levied by the British Parliament and they have been burthened with enormous exactions imposed by an American Congress; they refused to pay a trifling duty on a few articles and have submitted to oppressive tariffs on every commodity of daily use; they were impatient under the ancient and honoured rule of old England and fell under the crafty and greedy dominion of New England and New York. These are the blessings which the Southern States have derived from the revolution of 1776. They did little more than change masters. Who can fail to see in the existing war a Nemesis that is equally scourging North and South? Individuals are punished in the next world for their crimes as nations in this.

Have the revolted colonies of Spain in North America fared any better than ourselves? Has their revolution been less obviously a blunder? The present pitiable condition of the colonies that revolted compared with that of the few that did not revolt furnishes a significant answer to the question. Cuba and Porto Rico are marvels of prosperity; Mexico is the scorn of all nations. The evils of Spanish rule were blessings compared with the misery that revolution has inflicted on the Mexican people.

The experience of South America, of Chile, Peru, and all the Spanish provinces tells the same unhappy story. One Country only of all that great continent is strong, prosperous, and happy, the Country in which there was no violence, where the separation of the Colony from the mother Country was not stained with blood but was affected without disorder by moderate and peaceful councils. The harvest of revolution, murder and rapine, have been reaped without ceasing every where else.

Such has been the fortune of revolutionary States heretofore on the American Continent. Whether the bloody controversy between the North and South will differ from other similar disputes in its consequences remains to be seen. What good can come of it? If the

North fail, their ruin must follow. If they succeed in the war they will be rulers over insurgent provinces ready at the first opportunity to renew the contest. The restoration of the Union is an impossibility. There must succeed to it another government with standing armies, enormous taxes and despotic power beneath whose influence Northern liberty will wither and perish. The injury to the South is not less certain. Should their efforts fail to establish a Southern Confederacy, the destruction of their form of society must be the consequence. If they are victorious in the conflict the seeds of hostile interests among themselves will be sown at the beginning of their career. They have been contending for free trade during forty years and foes to free trade are already at Richmond. It is already, hopeless. They are resolute to hold their slaves against Northern anti-slavery, and an anti-slavery interest will be born almost with the birth of the Southern Confederacy and will grow up speedily in the Southern States. The whole controversy substantially is one between the white man's labour and the black's. The prosperity that we promised ourselves in our Southern confederacy will bring to our shores hordes of emigrants from Europe and the North and the conflict of white with black labour will come with them. Their advent will precipitate the change that has already begun. Already in all the cities of the South the white man is displacing the negro in almost every department of labour. The competition will increase ten fold untill the black is driven to the swamps and marshes of the coast and rivers. There will be other causes assailing the stability of the new Confederacy. Can we hope that in the South there will be no adverse parties, no feuds, no ambitious unprincipled leaders to excite and nourish them? Even now and hitherto there has been little cordiality between adjoining Southern States little even between portions of the same State. There must be disputes in families. There will be quarreling among States. Perhaps after all we had better have taken Mr. Jefferson's advice and kept the New England States for that useful purpose. They are singularly well fitted to fill the place. All that is certain in the future is the unhappy certainty that the progress of the North American States in all the arts of peace has been arrested for generations that revolution will be with us what it has always been elsewhere, a general disaster, a crime and a mistake. We promise ourselves immense prosperity under a new Confederacy. I am content with the advancement of the South.

But whatever one may think of Revolutions and their evils he will readily admit that when once begun they should be conducted with honesty, prudence and vigour. This has not been our mode of proceeding. The convention assembled at Montgomery to form a government was guilty at the outset of an act of political dishonesty. Their only true function was to form a constitution and submit it to the Confederate States. When the constitution so submitted was adopted by the States, the election of President, Vice President, and Congress should have gone directly before the people to whom alone the right of election belongs. Instead of this the Convention usurped the government, elected a President independently of the people and voted themselves a Congress, under the name of a Provisional government. They deprived the Confederate States of the benefits that would have resulted from a settled and regular administration of their affairs. They placed the South in a false position with other nations. Europe would not treat with the unstable authorities of a Provisional Government. Such a government lacked every where the prestige and authority of a government regularly established with due constitutional forms. Above all, it showed a reckless readiness to sacrifice right to a supposed expediency by men whose clamours for right against expediency had filled the Country for years. They failed to see that a strict adherence to principle is always the highest expediency.

The establishment of a Provisional government set at naught the fixed bounds of constitutional freedom and all the authority and precedents of the past. No convention before had assumed the government and so egregiously mistaken the duties imposed on conventions. The nature of a convention is clear. It is not a body of unlimited powers; that would be a despotism. It is not a dictator. The dictatorship is unknown to our representative form of government. The nature and duties of a convention are obvious. They are as distinctly definable as those of legislature, a judge or a governor. These authorities have their special departments, the legislature to make the laws, the judge to interpret them, the governor to see them executed. A convention is constituted neither to make, interpret, nor execute law. Its sole end is to form the government which performs these several functions. The only power entrusted to a convention by the people is the government making power. When a convention has framed a constitution for the people it has done its work. The only duty left for it to perform is to dissolve itself, to adjourn finally.

The purpose of a convention is evident not only from the essential nature of constitutional government but from the whole history of conventions. It is seen clearly in the proceedings of the convention of 1787, and in those of 1788, called by every State, and directed by the wisest and best men of the Country, by Washington and his compatriots.

The gentlemen at Montgomery proceeded differently. They were wiser than the men of the Revolution. They appeared to think they were the only men in the South able to conduct its affairs. They were afraid to trust the people lest the people might differ from them in opinion and elect others to occupy their places. They determined to govern however irregularly. The first step in their career was to disregard the limits and landmarks of constitutional freedom established by the ablest men of the Country. What followed was in keeping with their first measure. They sat in their self constituted Congress with closed doors. What was done or said, no body could tell. Feuds sprang up among its members. The people knew nothing about them. Who was right or who was wrong or what they wrangled about remains a profound secret. Is it surprising that the fortunes of the Southern Confederacy have not prospered more, abroad and at home, under such auspices?

So much for the political honesty of our leaders. Their measures have been worthy of their principles. A series of practical blunders marks their course. The ordinance withdrawing South Carolina from the Union was passed in Convention at Charleston on the 20th day of December. Five days elapsed and Fort Sumter remained unoccupied. At the end of that time, Col. Anderson moved over from Fort Moultrie with his garrison and took possession of the stronger post. It became necessary to retake it and thus furnished the pretext which the Federal Government was anxiously seeking for appealing to the passions of its people and exciting a war. The pretext was eagerly seized and war ensued accordingly.

It happened in this way that the first scene of the great military drama in the United States was acted in full view of Charleston.[5] Fort Sumter, about three miles off, rises out of the sea on an artificial shoal of stone, midway nearly between two sandy islands, Sullivan's and Morris', which mark on the North and South, the entrance to Charleston harbour. On these islands numerous batteries had been built. After a long and fruitless negotiation to induce the Federal Government to withdraw its troops, it was resolved to bombard the fort. Before daylight, on the morning of the 11th of April, a signal gun from Fort Johnson followed by other guns in quick succession announced to the expectant citizens that the conflict was begun. The streets were soon crowded. Multitudes assembled at every point where the fort was visible. The wharves, the windows overlooking the scene, the roofs, the tops of chimnies, were all occupied by the various batteries and the white jets like steam that told where the shells burst over the fortress and showered their fragments down on the devoted heads of the garrison. The canonade continued all day and at intervals during the night. Early the next morning it was anounced by men and women rushing through the streets that Sumter was on fire. Black clouds of smoke rose from the fort and rolled away Northward, towards Sullivan's island. The flames shot up high over the walls. Occasional columns of smoke indicated the explosions of shells and cartridges in piles and heeps. The barracks had been fired by shells or hot shot. The garrison were in danger of suffocation. Their magazine was threatened. Their strength was exhausted and surrender was unavoidable. About midday the firing ceased and a white flag was displayed from the walls. On the day following, the 13th, Major Anderson, was permitted with all the honors of war to leave the post, into which he had stolen three months before to the lasting detriment of the Country. The wonderful part of the story is that after a canonade of two days duration not a man was killed on either side. It was so wonderful, so contrary to those entertained at the North from the terrible fire of Sumter that nobody there would believe the story. Even now convictions are piously cherished by Clergymen and their congregations that hundreds of their "Southern brethren" were slaughtered in the conflict.

The bombardment of Sumter growing out of our own neglect, and forced on as it was by the crafty contrivances of the Government at Washington made war inevitable. It was indeed inevitable without it. Preparations for war should have been made accordingly. Stores of arms, ammunition, clothing, military equiments of all kinds should have been provided. Our sagacious Southern leaders thought differently. They acted under a pernicious delusion that there would be no war. One gentleman high in Official Station declared that the most delicate stomach might drink all the blood that would be shed in the quarrel. They professed to say in one breath that the South was essential to the well being of the Northern people and that the North would permit a necessary good, one of vital importance to them, to be taken away without striking a blow—that a strong and selfish people would yield every thing without a contest. They reversed the old maxim and believed that right was might. They did more. They assumed that right was always yielded by a foe without opposition to its just claims. Our Southern leaders either believed the paradox and were blindly ignorant; or they did not believe it and were willfully deceiving the people. In either case they gave admirable evidence of their high qualifications to conduct a great and perilous enterprise.

Acting under the delusion that there would be no war our leaders made no preparation for war. Month after month passed away and they did nothing. They made perpetual mistakes but we comforted ourselves with the assurance that some how or other good came out of every blunder however enormous the blunder might be. It was so with Sumter; it was so with every thing. The greater the mistake committed the stronger the evidence afforded that Providence was on our side. Under this encouraging conviction we went on blundering still. Why should we not when every folly was turned into a benefit? We placed forts at Hatteras. The forts were captured and the garrisons made prisoners. Again with similar results, we erected batteries on the Tennessee and Cumberland, on Roanoke Island and at Port Royal. Competent judges had examined the inlet to Port Royal sound and decided that it could not be defended except at the expense of millions of money and years of labour. Nevertheless the defence was attempted. Sand batteries were erected on Bay Point and Hilton Head. A number of large cannon were provided and placed in position. They made a formidable appearance to inexperienced eyes. The planters and troops were persuaded that the forts were impregnable. It was an idle delusion. A canonade of a few hours by a Federal squadron under Captain Dupont compelled the Confederates to evacuate their post.[6] The island might have been so surrounded by the enemies gun boats as to cut off all retreat. It was not surrounded fortunately and our troops made their escape. The fault was not theirs that the place was not defended; it was indefensible. They attempted an impossibility and failed necessarily. It was another blunder of their leaders. What the special benefit derived from this particular mistake may have been it was difficult to see. To the people of St. Helena parish and the adjoining country the disaster was incalculable. They lost every thing, houses, plantations, negroes, furniture, clothing. They became fugitives, not always welcome among their neighbours. We at a distance from the scene improved the occasion to show our patriotic devotion at the expense of our suffering friends. They abandoned their houses; we asked why they neglected to burn them. We gave the most convincing evidence of the ease and equanimity with which we are able to bear the losses and calamities of our neighbours. We decided for them that they should have destroyed every thing. Not a roof should have been left standing to shelter the enemy. Whether we would have practised what we preached is not easy to determine. But it was easy enough to assume that we would, and we talked accordingly.

The panic produced by the defeat at Hilton Head was not confined to the adjoining islands. It extended to Charleston. The enemy were reported to be at Church Flats about fifteen miles from the city. The news was carried by men on horseback at full speed through the streets of the city. A rumour that a brigade of the enemy had alighted from balloons would have been hardly less worthy of credit. But every body believed the report. The troops marched from their encampment, proceeded a mile or two and marched back again. The rail road cars were crowded with flying multitudes seeking shelter in the Country, abandoning their houses but not burning them. Not a dwelling was set fire to notwithstanding the lessons lately taught us by the neglect of the people of Port Royal and our animadversions on their neglect.

We made other mistakes. It was the common belief that England and France would not tolerate a blockade of the cotton ports. Cotton is king was proclaimed exultingly by thousands. They believed the words to be something more than an empty phrase and forgot that, if cotton were really king, we are warned by the highest authority not to put our trust in princes. England and France disregarded the claims of our monarch and showed him no sign of recognition. England had a policy of her own to subserve and followed her interests according to her own judgment without respect to him or us. To a large party in England the cessation of supplies of cotton from America was boon as welcome as it was unexpected. The party that had long laboured to build up the cotton growing interest of India and who found the better and more abundant cotton of the United States an insuperable obstacle, rejoiced to see the obstacle suddenly removed. Blockade and war in America promised success in India — a success that nothing else could bestow. If cotton is king, the English desire a different dynasty from the royal house nursed by Slavery.

They would gladly set aside the reigning American family for one of Eastern origin. The blockade of the American ports gives the opportunity. Let the blockade, they say, continue by all means. The people of England remembered that the cultivation of Indigo had been transfered from America to India. Before the Revolution, the indigo consumed in England was made in South Carolina and Georgia. Since the Revolution, it is produced in Bengal. Why not with cotton as with indigo?[7] Who will believe that cotton of any quality may not be cultivated in a Country where the staple has been grown from time immemorial and when the finest muslins are the products of Indian looms. Nothing is wanting but the stimulus of capital and opportunity; the first is furnished by England in profusion; the last, by the American War. It may be that the advantage hitherto enjoyed by the American planter grows out of his organized Slave labour. The war may destroy Slavery. Let the war continue between North and South. These were the views of large parties in England.

Our faith in a phrase has been boundless. Cotton was not only to controul every power abroad but to fill the Confederate treasury at home. A scheme was contrived for what was called a cotton loan. Not a bale was to be borrowed or lent. The name was more claptrap, a tribute to the supremacy of cotton or a snare to delude the people. Instead of our planters lending to the government money of which they had none they were to lend the amount for which a certain quantity of cotton would sell. What could be expected from the plan, it is difficult to conceive. If the planter had not a dollar in money it was easy to understand that he could not lend money but neither could he lend the proceeds of his cotton if the cotton remained unsold. The Treasury overlooked the important consideration that a sale requires a purchaser. When the time arrived the purchaser was missing. There was no sale. There was nothing to lend or borrow. King Cotton again deceived his subjects.

Once more we exhibited our confidence in the capabilities of the great staple. We imposed an export tax on cotton to pay the interest on the public debt. Our profound conviction of the omnipotence of cotton induced us to abandon the received maxims of political economy and our own practice of seventy years. Nor was this all. The duty was made a discriminating duty. It was a duty on cotton and on nothing else. Why other exported articles should not be taxed as well as the great staple of the Country; why rice, tobacco, naval stores, grain, or lumber, should not be subject to a duty also, nobody could explain, except upon the principle that "cotton is King" and that to be taxed was a royal prerogative. It is somewhat anomalous certainly for a monarch to be taxed at all but we had unlimited faith in his ability to do any thing and to tax him was only another way to show our confidence in his power. But as there was no cotton sold for the loan so there was none exported for the tax, and the cotton loan and the export cotton tax were failures alike.

It was somewhat singular that a new system of burthens on commerce in the shape of export duties not known in the United States, should be devised in the Confederacy. To the export duty we added an elaborate tariff on imports. It is not so high as the Morrill tariff but it is higher and more complicated than any previous to the war of 1812. We have been clamouring for free trade for forty years and refuse to establish it when we have the power. Has our clamour been a pretext and a falsehood? And what has the tariff policy produced. The duties received have not paid the cost of collecting them. The only benefit derived from the tariff is that the custom House officers have received their salaries. The proper reply to the blockade of the enemy was the offer of free trade to all the world except our foes. It would have enabled us with better grace to assure the people of Europe that our controversy with the North turns as much on unjust taxation as on Slavery. We have so declared, but who in the face of our tariff and export tax can believe the declaration? Our professions of free trade have been falsified by our practice.

I will not dwell on the blots in our Statesmanship. It is more agreeable to note the military exploits of our gallant citizen soldiers; the courage, the skill, the noble devotion of such men as Lee and Beauregard and Johnston and Bee and Barstow and Evans and Price and Van Dorn and a host of others of whom their Country may well be proud. The ardour has never been surpassed with which all classes rushed to the field and bore without a murmur the hardships and diseases of military life, while they encountered its dangers with joyous alacrity. Their courage was only equaled by the readiness with which they yielded to the judgment of their leaders. Whether a more active campaign might not better answer the ends of the war they left for those to decide on whom the Country had imposed the duty. The zeal of the volunteer was tempered with a just respect for authority. As the orders came the soldier was prepared alike to fight, or march, or encamp. It was a noble example of combined ardour and obedience. More generous spirits from commander to private have never before been marshalled to defend a Country's cause. The women of the South have been equally or more enthusiastic. They devoted themselves to the wants and comforts of their countrymen in arms. They praised and encouraged them; they formed societes to make and distribute clothing and comforts; they nursed the sick and wounded; they contributed to their spiritual wants; they urged and promoted temperance; they laboured with untiring assiduity in every way to cheer the soldier in performing his duty. All ranks and classes, the rich and poor, the old lady of eighty and the young girl at school, animated with unwavering devotion to their Southern home.

The Soldier very properly obeyed the mandates of the Provisional government in conducting the war. But it has been doubted whether a more active and enterprising course of action was not the proper one. It was said that even defensive war might have sought to drive the enemy out of Virginia and to improve a great victory when once achieved. This is the manner in which all great Captains have carried on war. Our commander in chief pursued a different policy. He arrested pursuit after victory, wasted the energies of his troops in camp with weariness and disease and gave the demoralized foe time to recruit his ranks and recover his confidence.[8] He contented himself with placing a body of troops to face the enemy wherever the enemy happened to appear. But he never struck a blow except to repel a blow. If an attack was made, it was to be repulsed, but that was enough, no pursuit was permitted of the flying foe. It was certainly a very simple kind of strategy and yet it never seems to have suggested itself to Alexander, Caesar, or Napoleon. Neither Hannibal in Italy, nor Scipio in Africa, ever thought of it. The discovery was reserved for the genius of President Davis in the nineteenth century. It escaped the notice of every other great chieftain from the time of the Trojan War to that of Napoleon. This was the talk of the day at street corners. I am not a military man and unable to decide between the President and his critics.

It is difficult to understand why the Statesmen of Europe, of England especially, should have hesitated as they did to embrace the opportunity so unexpectedly offered for dividing the great Republic. One more half century of undisturbed progress must have made the United States the dominant power of the world. A greater tyrant than this American Democracy would have proved — a more arrogant and insulting dictator—the ages of the world have never seen. The only event that could prevent the evil which threatened the nations of the World was the breaking into hostile and irreconcilable parts a power already prodigious and advancing with the strides of a giant. The opportunity was offered to the Statesmen of England and they stood shilly shalley, playing a little, paltry, game of neutrality and making fine speeches of hollow sentiment, of sympathy and regret at the occurrence of a schism which every one knew they must rejoice to witness. It is true there was some conflict of opinion, of sentiment, even of interest among their own people, enough to tie the hands of an ordinary ruler. The Statesman who was head merely of a party, anxious first to keep his place and next only to promote the present or future welfare of safety of his Country, might hesitate and doubt what course to pursue. But would the elder, or younger Pitt, or Canning, or even Castlereagh, have paused for a moment to secure the maritime superiority of England for an unlimited time against an aspiring rival?[9] It was the generous as well as the politic proceeding to recognise the Southern Confederacy at once. They were the weaker party in numbers, wealth, and military preparation. They had taken up arms to defend their liberties against treacherous friends and unscrupulous enemies. Surely England ought to have been ready to receive them into the rank of nations as promptly as she had received other countries with smaller claims on her sympathies—degenerate Greeks and revolted Spanish colonies. But Lord Palmerston and Lord John Russel [*sic*] were at an age when men move only while rest is no longer possible.[10] They shrunk from all large and liberal views of a great political question and England was content to look on with indifference at a conflict waged by a kindred people for their rights.

In the early part of November the Northern government began a series of predatory expeditions on the Southern coast. The first under Sherman and Dupont disembarked at Port Royal.[11] They presented to the world a striking evidence of the ease with which men strain at gnats and swallow camels. They were prosecuting as felons in New York, the captured privateersmen of the South, and were seizing all the cotton and other property of widows, children and non comabatants, on the islands of South Carolina, contrary to every usage of civilized war. The robbery has been approved and applauded throughout the Northern States. They talk with exultation of cultivating the plantations of Port Royal on Federal account as a sort

of financial appendage to the Washington government. The rights
of the owners are utterly disregarded. Northern men in the Federal
service engaged formerly in surveying the coast served as guides
to the marauding parties. With their wives and children they had
spend months in the families of planters, had eat dinners and drank
wine and now they acted as pioneers of plunder to the scenes of the
feast. They were better able to discover the stores of old Madeira
from having frequently joined the owners in drinking it. Their first
question asked of the servants on entering a house from which their
cannon had driven the owner was — where is the wine kept? Sometimes they succeeded in making prize of it, in other cases, the robbers
were disappointed by its removal or destruction. There was something indescribably mean in the conduct of these parties but very
characteristic of the people whose officers they are. They are a thrifty
race, not scrupulous about the means if their end be attained.

It was about a month after the invasion of Port Royal that the
great fire occurred in Charleston — the greatest as to extent of surface
ever known in America.[12] It reached across the city from Cooper
river to Ashley. Its length was a mile, with an average width of two
hundred and fifty yards. It began at nine o'clock in the night on the
eleventh of December and burnt until ten the next day. The day of
the eleventh was calm. With the fire a violent North East wind
sprung up. The fire commenced at the eastern end of Hasell street
near the river, in a nest of wooden buildings. A similar nest for some
future conflagration is getting ready on Gadgen's wharf. The flames
swept along, an avalanche of fire rushing on with a speed and fury
that nothing could resist or retard. The flakes carried by the wind
set fire to houses a long way in advance and kindled new flames in
various quarters. In the line of the wind, opposition became useless.
The people at least restricted their efforts to limit the spreading of
the fire on the right and left. The strong wind acted like a blow
pipe on the flames. It is common at the close of a fire to see large
beams charred and half burnt still smoking in the ruins. Here we
saw none. Every particle of wood was turned into ashes. Hundreds
of the inhabitants lost every thing, even their clothing. The city on
the succeeding day was a scene of desolation. The people wandered
about, like men in a dream, among the ghastly skeletons of their
homes, the grim, dead, chimnies with their dreary grates now hearth-
less, the broken walls of humble tenements and stately mansions

involved in common ruin, and the grander remains of churches and of the Catholic Cathedral. It was difficult for the gazers to realize the truth while they looked at it. I saw one poor old woman groping about the ruins of a house, engaged apparently in looking for something she had lost. It was the comfort and happiness long enjoyed and now gone with no prospect of returning. She told me with tears in her eyes that the house had been her pleasant home for thirty two years. It was destroyed and with it every thing she had in the world. Miss Pinckney, the daughter of General Charles C. Pinckney, in her eightieth year, was driven by the flames from her house on East Bay near Cooper river. She took refuge with her relatives in the mansion of Mrs. Rutledge on the opposite side of the town near Ashley river. The fire found her in her place of refuge before morning. Twice in the night she was a fugitive from the flames, yet she bore the fiery trial with the calm courage of a veteran in battle.[13] The great calamity of Charleston was not without its accompanying good — it called out warm sympathies and generous charities from every quarter of the confederacy; and gave great joy to the Northern people. They exulted over the event; a manifest judgment of Providence on the home of rebels and traitors. They believed that Heaven had put the torch to Southern homesteads to avenge the abolition party and support their cause.

In character with this sentiment a few days after the fire a fleet of vessels loaded with stone appeared at Charleston bar. The fire had destroyed in part only; the fleet was to do the work effectually and blot out the city from the list of commercial places. The blockade was to be turned into a barricade of stone at every outlet of the harbour.[14] It was adding one more to the list of warlike appliances in the crusade against the South in perfect keeping with all the rest, with the handcuffs carried into battle for expected captives, the chaining of privateersmen, the arraigning them as felons in Court, the plundering of private property at Port Royal and elsewhere. Our enemies have not gone so far back in the practices of uncivilized war as to resort to the use of poisoned weapons. Perhaps they may have some scruple of conscience, or they doubt the efficacy of the measure, or they feel some apprehension of public opinion in Europe. There is no reason, however, for such apprehension so long as a Lord John Russel [sic] controuls or influences public opinion. He remonstrated with Mr. Seward on the barbarism of the stone barricade and was satisfied with Mr. Seward's assurance that the stones were thrown on the bar of Charleston only to be taken up again when the war should be ended. He might have added that all the killed should be restored to life at the same period. One assurance would have deserved quite as much confidence as the other.

Chapter Thirteen

Old Letters

For some days past I have been living among ghosts, among the shadows of events long past and of persons dead during many years. It was apprehended that the enemy might pay Charleston a visit. Our Northern brethren have an especial hatred for the city. It is a nursery of treason, a trumpeter of sedition, a nest of rebels, an exact counterpart of the Boston of 1774 that insulted the dignity of King George and threw his tea into the river. The people of Massachusetts do not appreciate the resemblance. They threaten to burn the imitator of their own good example, to sow it with salt, to barricade its harbour, to make it a desolation like Tyre or Carthage. I proposed to myself to anticipate them in a small part of the work, to save them the trouble of burning my papers at least by burning all myself. I had a large collection, the papers of others as well as my own. I reviewed them hastily before committing them to the flames. They have had the power of cabalistic signs or written incantations. They have been able to draw spirits from the vasty deep, the shades of old friendships closed by death, of departed hopes and fears, joys and sorrows, successes and disappointments. I see among them visions of time wasted, opportunity neglected, kindness or love not properly appreciated nor received with sufficient gratitude and neglects or wrongs unduly magnified or resented too long and earnestly. But the whole brood of sweet or bitter memories have come before me in an altered aspect, arrayed alike in the dull gray garb of time long past. The sorrows have been soothed, the joys have long ago lost their gloss, the disappointments their poignancy, the mortifications their sting. I remember with surprise how much pain one event inflicted and how much pleasure I received from another. Like the storm and sunshine of the year past, they are now alike unimportant.

It is curious to see how much of one's life is occupied with money concerns. Mammon dictates a large portion of every man's correspondence. Something is to be bought, or sold, or received, or paid, or lent, or borrowed. The great family of duns are attendant on all doors. They are of various humours, the gentle, the earnest, the importunate, the peremptory, the pert, the impertinent, the insolent and insulting. It is a vile brood in their mildest moods. Nothing can differ more than the man's tone who invites you to buy his goods and wares, his farm or merchandise, and when he asks or demands payment for the debt he has persuaded you to incur. In one case he is oil, in the other vinegar. In one, he presents an illustration of the suaviter in modo, in the other of the fortiter in re. The trader who has received you at his counter, for six months, with persuasive smiles and obsequious bows presents his bill at the end of the time with sour solemnity. He has a standing reason for being importunate; a large amount to raise, notes in bank to meet, his stock of goods to replenish, an old firm to close. Sometimes hints are dropt of an Attorney's interposition. Sometimes you are actually turned over to the gentleman of the bar. The gentleman of the bar adds to your correspondence by sending you a diplomatic note expressing a hope to enjoy the pleasure of your company some time before return day. For this you pay two dollars. It is the price of bar courtesy established by those who best know its value. The dun from whatever quarter is a nauseous drug even when taken in homeopathic doses. When it comes, once in a way, from time to time only, its aspect is odious. But a mass of duns, the accumulated horrors of forty years exhibited in a series of letters, is a spectacle to turn one to stone. Nothing could enable us to bear the sight of such a Medusa, to look on "a monster of so hideous mein" but the comfortable reflection that it is a shadow only; that the demons are exorcised; that time has placed a great gulf between them and us.

I have not been without my share of the correspondence that includes the dun in all its manifold shapes. They crop out from my papers like boulders of granite in a green field. But among the letters of an old friend and relatives they exhibit their most hateful forms. It fills me even now with sorrow to go over the memorials of evils encountered in this way by one so kind and good. Here they are among his papers—the demands in various aspects for the payment of debts lightly or hopefully incurred. It is so easy to go in debt. It is made so easy by the cunning craftiness of the seller. The demon of credit is such a deceiver. He makes a year to come to seem a century. But at its end, it is so short. Nothing has turned out as was hoped. The harvest has failed. The price of the great staple is low. Then comes the demand for money more and more pressing according to the humour of the creditor. There is no better test of a man's character than the manner in which he asks for his money. The roughest and more unsparing of my old friend's correspondents was one who became a millionaire and moved his wealth to a Northern State. It would seem from his letters that the sound of the last trump could not stop though it might drown, his demand for money or produce. Pay me that thou owest speaks loudly in every page. One may see from a single letter how and why it was he became rich. On the heel of the letters came the Attorney, the judgment, the execution, the sheriff's sale, the scattered household, the abandoned hearth stone, the broken heart, the destitute children and the world's cold charities. I find all these things in the papers of my unfortunate relative, a well meaning man, easy in temper careless in disposition, ignorant of business even to the overpaying of his creditor's Attorney. He had a large family and very moderate means. What days and nights of sorrow the papers tell of. How plainly they show the early hope changed into despondency, the despondency deepening into despair, and all this, so distinctly revealed, is told without one word from himself but is gathered indirectly from the words only of his correspondents. We see the effects in the causes. And this and a thousand other similar domestic tragedies are the necessary consequences of the credit system which all States protect and foster. Why they do so is easily understood. The credit system is the system of the powerful. Laws are made by the strong. They have given to the creditor in many countries the most cruel control over the liberty and life of the debtor; to chain him, to imprison him, to sell him. The debtor has been treated as a criminal, whereas he is for the most part an unfortunate only. He is a culpable defrauder in the law's estimation when he is really the party ensnared. The fault is on the other side. The credit system is the offspring not of solicitation among buyers but of competition among sellers. They give credit to effect sales. It is done for their own benefit not that of their customers. Remove the competition and credit ceases. Cash is required just as it was in Charleston during the blockade. When the scarcity of goods destroyed competition credit sales of every kind were at an end. Cash was demanded for every thing. Yet the laws lean to the creditor's side always as if he were all times the innocent and injured party, as though the credit system with all its consequences and evils were not his own work for his exclusive advantage.

But money although a prominent is not the only topic to be found in a life's correspondence. The most ancient paper in the collection which came under my examination speaks contemptuously enough of such considerations. It is a letter dated nearly a hundred years since, in February 1766, and written in "Charlestown" from Childermas Harvey to Thomas Wigg of Indian land.[1] Indian land was the name applied at that time to all the main land in the neighbourhood of Port Royal. It had been the territory held by the great tribe of Yamassees which the war of 1716 drove into Florida. Mr. Harvey after a few remarks in the usual forms of letter writing adverts to certain matrimonial schemes the hopes and dreams of youth. He is enthusiastic in describing the charms of the beautiful Miss Barnwell. He is evidently, from some of his expressions, a very young man. He laments his inability to visit Port Royal as he had promised his friend to do but hopes to get there soon, if his friends permit. He then goes on to say in reference to a certain garment that Wigg it seems had borrowed on a visit to his friend—"You remark that you have worn my breeches out and desire me to get another pair on your account. I did not think, Tom, you would have been so particular with me. Damn the breeches! they were not worth mentioning. Pray, Mr. Tom, let me see no more such formality from you as you may expect none from me." The difference is immense between this and the letters of the griping creditor who became a millionaire. In another letter two years after, Harvey informs his friend Tom that he is about to undergo a painful and dangerous surgical operation. He has directed that if the result should prove fatal some memorial should be sent to his correspondent of his sincere friendship. There is no farther trace of the writer and probably the operation ended as he apprehended. Two short letters comprise the whole memorial that has prevented his name from perishing from the earth.

My own correspondence embraces a variety of forms. It changes from time to time as my position was changed. I became a member of the State legislature and a letter informs me that a candidate for a certain office "has not the honour of a personal acquaintance with me but would be none the less grateful for my vote and influence." Or a personal friend claims my aid in support of some excellent fellow in whose election he takes a particular interest. This sort of solicitation which could not be escaped was what Hampton was accustomed to call "scalping." He was always ready to scalp or be scalped in behalf of a friend.

The scene is shifted and the tone of my correspondence alters accordingly. I am a master in Equity, custos rotulorum, and grand Almoner of a District or parish with a charity fund to distribute and controul. A popular leader writes in behalf of an amiable octogenarian, a pensioner on the fund, asking a small addition to the old man's allowance, or he recommends a widow and six small children, or a veteran who has done service in the war of 1812. And all this he does from pure benevolence with no view to any personal benefit. Another gentleman writes to obtain a loan from the fund. He has heard that a certain bond was about to be paid and the money to be reinvested. Can't he get a few hundreds or a thousand dollars? The crop is bad or some casualty has befallen his affairs. He will give the most ample security and be forever obliged.

I am Collector of the Port of Charleston. There are subordinate offices at my disposal. I receive a hundred applications backed with certificates bearing numerous signatures stating the qualifications of the applicants. They are among the most exemplary and excellent of men. But there is no vacancy, the Collector has no power to make appointments without one and no disposition to turn the incumbents out of office to put others in. He is thought to be very unreasonable and the applicants request their letters to be put on file. It is done accordingly. At last an officer dies. Before he is buried there is a frantic rush for the vacancy. The filing has been regarded by each applicant as a solemn promise that he should be appointed before any of the rest. One of the hundred receives the place and the ninety nine consider the Collector as faithless to his pledges.

My letters, while in Congress, took a wider range. There is still the same zeal among my correspondents to serve the public but it is in higher departments. One desires a son to be educated at the public expence in the West Point Academy. If he has been there himself it always makes an additional reason why his son should go there too. Another would have his boy in the Navy for which he has every qualification that nature can give. Another wants an account passed at some department, or a patent granted, or a scheme promoted, or a law passed, always for some personal advantage or an act repealed. Others of my constituents commune with me on the State of the nation, its threatened dangers, the violations of the constitution, the encroachments of the North, the violations of Southern rights, slavery and the tariff. One old and venerable citizen has a claim on the government for Revolutionary services performed by his father or Grandfather in the shape of large loans of money to the old Confederation. There is no sufficient evidence of the debt, none, at least, that satisfies the Treasury department. But there is not a doubt in the mind of the claimant. It has been talked about in the family without ceasing for half a century. There is no paper evidence but an old neighbour who died ten years since knew all about the transaction. It is intimated that nothing was wanting but activity in the representative. My predecessors had been negligent. Of me better things are hoped and expected.

There was one part of my old correspondence over which I went with a pleasure unqualified except by the remembrance that many of the writers and the persons of whom they speak, the brave, the generous, the frank and friendly are no longer among living men. The letter among these of earliest date was from George Butler, the eldest brother of Pickens Butler late of the United States Senate.[2] It was written in the summer of 1809, he being at home in the Mountains and I at Columbia spending the summer vacation in College. He tells of his excursions in various parts of the mountain region, and of the beauty of certain young ladies whom he had met in his travels, inquires about his books and talks of the studies of the coming term and the approaching end of his college labours. He replies to a letter received from me and remarks on my unreasonable complaints of wearisomeness and ennui in our deserted college halls. It seems I must have thought it scholarly and philosophical to be sentimental and lackadaisical on idleness, the vanity of human pursuits, and the quantum est in rebus inane. Butler was just the man to have no sympathy with any such nonsense. He was as solid and inaccessible to fanciful troubles as Flat Rock or Caesar's head. He could not understand why a man should sit down to complain about the ills of idleness when it was any moment in his power to cure the disease by becoming busy and employed. He knew how easy it was to expel the demon of ennui or spleen. "Throw but a stone the giant dies." He was aware of the remedy, was always ready to use it and expected others to do so too. In the war of 1812 he held a Captain's commission in the army of the United States and the service could boast I am sure, no braver or nobler spirit. He died very soon after the close of the war.

My next oldest letter is from my classmate and chum Thomas Julius Dupont. It was written in New York where he had just arrived on his way to attend the Medical lectures of Philadelphia. The ship in which he sailed from Charleston reached New York harbour during the night and came to an anchor a little below the city. He rose early in the morning of the next day before the vessel had got under way and on reaching the deck was amazed and delighted with the beauty of the surrounding landscape. On the North he saw Governor's Island, the broad city with its numerous spires and distant hills along the Hudson. On the South the woods and white cottages of Staten Island; eastward the homesteads and orchards of Long Island and opposite to them the low green shores of New Jersey. His temper was enthusiastic. He mounted to the Companion way of the ship and burst out into a rhapsody of admiration and poetry. The scenery is beautiful in itself. He had come within a few days from the swamps and sombre pines, the sandy plains and broad marshes of the Carolina sea coast and the scene was still more lovely to his eyes. When he had finished his exclamations he found all the passengers and the whole crew, the Captain, sailors, Steward and cabin boy, assembled around him and in a broad grin at a display of enthusiasm they had never seen or heard of before. I had other letters from him while at his studies which he pursued with as much assuidity as the most prosaic of medical students. He discusses in them the principle of life as expounded by Rush, the great medical authority of Philadelphia;[3] explains the Brunonian system at that time fashionable with medical students and is eloquent on the attractions of medical science in general and the accomplishments of its professors in Philadelphia especially. His room mate was William Waring a graduate of Columbia the class before his own. He speaks with high praise of Waring's zeal and progress and predicts for his fellow student eminent success in their common profession. The prediction was fulfilled. Waring became a distinguished and successful physician in Savannah. He was remarkable, for his great ability in eating as well as in medicine; he had the thinnest figure and the greatest appetite of his times. If he had an equal in the last talent, it was Dr. Brazier of Columbia of whom it was said that he could eat his length in fish at a meal. But the Columbia Doctor was a man of portly proportions and capacious stomach; Waring was thin as a lath and apparently with no stomach at all. My friend Dupont had every virtue and attainment to ensure to him also great professional success. But he was never strong. His health failed rapidly and he died early in his career of a long standing chronic complaint. He left one child, a daughter, the wife of Mr. Pelot of Charleston.

These two correspondences ceased in a short time. The third is of much longer duration. It embraces a period of fifty years.[4] I will give a few extracts confident that my readers will wish that I had given more. The first letters of the series were written from the Euhaw or from Coosawhatchie, the capital of Beaufort District, containing the Court house, the jail, a dozen lawyer's offices and half a dozen dwelling houses. Other letters came from Erin or Rockspring, summer retreats in the neighbourhood of the village. A summer retreat was a necessary of life with the people of Coosawhatchie. To live in the village two summers was an impossibility for all white men with one exception, just enough to prove the rule. The exception was Mr. Bassilieu who kept a shop and furnished gentlemen of the bar with board and lodging. He was able to dwell with bilious fever and country fever as Indian conjurers handle poisonous serpents without harm. His mother must have annointed him when an infant with some patent medicine of rare virtue or medical charm. He was a wizard so far and yet he seemed in all besides a plain and simple hearted man. To all but him a summer in Coosawhatchie was death. It was unnecessary to try a felon guilty of a capital offence. All that was required was to put him in jail during May to wait the November Court. The State paid for a coffin and saved the expenses of a trial and execution. The lawyers at last became restive under the loss of fees. They importuned the State to remove the jail and Court house to a healthier spot. It was done and the criminal now escapes the law no longer by the aid not of malaria, but by the help of lawyer alone. With the removal of the Court, Coosawhatchie ceased to exist. The wonder now is how it ever existed at all. But in the time of my youthful correspondence, it was in its palmy State. In the winter it had forty inhabitants; in the summer one. The rest betook themselves to the piney woods where Erin and Rockspring were among the pleasantest places. In our letters Rockspring rose to the dignity of Rupefontem [?] alone.

My correspondent [James L. Petigru] was a native of Abbeville and a pupil of the celebrated Dr. Waddel whose school at Willington was as famous in Carolina, to compare small things with great, as Eton or Westminster in England.[5] To Waddel's all ingenuous youth from every part of the State flocked to be educated. My friend went with the rest to be initiated in classical lore. The learned Doctor appreciated his scholar's abilities and desired to make the disciple his coadjutor and successor. But ambition and the love of learning carried the Student to Columbia. There he supported himself by teaching and in due time was graduated in the College with the highest honours of his class. From Columbia he removed his scene of action to St. Luke's parish by the advice of Judge Huger and other friends. It was then that our long letter correspondence began. He studied law for the future, kept a school for the present and, while he pursued his double labours, lived in the family of the Revd. Mr. Sweat....[6] "with the garrulity of a woman, the ideas and language of a man."[7] He laments his lost zeal for study and is almost inclined, he says, to wish that he was "fairly within the vulgar pale, lording it over a farm, talking of venison, drum fish, cotton seed and politics. This is the State in which a man quickly vegetates and like other vegetables is governed by steady principles and led to dissolution by regular gradation without the annoyance of passion or eccentricity of mind." He evidently had come to the conclusion that our low country planters have a leaning to the school of Epicurus, to the philosopher's mode of living at least if not to his studies.

One of the longest and most interesting of these early letters was written on a visit to Charleston during the war of 1812. "I was amazed," the writer says, "at the sight of our friend James T. Dent who is here expecting an appointment from Washington. You may remember his steady attachment to the maxim of Creech's Horace.[8]

'Not to admire is all the art I know
To make men happy and to keep them so.'

He has been wandering about carelessly, improving his knowledge to the detriment of his purse. But while one's capital is not yet gone and his hopes are young there is nothing to prevent pleasure. Nobody has met me with more cordiality than Mrs. Calder at the Planter's hotel. The good lady took hold of my hands, called me her son, and what was extraordinary, remembering I had left her house on a former visit at the time of her son's death, she bursts into tears and declared she could never be restored to her tranquility again. She looked indeed very much reduced. Nevertheless the hostess at length predominated and she joined with much glee in some of Frank Hampton's broadest jokes. Frank is another of the old fraternity that

I find here. There is this to be said of Frank that I see no difference in him now, in his prosperity, a gay and gallant office.[9] He is the same only greatly improved. I met Bull too and was positively astonished. I am as much pleased at his good fortune as I was surprised at his sudden appearance. He is considered the Governor's private secretary though it has not been formally announced. It is a snug post and opens the world to him in a very advantageous manner. There are no pique or misunderstanding betwen him and General Allston.[10] The boy grew restive and as the method agreed on between the parties precluded coercion, Bull refused to receive the salary any longer and left the place 'contrary to the General's wishes.' Bull has gone from college to be a private tutor in Allston's family and the boy alluded to, an only child, was 'too much petted to be subject to the rod, the grandson of Aaron Burr.' I am about to be admitted to the Bar," my correspondent goes on to say, "with my old class mate (at Waddel's) Tresevant who will make, or I am deceived, a vey good attorney. I am in comfortable quarters with Bob Taylor at Mrs. Bee's who has more of the milk of human kindness than I used to think possible for any housewife. I cannot make a like return to the hero-comic story of your letter but I can tell you of a damned rascally thing of recent occurrence. A privateer, the Revenge, Capt. Butler, put into this port two weeks ago. The common sailors had divided more than a thousand dollars apiece. And this overflow came by robbing a Spanish vessel. They robbed her crew and passengers not only of all their money but of every rag of clothing except what was on their backs. The pirates strutted through Charleston proclaiming this deed, displaying their gold watches and fine clothes and not a soul took any notice of it, till at length the crew got to fighting among themselves and one went and informed. Even then the marshal arrested none but the Captain and, as it said, has retained no evidence against him. Thus to the dishonour of our name these pirates will in all probability go off with impunity." In another part of his letter, the writer speaks of having seen General Tait at the Planter's hotel where the General lived, and remarks that he "never met him without being struck by his misfortunes and by the calmness with which he bore them."[11] Tait was a man very much beyond the common order. He had served through the American Revolution in Robert's regiment of artillery, with the commission, I think, of captain. At the close of the war, or when popular excitement grew strong in France, he was led by an adventurous spirit to offer his sword to the new Republic. But the French were more ready to lend swords then to borrow them and had plenty of aspiring spirits among themselves without taking them from abroad. His fortunes were not prosperous. He was in service however and was one of the officers in command of the expedition under General Humbert that landed on the Coast of England . . . . [12]

They hope to be transferred from the Solicitor's place to the judge's bench. Our friend becomes immersed in politics. In the city a violent feud raged between parties headed by Geddes and Hamilton. The controversy threatened the peace of the city. Once or twice the belligerents exchanged brick bats and hard words. After a time the great Nullification dispute began, and the Attorney General is constrained by the requirements of party to resign and be made a candidate for the Senate. "We are about," he says, "beginning another canvass which will be even more exasperated than the election of Intendant. I am in for it according to my usual luck. They have impressed me for a Senator — nothing less than impressment. I resisted stoutly and bawled lustily for help, but none would help me, so nothing was to be done but to take my place in the team. If I am elected," he adds, "I shall see much of you in Columbia for I suppose your election is certain since Beaufort, it is said, is willing to go the whole length of Governor Miller's course — 'Ballot box, jury box, cartouch box.'[13] I wish Elliott were hard where his soundness would be more appreciated than it is among your insurging people. Strange too that Beaufort the most exposed place in the State should be most eager to rush into danger. But many ingenious gentlemen of my acquaintance are seriously of opinion that the same Yankees whom we now accuse as shameless robbers would desist from hurting us as soon as the Union is dissolved; that we should only have to do like an indignant gentleman who turns his back on a man he dislikes and lives beside him for the rest of his life without speaking and without fighting." This was in 1832. Many ingenious gentlemen were of the same opinion in 1860 and the present desolation of our South Eastern coast is a striking commentary on the sagacity of my correspondent's remark and the thoughtless improvidence that produced it. I am afraid the present condition of Port Royal and Edisto made no part of the consequences expected from Secession by our present rulers and has been as surprising as ruinous to the sufferers.

The controversy of Nullification divided many friends. It produced no interruption in our intercourse. "You and I, he says, will never dispute much on politics and not at all on any thing else. There is less difference between us than between some who are on the same side. Nevertheless we differ more than I ever supposed we would about any thing. I am devilishly puzzled to know whether my friends are mad or I beside myself. Let us hope we shall make some discovery before long which will throw some light on the subject and give the people the satisfaction of knowing when they are in their right minds. When poor Judge W—— used to fancy himself a teapot, people thought he was hypochondriac. But there are in the present day very good heads filled with notions that seem to me not less strange. That we are treated like slaves, that we are slaves in fact, that we are worse than slaves and made to go on all fours, are stories that seem to me very odd and make me doubt whether I am not under some mental eclipse since I cant see what is so plain to others. But I am not surprised that the people have been persuaded that they are ill treated by the government. Old Hooker says 'If anyman will go about to persuade the people that they are badly governed he will not fail to have plenty of followers.' And I am inclined to think that the better the polity under which men live, the easier it is to persuade them they are cruelly oppressed."

"You say," he remarks in another letter, "that in Beaufort you are all trying to become every day more religious and more States rights. The connection between the two pursuits is not so obvious at first sight as it becomes on a closer inspection; for as it is the business of Religion to wean us from the world, the object may be well promoted by making the world less fit to live in. And, though I do not myself subscribe to the plan, I am fain to confess many excellent men have thought that the making of a hell upon earth is a good way of being sure of a place in heaven. But I am tired of harassing myself with public affairs, and wish I could attend more closely to my own and had more of the taste for gain, the sacra fames auri. But I am afraid the bump of acquisitiveness is omitted with me unaccountably and that I might as well try for music or dancing, or for State rights and faith in Jefferson which seem admirably calculated to save one in this world whatever it may do in the next."

The last letter in this portion of my correspondence begins with a declaration that the writer is about to give me the most convincing proof of uninterrupted friendship by asking an important favour — not one within the ordinary rules of kindness or he would not begin in a manner so solemn. "But," he goes on to say, "as it is really a very serious affair, I owe it to the sincerity of my feelings to open the matter in such a way as to enable you at a glance to see the extent of the sacrifice I am requiring you to make. And now to the point." The point was that an old lady under his especial care desired to get from Charleston to her residence in the Country. She had a reputation for not making herself agreable to her friends. He could devise no way to accomplish the end he wished but to consign her to my care by Steamer. The steamer would deliver her at Beaufort where I could meet and take her in my carriage whither she desired to go. The plan was carried into execution. I received the ancient lady on the wharf, took her to her plantation, was pleasantly entertained, found her intelligent and agreable, read in the evening by her request a few of her favourite Psalms and went on to Coosawhatchie the next morning without being particeps criminis in a single case of murdered reputation.

My correspondent was not only the architect of his own fortunes but of all those among his friends who came within reach of his influence and care. His sisters were carefully educated and advantageously settled in life. His brothers were assisted on the road to fortune in various ways. His time, money, legal ability and acquirements were always at the service of his friends without reserve. One of his brothers he placed in the navy during the war of 1812. The young midshipman made his first voyage in going from Beaufort to Charleston. I was a fellow passenger and never beheld a case of more desperate sea-sickness than that suffered by the embryo naval Captain. He lay on deck utterly heedless of all that was passing. His hat fell one way. He kicked off his shoes in another direction. If he had been picked up and thrown overboard he could hardly have roused himself from the deadly apathy. He made a brave and efficient officer and gradually climbed up to the post of commander. After forty years service he fell into the hands of the Relief Board, that singularly anomalous body invented by "poor Pierce" to kill off certain officers of the navy that room might be made for others. My old friend the midshipman of 1812 was one of the victims condemned without a hearing. It was a vile injustice at variance with every maxim of the government and every principle of law or right. I took occasion to say so in one of the public journals and my communication drew a letter of thanks from my correspondent such as a deep interest in his brother's affairs would prompt and my good intention only could deserve. He declares that if he succeeded in getting a court martial which he meant to demand the people would wonder that the Board could have committed a mistake so utterly discreditable not only to their integrity but to their understanding. The letter is characteristic of the writer in many ways and the whole proceeding of the board about which he speaks was in keeping with the government that devised it.

For the last twenty years my correspondent and I have been near each other, in the same city, and our letters have been few. The last I have received was written at his farm in the up country during the hot July in 1860. "I have a liking," he says, "for trees. I call them after my friends. Such a one is from A. Huger, another from Allston and another from Grayson till my avenue comes to fill the place of a portrait gallery. I have just met with a great misfortune. Three overcup oaks the pride of my eyes have been mutilated by a vile African to add a contemptible patch of ground to his field. 'Aliquid monstrosum semper Africa profert.' Brooding over this misfortune I found some consolation in recollecting a promise you made me of a cork oak. I now send all the way to Charleston for that and a few similar objects. It is awfully hot, he adds, and dry. Oh fortunate nimium Agricolae is a poetical licence where they gasp for rain as the planters are now doing. I find little to talk about. Some folks incline to politics. But I am tired of a 'tame cheater' and fail to even get angry with dull fellows who want a revolution for variety."

This last letter written as it was from the home of his birth makes a fitting finish to what may serve as a general sketch of a life, of its youthful aspirations after knowledge, its loves and friendships, its schemes of worldly advancement, its disappointments and disgust, its resignation to the unavoidable, and its return to the scenes of boyhood and youth, our natural and appropriate place of refuge from the pursuit of the world's cares and vexations.

> And as the hare whom hounds and horns pursue
> Pants to the goal from which at first she flew
> We all have hope our long vexations past
> Back to return and die at home at last.[14]

What a charm of tenderness there is in this and some others of Goldsmith's comparisons; in that, for example which refers to the Country Pastor's active sympathies with the fortunes of his flock and the serene piety that predominates over every worldly feeling.

> To them his heart, his love, his griefs were given
> But all his serious thought had rest in Heaven
> Like some tall cliff that rears its awful form
> Swells from the vale and midway leaves the storm
> Though round his breast the rolling clouds are spread
> Eternal sunshine settles on his head.

How very beautiful that again in which the poet describes the pastor's solicitudes and efforts to win his flock to virtue and devotion—

> And as a bird each fond endearment tries
> To lure its new-fledged offspring to the skies
> He tried each art, reproved each dull delay,
> Allured to brighter worlds and led the way.

I believe the figure is original. It may be thought to have some relationship with the Saviour's pathetic address to Jerusalem "How often would I have gathered thee together as a hen gathers her chickens under her wings and ye would not." If so the passage was never so happily imitated or applied. The portrait acquires an additional charm from the fact that the subject was the poet's brother who married for love and began life on a curacy worth forty pounds a year.

I have passed the ordinary limit of human life, the three score years and ten allotted to humanity. I have witnessed the demise of the Great American Republic. I may with special reason add one more voice to the millions that have already proclaimed the vanity of human expectations. We read carelessly in youth the assurance of the wise that all is vanity, but we attach no definite meaning to the declaration connected with ourselves. All may be vanity of vanities with those who have gone before us. Solomon in all his glory, his wealth power and wisdom, may have found life's promises deceptive but it shall not be so with us. Our pet schemes and youthful expectations will not delude us. They, at least, shall prosper. No cold realities can ever disperse our illusions. And so by this cunning device of our nature we all in turn rush after our several visions that turn deserts of sand into lakes of living water and the world's machinery goes steadfastly on without a pause. But we come to see the reality at last like all who have gone before us. When seen it is so little attractive that sanguine as we may have been at the beginning no one is willing to repeat the past—to live over the scenes of disappointed hopes, evil thoughts and deeds, indulged appetites and unrestrained passions. We would republish the volume with amendments but never with the errata and defects of the first edition. We prefer to leave the scene to those who follow as hopefully at the beginning and as despairingly or resignedly at the end.

With no reference to a future State, but as a calculation of chances for this world's happiness merely, it is better, as far as my experience goes, to keep innocency and to take heed to the thing that is right. Piety and virtue are not exempt from life's calamities. The purest and saintliest of men repeat the declaration "vanity of vanities" as well as the worst. But it is not uttered in the tone or temper that belongs to the complainer who has made sacrifices of truth and virtue on the altars of his false deities and finds the gifts of his gods to be worthless. The good man has one hope that does not deceive and that bears him company to the grave, that cheers him in sorrow and gives him courage in adversity.

> What nothing earthly gives or can destroy
> The soul's calm sunshine and the heartfelt joy,

is indeed virtue's prize. It is not a poetical rhapsody but sober truth taught by experience. Whether by the poet's "virtue" we are to understand the Christian's faith and practice or that more vague and imperfect belief that guides the philosopher and purifies his life, it is equally true that virtue even in this world is happier than vice; that honesty is really the best policy; that to do good and ensue it is the part of worldly wisdom as surely as it is of those nobler aspirations that look beyond this life to another. I bear this testimony of a life's observation in behalf of piety and virtue.

Appendix

The War Diary of William J. Grayson

The manuscript of William J. Grayson's War Diary is in the South Caroliniana Library at the University of South Carolina. It was published by Elmer L. Puryear in the *South Carolina Historical and Genealogical Magazine* 63: 137-49, 214-26, excluding passages on the South Carolina Convention and the death of Charles C. Lee, printed here for the first time. The manuscript covers only the period May through November, 1862. Grayson may have intended it to be part of his autobiography.

The War Diary of William John Grayson

MAY 10TH [1862]. The battle of Shiloh is announced today in
the papers. It was a brilliant victory on the first day. On the second,
the victory faded away into a drawn battle and many of its fruits
were lost to the Confederates. The plunder of the Federal camp
disorganized the victors for a time and arrested the progress of their
arms. The stores of good cheer were abundant; the Confederates
were hungry and thirsty. They turned from fighting to plundering
and sacrificed their laurels in some measure to the indulgence of
their appetites. They drank and fought with equal vigour but with
different results. It is not the first time that a Southern army has
suffered a victory to be turned into a drawn battle from the same
cause. At the battle of Eutaw in 1782 the American army drove the
enemy from the field of battle to their camp and beyond their camp.
Every tent in the camp was provided with a table on which good
liquor and food were set out ready for the refreshment of the British
troops. The victorious onset was arrested at the tables. The Americans charged the dishes and bottles with great success but in the
meantime their opponents rallied, returned to the fight and compelled
Greene to retire from the field and postpone the half won victory
to a future occasion. The honours of the first day at the battle of
Shiloh are due to Johnston although it devolved on Beauregard to
announce the victory. Johnston was killed at the close of the day.
At his death from the insubordination of the troops or the prudence
of his successors in command the fortunes of the day were checked
and changed.

MAY 12TH. The price of everything grows apace. I gave ten
dollars today for a bushel of salt at Bennell's mill. Bacon sells for 45
cents a pound, butter for 75 or 80, lamb for 37½, tea for six dollars,
coffee for 75 cents. Every article of clothing is of double, triple or
quadruple prices. But we still have old clothes to wear and something
to eat. We are not yet reduced to rats and horse flesh. Fat mules
go about the streets unmolested. We have not approached the pri-

vations which others have suffered in defense of their liberties and nobody complains of the small sacrifices they have been obliged to make.

MAY 13TH. Our troops have evacuated Cole's island and Battery island at the mouth of Stono river. This is another example of weakness and vacillation in our military rulers; one erects a fortification at enormous expense and another destroys it. Our waggon has a team hitched to each end and they draw in opposite directions — what will become of the waggon? We held the batteries during winter and Spring and at the beginning of the sickly season the troops are removed to places subject to malaria — to the worst enemy they can encounter. Country fever is more deadly than bullet or bayonet.

MAY 14TH. The negro crew ran away today with the Steamer, Planter, and carried her to the enemy.[1] They went off from under the nose of the General's Headquarters, within sight of the guard. The Captain and other officers had gone to their several homes and were quietly in bed. Nobody was left on board but negroes; no guard was provided although idle soldiers filled the streets and the boat was engaged in transporting military stores and cannon, five or six of which were on board. The blacks put up the private signals and passed all the forts without question. A few hours after this event, as if to go from extreme laxity to extreme rigidity, the authorities declared martial law. It has made no change except to annoy the citizens. From no precaution at all we have rushed into every sort of useless and harassing regulation. Market carts are not allowed to pass the city bounds; market boats are compelled to stop, not at the market wharf, but, at Morland's a mile from the market. Passports are required for all persons leaving the city. Women and children are advised, almost obliged, to quit the city and two hours only in the day are allowed for obtaining tickets to leave. An immense crowd assembled at the Provost's office this morning; not one in ten was able to obtain a passport. Requests from the multitude to prolong the time were made in vain; petitions and complaints were treated with contempt. The provost and his subordinates were as inexorable as the ancient judges of the infernal regions. There was one alleviating consideration to console for the citizen. The city was threatened with an attack from Lincoln's soldiery. The domestic tyranny would serve as a preparation for the stranger's oppression. We should get accustomed by times to being skinned. If Providence should afflict us for our sins with the foreign despot we should have gone through a training in our home school. It will afford some relief from the ennui of our captivity if it comes, to compare the two doses, the city brewed and the Northern deception, of vexatious annoyances.

MAY 16TH. The Provost finds it impossible to enforce the absurd regulations with which he began. It is made possible to get a passport without running the risk of being squeezed to death in a crowd. Ladies and children are even permitted to leave town without a passport and it has been discovered by our sagacious rulers that the fittest place for a market boat to land is at the market wharf. We are thankful for this unexpected advent of common sense to our councils and enjoy our liberties with thankfulness.

MAY 20TH. Norfolk, it is reported, has been evacuated by the Confederate troops and the Merrimack has been destroyed. There ends for the present all hope of a Southern navy. The loss of Norfolk involves that of the Navy yard at Portsmouth with its dry dock and ship building facilities. Yet, I believe, the destruction of the Merrimack produced a deeper mortification in the South than all the other losses that attended it. There had been among the people the most exaggerated expectations excited by the appointment of Com. Tatnall to command her.[2] The only fear was that he would be too rash; that he would assail Washington, attack New York, or bombard Philadelphia. Nothing was thought too adventurous for a commander so noted for daring. But let no man be counted happy until death has closed his account with fortune. The Commodore did nothing but blow up the ship. Whether it was his fault or his misfortune will not materially alter his position with the people. Whatever the reasons may be for destroying the vessel, her end was unfortunate for all concerned in it. Suicide is not a meritorious departure from the world for either men or ships and the actors never escape grave imputations. The old commodore's laurels have been tarnished by his misfortune, we will think, and not by his fault. But the world seldom cares to inquire which cause is the true one. To be associated even innocently with such a calamity to the Country ensures to the party the evil eye of the people.

JUNE 2ND. The first consequence from the abandonment of Cole's island is the entrance into Stono of the Yankee gunboats and their shelling the islands on either side. The inhabitants of James Island and John's Island have fled from their plantations and the cattle are eating up the half grown crops. Our general having created the necessity of getting out of the enemy's reach by opening the inlet to his marauders now commands all negroes to be removed. It is more easily said than done. Ripley after seeing his plans counteracted has been ordered to Virginia. Two regiments go with him. General Mercer from Savannah takes his place in the city. New brooms sweep clean. We shall see how the adage applies to the new general. Ripley had outlived his popularity. There is but one step, in such cases, with the good people, from hosannahs to cries of crucify him. Pemberton, our major general, is regarded as irritable, petulant and rude. He scorns civilians and militia generals and has no great regard even for the clergy out of the pulpit. One reverend gentleman called at headquarters to intercede for two young men who had got into trouble in camp. The appeal for mercy was contemptuously rejected. The commander in chief, as the divine expressed it, threw up his nose in the air like a wild ass' colt and refused to listen to any intercession for mercy. The decision may have been sound but the manner was ungracious.[3] If he sends the enemy to the right about with as little ceremony we shall nevertheless be satisfied with him. With such an atonement even the clergy will pardon his brusquerie.

JUNE 3RD. The enemy has landed at Legare's place on the lower end of James Island under cover of his gun boats. A small party of Confederates advanced to meet them and a skirmish ensued in which we lost a few men killed, wounded and missing.

Ryan's company captured twenty of their opponents. There was much firing and a great deal of noise during the day and a greater part of the night succeeding. But nothing decisive was attempted to drive the foe from the island. It would be unreasonable to expect vigour or activity from raw troops. When the war shall have lasted two or three years and regular armies are formed, we will see soldiers more fitted for service because better disciplined than volunteer corps can be. At present our troops so long accustomed to be political masters are not always submissive to the arbitrary tone of military rule. There is an uneasy feeling in the city. It seems to be doubted whether the commanding general means to defend it and whether, like Norfolk, it may not be abandoned without a contest. But surely some port should be kept open for communication with foreign countries and a supply of arms and ammunition. It is a mistake to suppose, as people generally do, that in the Revolution of 1776 we were cut off from all intercourse with neutral nations and that a similar condition could be borne now as they suppose it was borne then. Some portion of the American coast was always open to European adventure and the arrival of guns, powder and clothing, during the Revolutionary war. This is an absolute necessity in the present as in the former conflict.

JUNE 4TH. People are moving in crowds from the city. Carts are passing at all hours filled with furniture. The talk in the streets is when do you go; where are you going. Every one take care of himself and the enemy take the hindmost, seems to be the prevailing maxim. My younger folks are gone; some to Newberry; some to Anderson. My wife and I remain. I am averse to play the vagabond at seventy-four. Besides if Charleston falls what part of the country can be safe from the marauding parties of the enemy.

JUNE 6TH. The report today is that Mercer goes back to Savannah and General Smith is to take his place. So the generals are kept moving if the troops do nothing. It is to be hoped that the change of Counsellors like their multitude will bring us wisdom and safety. So far we see very little. The evacuation of Cole's island proves to be the source of infinite evil. We have opened the door to the enemy and invited him to come in. He never attempted to enter Stono while Cole's island was occupied. It would have been very difficult from the intricacy, shallowness and shifting nature of the Channel. Now his gun boats occupy the river as they please. The military authorities have begun to make bomb proofs in Meeting street near the ruins of the circular church and are impressing all negroes. The blacks seem to be considered as contrabands on both sides alike. The Federals seize them and put them to work; the Confederates impress them for the same purpose. The owner's rights are postponed in either case. Throughout the country the paramount law of the land is the law of force. The public journals are silent, adherents of the ruling faction are afraid to speak out. The greediness for office and pay is prevalent everywhere at the South as well as the North. There are disinterested men in our Country but we must go about with a lantern to find them. Certainly our chief men, President, Governors, generals, are not of the number. Washington during the Revolution refused all compensation for his services; what leading man of the present day has imitated the example. They all take whatever they are able to pocket from the scantily furnished public purse.

JUNE 8TH. The bomb proofs or rat holes begun two days ago are abandoned. So we go with feeble vacillating councils, a ship tempest tost with irresolute or ignorant pilots in command.

JUNE 10TH. A skirmish began today on James Island. General Smith made an attack on the Federal force but with very little effect. We had fifty or sixty men killed or wounded and made no impression on the enemy. Doubts are entertained whether the government intends to defend the city. Their stores are ordered away. The banks are moving by the general's advice. I hope he will not bestow all his roughness on his civilian friends but expend it freely on his military foes.

JUNE 12TH. The bells, today, were taken down from the steeple of St. Michael's Church to be sent to Columbia. One that I saw in the Portico bears date 1765. They have crossed the Atlantic three times. Sent to this country originally from England, they were carried back at the close of the Revolution by the British troops. Restored to the Church by the exertions of private [citizens], they are now hurried away from apprehension of another enemy less scrupulous than the former plunderer. I don't know whether the Federals have stolen Church bells but they have given abundant evidence of their entertaining loose notions on the rights of private property and have turned churches into stables for the convenience of their cavalry. We could hardly expect much respect from them for church bells whether as private or sacred property.

JUNE 16TH. The enemy attacked our battery at Secessionville today, at day light, and were repulsed with terrible slaughter.[4] The battery was held by a handful of men under the command of Major Lucas. The attack was almost a surprise but the defense was heroic and thoroughly successful. The enemy were led into action by three generals. Their number was not short of three thousand sustained by their gun boats and batteries. Their discomfiture was total with a loss, it is conjectured, of a thousand men. It cost the Confederates a number of valuable lives. Among these are some of my old and valued acquaintances, Henry King, John Edwards and others. The cause cannot fail which is consecrated by such sacrifices. But alas! for the hearts of mourning mothers, fathers and friends. We are all too apt to enlist Providence on our side in every quarrel but we may at least hope that he will not prosper the arms of men who come a thousand miles to ravage the homes and spill the blood of Southern men under the false pretence of restoring a Union that all the world sees is past restoration.

JUNE 19TH. There has been no movement since the fight of the 16th, but there are a thousand rumours. One is that a great Federal fleet is preparing in the Chesapeake to attack Charleston; that foreign consuls are warned to prepare for the safety of their people; that a French frigate is off the bar to assist in that purpose; that an English frigate is expected with the same view. The great canard has grown from the fact that a French frigate is below with the usual dispatches for the French Consul. It is announced that an English vessel is stranded on Sullivan's island in attempting to run the blockade. She is said to have a thousand barrels of powder much wanted in the City and a large cargo of other articles of value. Anything is acceptable where every thing is wanting. The vessel has reached the city and proves to be the Memphis.

JUNE 20TH. It is impossible to get a correct account of events that pass almost in your presence. A hundred accounts are given of the attack on Secessionville, all from eye witnesses, and yet no two of them alike. It is said that Sir Walter Raleigh saw a tumult at the foot of the tower where he was confined as a prisoner and received an account of it from a half dozen bystanders no two agreeing and all differing from his own version of the story. He concluded therefore that little reliance can be placed on historical narratives. I am afraid they are collections of monstrous falsehoods, a grain of truth perhaps in a bushel of chaff. In this case our own stories differ from each other and the Yankee narrative is at variance with them all. No Confederate general, it seems, was on the field at the beginning of the flight, not at any time, except it be near its close. It could not have been conducted better however if a dozen brigadiers had been present. History will assign all the honour nevertheless to the commanding general in the neighborhood.

JUNE 21ST. A gentleman owning a farm in St. Andrews represents the conduct of our own troops as infamous. They pay no regard to the rights of property and plunder him openly in his presence, careless of threat or remonstrance. These are the characteristics of a democratic soldiery who elect their own officers, among whom private and captain or Colonel are on terms of familiar fellowship, crack jokes together and slap each other on the back in a hearty way. War with these people is a season of license. The camp is a barbacue ground with the additional convenience over ordinary barbacues that the parties assembled may plunder any neighbour's house, shoot his pigs and help themselves without scruple to whatever they may fancy in his field or garden. On John's island, during the winter, every house abandoned by the planter was gutted by our troops and the furniture that was not carried away was wantonly destroyed. Pictures served as targets for pistol shots or objects for bayonet practice; the window sashes were smashed and the doors, window shutters and out houses converted into fuel. One gentleman of John's island saw his chairs on the rail road cars. No destruction of Lincoln's men could be more complete or unsparing. We are realizing the adage that the laws are silent among arms even where the arms are in the hands of our own people.

JUNE 25TH. It is reported today that a negro has come into our camp from the Federals on James Island. He is a Georgia runaway who has seen enough of his Northern friends and is desirous of returning to his master. He had been employed by a Colonel of the enemy to attend to a horse and took the opportunity of riding the horse to water to ride off to the Confederate camp. With nominal wages and these paid by Lincoln's government, the negro performs the same duties to his Northern as to his Southern master. He enjoys the great advantage too of being called not a "slave" but a "servant." The return of the runaway to his former condition indicates sufficiently the benefits of the change. He reports that the enemy carried from the field on the 16th six hundred and forty killed and wounded; this number with those buried by our troops and the prisoners taken will fall little short of a thousand. In these murderous conflicts both parties aver that they are doing their duty and both have devout men and pious chaplains who exhort them to perform it faithfully. It tempts us to believe that the moral sense is no infallible guide in questions of ethics and that Christianity is not a successful teacher of peace on earth and good will towards men. Here are men who come a thousand miles from home to cut their neighbours' throats. They do this to honour their flag, to restore amity and the Union, and to obtain a farm of rich cotton land on Edisto island. There is a levity exhibited in their letters picked up on the battle field, a malignant mockery of all that is sacred mixed up with a sour spirit of hatred that savours of European Red Republicanism and New England rancour combined. Our worthy friends of Massachusetts treats us [as] they did the Indians, witches, quakers, Baptists and other heretics of earlier times. There are many pious Christians but not a voice is heard in favour of peace. So far as we can judge from their acquiescence in Sewardism they have fallen into the strange delusion that Christian Charity is consistent with rape, rapine, and murder. The pray and preach not for peace but for the more earnest prosecution of a bloody war and the enactment of general confiscation acts. If any disapprove these things, they do nothing to oppose them. They are not of the class to which the brave apostle belonged who fought with beasts at Ephesus. The beasts at Washington have it all their own way and the Christian brotherhood at the North not only quietly look on while the brutes rend and devour but stimulate their appetites to fresh exertions. These things try the faith of good Christians. An old friend remarked to me yesterday that Christianity is a failure. It inculcates peace and love but has made no progress in changing our nature; was is still as rife in the world as in the palmy times of paganism. But this is a sorry conclusion for a Christian to arrive at and not a just one. The religion of love is not without its fruits even on the field of battle. The wounded enemy now is not commonly put to the sword. He is received in the hospitals of his foe. His wounds are healed and his wants supplied. He is not made a slave nor are women and children sold sub hasta by the conqueror now as in ancient times. In spite of even Butler's brutality let us hold fast to the faith and confide in its future mitigating influences in the world of Christian faith and morals.

Another large steamer, the Hero, has arrived with a cargo of goods. She grounded on the bar coming in. The crew took to her boats and made for the shore leaving the officers on board. But the tide rose and lifted the vessel. She steamed in past her fugitive boats and came up to the City with no damage but the loss of a few goods thrown overboard to lighten her.

Evans and Drayton are ordered to Virginia with a number of the troops from between Charleston and Savannah. There has not been much activity among our commanding officers along the coast. Their policy is not aggressive. The rule seems to be never to attack the enemy at our door until he attempts to enter it and not to pursue him farther than the threshold when he retreats. The ardor of subordinate officers, it is said, is checked by their superiors. We who are spectators only at a distance are advocates of greater energy. A distinguished gentleman, previous to the attack on Sumter, urged the Governor vehemently and repeatedly to begin it. The governor harassed by his pertinacity, at last offered him to command, with permission to begin the war at his discretion. The importunate gentleman declined the offer. While criticising our leaders we should probably receive a similar offer in the same way.

JUNE 26TH. Preparations are made for obstructing the harbour. The people seem to have little faith in the attempt. It would be better perhaps to multiply forts in and above the city, that if the enemy's gun boats pass the fort below they would still be under fire. It ought not to be understood as it formerly was that if a gun boat approaches the city a surrender must follow. Vicksburg has settled that question. In New Orleans, instead of vain attempts to obstruct the river, had erected strong forts near the city, she would have escaped the brutalities of Butler.

JUNE 27TH. A gentleman from Richmond tells me a shocking story of the scenes exhibited on the way in the transportation of the dead from the field of battle to their friends at home. The condition of the bodies, the offensive smell, the careless manner in which they are handled on the road and left exposed at the depots, make their passage anything but pleasant to all who come near them. There is not one man in a hundred who would not avoid any such disposition of his remains. Major Wheat of the Louisiana troops in the battle of Richmond requested, in his last moments, to be buried in the field of battle. It is what every brave soldier will prefer. Let the fallen be buried where they fell. Let friendship erect its monument there and the Country raise a general memorial to its illustrious defenders. It would add infinite interest to the battle field forever. The tombs and the names of the heroes beneath them would court the eyes of all who should visit the spot that will live in history like the field of Marathon. What cemetery could be so sacred and appropriate. I respect with warm sympathy the affection that would see the remains of the departed and join in the last offices of respect that are due to the dead, but it is better to restrain the wish when to indulge it is so painful to surviving friends, when it removes the deceased from his fitting resting place and when in almost every case it would be in opposition to his dying desires.

JUNE 27TH. While we revile the Yankees we imitate them. It is one of their peculiarities to be always inventing slang words and phrases which they thrust into the newspapers and wear to tatters. We never fail to adopt them. Some time ago, the term was "high falutin," next, "in our midst" now it is "skedaddle." We meet with it in all quarters, North and South. No troops run away or retreat;

they skedaddle. We use their manufactured words as we do their brooms and buckets. Every thing proves how provincial we were getting to be. Even war and revolution have not broken the chain of habit.

JUNE 28TH. The heart of the city is moved with a report that a great conflict is going on near the city of Richmond. Every body is alive with anxiety and expectation. Everybody has a word to say as to the proper mode of proceeding. It is the privilege of a free people to criticize its authorities, civil and political, to know every thing, to be familiar especially with military affairs. A story is told of Hannibal being once invited to hear a Rhetoricean discourse on the art of war. If the Carthaginian leader were a sojourner in our city he would meet an instructor at every corner. It has happened by some oversight of President Davis that the great strategists are not in the army. They are left at home to supervise the marches and battles of Lee, Johnson and Beauregard. Some of the gentlemen most prominent in hurrahing the people into the contest have never been able even to get into the ranks. All that they have been able to do is to given their opinions and advice freely on the conduct of affairs and on the characters of those who direct them. Unfortunately for the Country, the structures of these neglected patriots have no influence at headquarters.

JUNE 30TH. The English war steamer Racer entered Charleston harbour today and lies in front of the battery. Everybody has an opinion to express. One asks if she saluted the Confederate flag — of course she did nothing of the kind. It is conjectured by another that her arrival indicates an attack on Charleston and she comes to look after English subjects and interests. In another's judgment it indicates a change in England's policy and foreshadows her recognition of the Southern Confederacy. This notion is a very idle one. England's foreign policy consults her own interests only. She acts when these demand it and never before. She stood aside and saw Poland divided and Hungary crushed. She interposed in South America because she hoped to obtain great advantages from the trade of the Spanish Colonies when independent States. She desires Southern trade but will not risk her interests in the North. She will stand aloof from the South during her struggle and be cordial with her when the battle has been fought and the victory won; while we are struggling in deep water she will look on complacently and do by us afterwards as Johnson says Lord Chesterfield did by him — encumber us with help after we have reached the shore. She will not risk the loss of her Northern debts. There is nothing surprising in this. Whatever may be true of individuals, the conduct of Nations is always selfish. It is so at least with what are called free governments. An autocrat may be swayed by generosity or caprice to take part with the weak against the strong; nothing moves a Republic or limited monarchy but gain or ambition.

DEATH OF CHARLES COCHRAN LEE[5]

Every day adds another to the long list of those who have poured out their life-blood on the altar of their Country's independence. In the desperate conflict of Monday the 30th of June Charles C. Lee of the North Carolina troops was killed by a grape shot while leading his regiment to the charge of a battery. He was the Son of Mr. Stephen Lee of Asheville and nephew of Judge Lee of this city. Col. Lee was born in Charleston and educated at West Point. He became a professor in the Military School at Charlotte, took service in the Confederate Army at the beginning of hostilities and has been engaged in repeated battles with the enemy during the whole course of the war. He fought through the fierce conflicts of the first three days before Richmond and fell, on the fourth, a noble example of devotion to the cause of his Country. No better soldier has fallen in the great battles that have won we trust the freedom of the Confederacy. The military knowledge which he acquired at West Point was improved by practice and enlarged by subsequent application. He was indefatigable in assisting to train the troops of his adopted State and no finer troops than the North Carolina regiment are found in the Confederate Service.

Col. Lee was exemplary in all the relations of life. His manners were singularly winning. The most transient acquaintance was caught by their charm. How many affectionate hearts will bear witness to the tenderness of his nature, his true Spirit and gentle bearing! The father and wife and child too young to know its loss and numerous relatives will mourn over the untimely death of one so good, so brave, so young in his career of honour and usefulness. Surely such deaths are not in vain. The cause which they consecrate can never fail. Heaven we humbly yet firmly believe will bless to the Martyr's cause and Country a death so frought with sorrow to his household and friends. The sacrifice will not be fruitless. The blood of the patriot Soldier is the cement of the confederacy.

JULY 1ST [1862]. The city was roused at daylight by a canonade. It turned out to be a salute from all the forts in honour of the victory before Richmond. The city is deeply moved by the great news. A feeling of thankfulness prevails, a disposition to ascribe the glory not to our own strength but to Providence. There is less of a boastful spirit than there was last year at our successes—not less resolution to do and dare, but more sobriety and moderation of spirit. We talk more of what God had done for us and less of our chivalry and invincible arms. The "Mercury" does say something in its comments on the fight of the 16th of June about blood or race and of "noblesse oblige" but it is in a quiet way only. I don't know whether any were in the fight who had figured in the raids on the John's island plantations, but if there were the "nobless oblige" would none the less apply to the occasion. The Norman noblesse the bravest in Europe were its greatest thieves.

JULY 3RD. The enemy on James island have abandoned their posts on Grimbald's plantation. They left behind them many inscriptions on boards, some queer and some blasphemous, with the promise of returning at another time. They have got so little by their present visit that if they evacuate the island, they will be in no hurry to come back to it. The defeat in Virginia of the grand army will probably call to McClellan's assistance all the marauders of Stevens and Hunter. Another steamer arrived last night with arms and ammunition. The Nashville attempted to enter but was chased back to Nassau.

JULY 4TH. The accounts from Virginia continue favorable. McClellan is routed and its troops are striving only to escape from their enemy. It is curious to see the change in faces and talk as the fortunes of the war fluctuate. The man who spoke despondingly and almost despairingly a few days since is now as bold as a lion. He always knew we should succeed in the long run. He thinks recognition must follow very soon on the heels of our great victory; that the Lincoln domination will soon be at an end and that Seward will hang himself. Let a trifling reverse come and he will go again from the housetop to the cellar and predict a thousand disasters.

JULY 5TH. The troops in our camps on James Island are sickly. The supervisor of hospitals tells me he sends away from thirty to eighty a day. The enemy must suffer in still greater proportion. We lose many more from disease than the sword. But in war it is always so.

JULY 6TH. The Nashville has arrived at Ogechee with a cargo of war stores. This is the third arrival of ammunition and arms in this neighbourhood within a fortnight. It shows the importance of keeping a part of the coast open to vessels from foreign ports. Charleston is now the most important and ought to be held at all hazards.

JULY 7TH. One more English steamer has arrived. The profits of a successful voyage must be enormous and afford a tempting bait to commercial enterprise. What a despair it must be to the Northern adventurer that he is obliged to abstain from it, if indeed he does abstain from it. The men who engage in the slave trade without scruple would hardly hold back from traffic with their enemy if the gains are great. The rumour today is that McClellan has rallied his discomfited host under the cover of his gun boats, at Berkley, on James River. The Northern papers of the 30th are confident that their general is only executing some great strategical movement; that he will soon be in Richmond and "bag" the whole Rebel army. Both sides resort, in turn, to the same jargon to conceal defeat. Each of the contending armies retreat and call it strategy. On the present occasion the Federals even claim a great victory. Halleck informs his troops in the West that McClellan has taken Richmond and fifty thousand men as he reported at Corinth that he himself had captured ten thousand prisoners and fifteen thousand stand of arms. We are a great people — we other Americans as the French phrase it — we fight great battles and both side[s] win victories at the same time. The Federals are rising in reputation all over Europe for acts of infamy. I hope we shall not share with them the fame of lying. But certainly we indulge sometimes in enormous rumours. One in circulation today represented our army, on the most "reliable authority," as having taken seventy thousand prisoners.

Everybody wears a radiant face in the Streets. Certainly, they say, England and France will not interfere. One would think it reasonable that they should to a certain extent at least. The Federal Government has had possession for some time of the great cotton port and it produces no cotton for Europe. The promises of abundant supplies from the Federal experiment of seizing New Orleans have produced nothing. Foreign powers might now reasonably suggest an experiment of another kind; they might insist on raising the blockade of one Southern port and seeing whether the consequences to the cotton trade might not be more in accordance with their wishes and wants. There is no doubt that their ships will get cargoes at Charleston, Savannah or Mobile while under Confederate rule if they get none from New Orleans under Butler's domination.

JULY 15TH. The enemy have retired from James Island and gone, we suppose, to share the triumphs of McClellan on James River. It is reported that Pemberton has been ordered to resume possession of Cole's Island. He is in the condition of the fisherman in the "Arabian Nights" when he dragged out of the sea one of the genii in a vase in which a wiser man had shut up the potent spirit. But the fisherman had wit enough to induce the giant to go back into the vase. I am afraid Pemberton will not have as much ingenuity and will fail to coax the gun boats back to sea until he closes the inlet. He is illustrating the maxim that it's easier to do mischief than to repair it.

JULY 16TH. Col. Wagner and Lieut. Wardlaw were wounded today by the bursting of a thirty two pounder. The gun was an old smooth bore, rifled and fortified by iron bands. There are different opinions as to the safety of such cannon. They seem to me to be a clumsy contrivance as all make shifts are. It is a lamentable and discouraging event when our officers and men are destroyed by their own weapons. It is sad enough when they are killed by those of the enemy. But here the gallant Wagner who behaved with so much heroism at the desperate fight of the 16th and escaped unwounded is struck down in our own fortress by his own gun. There was one soldier killed and four or five wounded at the same time.

JULY 18TH. Lieut. Col. Wagner died yesterday and was buried today. I never saw at a funeral so profound a sympathy. The attendance was very large. The deceased was much beloved. He was one of those happily tempered dispositions that conciliate all men and never fail to convert an acquaintance into a friend. It is the gift of a warm heart and genial manners, a gift of nature not to be bought or acquired and of higher worth than wealth, power or place.

JULY 19TH. There is not in the Northern councils or among the Northern people the slightest sign of remorseful or reluctant feeling at the torrents of blood they are wantonly shedding in every Southern State. Their talk is of continued hostilities, of crushing the rebellion, of arming slaves, of subjugating the Southern people, of the universal confiscation of Southern property. They speak like men who believe they have irresistable power and feel no scruple in using it for the worst ends. We knew they were a people of inordinate vanity, vainglorious and boastful, selfish and unprincipled in the pursuit of gain, but they have outgone every idea we ever entertained of their arrogant disregard of justice and truth, of the rights and lives of their neighbors and former associates. Unlimited carnage, unrestrained plunder is their cry.

JULY 22ND. The two gunboats begun in May are rapidly advancing to completion. One is built by Mr. Marsh, the other by Mr. Jones. It was a good plan to begin them at the same time. They have been pushed on with rival skill and speed. Judges of such matters speak in unqualified terms of their excellence. They are said to be as strong as live oak and iron can make them. The North have enjoyed immense advantages during their contest with the South in various ways—in the prestige of an established government, in wealth, population, commerce, the mechanic arts, the virtual assistance of foreign states whose neutrality has been one of appearance only and in the prejudices industriously exerted by our neighbors against the Southern people. They may nevertheless illustrate the truth which teaches us that the race is not always to the swift nor the battle to the strong.

On the 30th of July I left Charleston with my wife and daughter on a visit to the upper part of the State. In Columbia I found everything wonderfully changed. I had not been in the place for thirty years and could hardly recognise it. The old State house is still in existence. Ainslie Hall's store is yet standing; but there are gardens and houses and churchs in various quarters where none existed when I was last there. In my college days the Methodist Church looking very much like a barn was the only place of worship that I remember except the College chapel. We rode about the town and admired it greatly. The view from Taylor's hill over the Congaree valley has great beauty. It has been said that Columbia is the prettiest inland town in America. It certainly has great advantages, a fine position overlooking the river, wide streets, spacious gardens, beautiful houses and handsome churches.

On the first of August we took the railroad to Newberry at seven o'clock; in Newberry we spent a week and then went on to Anderson where we continued three weeks. I was never before above Columbia and have been charmed with the Country beyond the falls of the rivers. It is a noble region, for the most part undulating, enjoying a fine climate and good soil and producing wheat, corn and cattle in abundance. It ought to be a country of great plenty. All it needs is proper cultivation. Hitherto, it has laboured under the general curse of perpetual emigration to more Southern or Western fields of enterprise. The farmers are discovering at last that they can do as well or better by staying at home. They are beginning to improve their lands with guano and other manures but as yet imperfectly. It is hard to persuade them that it is better to cultivate ten acres well manured than forty not manured at all. An intelligent farmer from the Northern boundary of Newberry tells me the average production is around twelve bushels of corn and nine of wheat; it ought to be double or more. The whole Country above Columbia would be a magnificent farming region if cultivated by skillful labour. It would have been highly improved before this if our people below had made their summer excursions in their own State and spent the millions they have lavished on the North in giving new charms to their own hills and mountains. You are born in Sparta, adorn it, is a maxim of ancient wisdom which we have long disregarded. Just and liberal views of the citizen's duty to his State would have led the wealthy to a different policy from that pursued and the aid of their redundant capital could not have been bestowed upon a finer people. The inhabitants of the upper districts are a tall, athletic, intelligent race, a magnificent yeomanry, capable of every success in arts and arms. Their achievements in the present was indicate their martial qualities and evidences of growing intelligence are visible in the schools and churches of every village. There are signs of progress everywhere. Very different, I regret to say, is the condition of our maritime region. There, no improvement is perceptible in sixty years, except in Charleston. Many of the parishes are not as flourishing as they were a half century ago.

There never has been much cordiality between the upper and lower of South Carolina and it is said the late fugitives from the coast have not been received everywhere with uniform hospitality. If it be so, it is not surprising. What better had the parish population any right to expect when for eighty years they have been wasting millions annually on Northern watering places and investing their money in Northern farms to the neglect of their own State. If we have not been received everywhere by the people above with open arms it is because we sought their arms from necessity not choice. We look for refuge among our own people when we can no longer find homes among those who have been always hollow friends and are now the most malignant enemies. We have adorned New England

and New York and neglected our own beautiful back country which needs capital and attention only to become a garden. Let us hope for better things in the future.

In passing up and down on the railroad we saw at every stopping place a gathering of upturned, anxious faces seeking among the passengers someone who could give them intelligence of friends and relatives in the army of Virginia. This was especially observable after a great battle had been fought, when disabled soldiers were returning home from the field of carnage. Then fathers and mothers and sisters were eager yet fearful to hear who were killed, who wounded and who safe in the terrible conflict. They betrayed in various ways the different emotions excited by the news. By some it was received with quivering lips, moistened eyes and tremulous tones of farther inquiry; with others every indication of feeling was resolutely restrained; while with the hearers of favourable intelligence only, who found that all their beloved ones were safe and had contributed by distinguished conduct and courage to the victory achieved, bright flashes of proud pleasure glowed on every face. Perhaps in the next contest their turn for sorrow may come for hardly a family in the South has escaped unscathed. The horrible was has swept away props and ornaments of almost every household. The devotion of the friends of the wounded has been without limit. Hundreds have gone on after every great Conflict to carry comfort and assistance to their wounded and sick. No consideration of personal suffering kept them back. I met on my way to Anderson, late in September, Judge Law of Georgia returning from Virginia. He and Mrs. Law had gone to the Succour of a son wounded in the battle of Manassas. The father and mother, he nearly seventy and she no longer young, had braved all fatigue and from Gordonsville had ridden on horseback twenty miles in pursuit of their disabled boy. More fortunate than thousands of other parents they found him doing well and were able to bring him home with them. He was in the cars by his mother's side, looking well though still walking on crutches.

SEPT. 9TH. The State Convention assembled today.[6] It has been called together by the presiding officer at the request of twenty of its members. The people seem to think that the Convention has completed the performance of its appropriate duties and should now adjourn. The convention thinks differently. Having discharged its legitimate functions it is disposed to undertake the charge of governing the State. We are a remarkable people we So Carolinians.

Every other State is content with the constitutional government of judges, legislature, and governor; we have no faith in them. Every other state is satisfied with one State Government; we must have two. It is not surprising that the Convention should undertake to supervise the constitutional government, it is so easy for men to persuade themselves that they are wiser than their neighbours; it will be somewhat strange however, if their neighbours should agree with them in opinion. If the people should acquiesce in; if they are content; if on their long back, they are willing to carry two riders, who can have a right to complain? I hope the equestrians, the old rider and the volunteer, may keep their seats quietly and not fall out by the way. They may kick and spur the poor beast they bestride without danger. He bears it peaceably enough. The risk is that the riders may disagree before they reach the end of their ride. They may wish to go different ways while their patient animal that carries them, however willing, can go but one.

But if not, if there should be any conflict of will between the two state governments, with which we are blessed, the convention is the master. It has great advantages already. It claims supreme power; the other does not. The Constitutional Government is limited, circumscribed, hedged in, by the articles of the Constitution; the Convention has no bound. It knows no rule to guide its exercise of power but the autocratic sic volo, sic jubeo. It has decided already that if one should be tempted to regard such sweeping claims to mastership as savouring of usurpation and despotism under a new name he would be greatly mistaken. The Convention has given three conclusive reasons why he should think otherwise.

Firstly, the Convention deny the charge; they assure us that they are not claiming or exercising despotic power when they assume unlimited authority over the State, because, as they say, their measures have been beneficial to the Country or, at the least, they have done no harm.

They have not abused power, and therefore, as they think, have not assumed it. They have been moderate and modest and will continue to be so and everyone knows that the character of a government depends on the mode in which it is administered and not on its form. Whatever is best administered is best. We have been accustomed to think but it is all a mistake that the French Emperor's power is not despotic if he governs well.

Secondly, the Convention admit the fact that they are a despotism and defend the claim. They are the people and hold the sovereign power. The Convention is not a body of delegates chosen by the people to modify their government, as a legislature is elected to make their laws, and for nothing more; the two hundred gentlemen assembled in the State house and called a convention are the people, the Sovereign people, and may do what they please. To this reasoning of the Convention there can be no reply. No one in his senses will dispute it. It is like an argument to prove that a part is equal to the whole or that a bucket of salt water is the ocean; it admits of no answer. The one who can advance one or the other opinion is a fit candidate, not for the State house, but for another building which the munificense of the people has provided for similar cases. A short residence with the Doctor of the Lunatic Asylum would be the only fit reply to the logic of these disordered reasoners. They ought to have adjourned from the old wooden State house to a brick mansion in another part of the city.

Thirdly, it is intimated by the Convention orators that, in some way or other, the Convention is the dictator of the State for the time being that too, by the bye, it regards as subordinate to its own legislative authority, which it repudiated in all other matters. Some unfortunate gentleman it seems, when the act or ordinance calling a convention was about to be passed remembered a piece of Latin and introduced it in substance to round a sentence. The Convention was directed to take care that the State received no detriment. It is an old Roman Formula and was used when a dictator was appointed. In Rome, the dictatorship was a device of the Senate used for concentrating all power in the hands of one of their members. It was used in great emergencies very often for settling disputes with the people by an appeal to the sword. With us, the phrase in unknown in the Constitutional governments of America and at variance with the Spirit of our institutions. Is there any clause of the State Constitution that authorizes the appointment of a dictator? The legislature is empowered by the people to call a convention. It can therefore call a convention — no more. A convention when called is a well understood assembly of delegates chosen for a definite purpose, not a new and untried body for unknown or unlimited ends or acts. If it goes beyond the definite purpose of its election, it is not a dictator but a usurper, a betrayer of its trust, a criminal deserving punishment no matter what its intentions may have been. But wonderful are the virtues of a phrase however empty. For the very reason that it means nothing it may be taken to mean anything. The "no detriment" phrase, like the "general welfare" flourish of the United States Constitution, mere words used to fill up a sentence, has been able to kick aside all constitutional government with its limitations and balances. Great was Diana of the Ephesians and great still is her modern representative, the goddess humbug, whether her temple be in Washington or Columbia.

For these three reasons and perhaps for others equally clear and cogent, the Convention is resolved still to keep its seat on the shoulders of the people. I hope it may not encounter the fate of its prototype, the friend of Sinbad the sailor, the old man of the Sea though one is almost tempted to think it deserves nothing better.

If a Convention is to be regarded, not as a body of delegates elected for a definite purpose but as the sovereign people irresponsible and unlimited in power then I earnestly hope that the present convention is the last that the State of South Carolina will ever see. A convention of such powers would be in substance an oligarchy and one as odious and dangerous as any that the world has ever seen from the time of thirty tyrants in Athens to the present day. Any body of men exercising all power is essentially a tyranny no matter by what name it may be called, and no matter how its powers are exercised.

OCT. 15TH. I returned to Charleston on the 1st of October and found the city, as I left it, full of floating rumours. It was to be attacked in a few days. Somebody reported to Gen. Beauregard that the cabinet at Washington had so decided. How the gentleman contrived to find out the cabinet secret nobody could tell or cared to inquire. The mist was too dense for any eyes to look through. The portentious goddess, Rumour, is not changed since Virgil described her. Head is still in the clouds. The effect of the ambiguous words that she scatters among the people is not as startling as it was a year ago. The rogue rumors do not drive crowds of our people to the railroad. They gather more quietly now or the excitable people are all gone. But the words are not too numerous or unreasoning.

We found the gunboats launched and nearly ready for service. They are the ugliest craft that the sea has ever borne since the time of Noah's ark. Their appearance is that of two huge turtles floating in calm weather on the surface of the water as we have often seen them. The boats are said to be strongly built and will be more fortunate, I hope, than our former experiments in iron clad ships.

Preparations are actively making for the enemy. Numbers of negroes from all parts of the State are at work on the fortifications. The floating obstructions in the harbour are a failure. They have been swept away as soon as completed. There is no plea in this case as in that of New Orleans of a flood without precedent which nothing could resist. In Charleston harbour there was nothing to guard against but the spring tides of semi monthly recurrence for which the science of the engineer should be able to produce a sufficient resisting power or to know that it could not be obtained. The science in this case did neither one nor the other.

There have been changes in the commanding officer of the post since July. Pemberton is gone to the West. Beauregard has taken his place. Pemberton from being very unpopular was rising fast in public esteem when he left the city. He had not been a favourite for the very reason that ought to have commanded the people's confidence. He cared very little for this politician's plan or that militia officer's suggestion in military affairs, and the volunteer counsellor went away his bitter enemy. But decision and firmness will generally succeed at last even if a little rough in their mode of processing. It was so with Pemberton. Beauregard is a great favorite. He is more accessible and not so apt to intimate that a meddler's pet project is an absurdity. In the position they occupy, the Pemberton mode of action is, perhaps, the better policy in the end. The general who listens to every body's scheme is tempted to vacillate in his councils. The return of Beauregard to Charleston seems to have restored Ripley to his old station.[7] The people's trust is strong in their united efforts and ability.

OCT. 20TH. The Adelaide has arrived from Nassau with arms and ammunition. A few days subsequently, the Minho after escaping the blockading squadron ran on the stone work near Fort Moultrie and has become a wreck. It is like a soldier who escapes through a perilous battle and breaks his neck over the threshold when he has reached his quarters.

OCT. 23RD. Today the news arrived of a skirmish at Pocotaligo. The enemy landed from their gun boats at Mackay's point and marched on the rail road to destroy it. He was driven back by Col. Walker after a gallant action in which the enemy it is said lost two hundred, killed and wounded. Our own loss was about fifteen killed and forty wounded. The disparity of force was very great. Our own number of troops actually engaged is reported to have been about four hundred men, that of the abolitionists as consisting of eight regiments, not less we suppose than from three to five thousand. I notice the old parish names among our wounded, Fripp, Jenkins, Chaplin, Sams, Stuart, Fuller, Elliott, brave men exasperated by the sense of personal wrongs received from the Abolition foe and indignant at the invasion of their native State. They will prove formidable adversaries in avenging the double injury done to themselves and to their country.

OCT. 29TH. All the world is agog for making salt. I see a number of boilers every where in operation and others preparing in all parts of the city adjacent to the water. The largest producer makes an average of forty bushels and is reported to make $500.00 a day clear of all expence. It is said that the salt of our home manufacture is not suited to the curing of meat—that it retains substances which counteract the effect of the salt. I know nothing of the merits of the question but Mr. Collman tells me he cured his bacon last winter with salt of his own making and the hams he is now eating from it are as good as any he has ever tasted. At any rate there seems a prevailing faith in the article since its price is increasing from day to day and new works are erected every week. When I left the city in the Summer, the price was ten dollars; it is now twenty and rising.

NOV. 17TH. Last night the city was alarmed by a heavy firing at the mouth of the harbour. The wharves and battery were crowded with inquiries. Nobody could tell what was the matter but conjectures were not wanting. This morning, it is reported that the Yankees attempted to land on Sullivan's island; that the Herald attempted to go out with another steamer and were fired on by the blockaders; that Ripley was exercising his men and keeping them on the alert, by beating the long roll and practising target firing in the dark. On Saturday, 15th, another steamer arrived. A company of six or seven men bought an old brig in May, loaded her [with] cotton, ran the blockade, sold brig and cargo in Barcelona, bought an English steamer, fitted her with assorted goods and have got back in safely. The Success is immense. It is no wonder that men devise such words as chance, fortune, luck, to characterise certain events—such events as are brought about by causes the chain of which we are unable to trace. We live in times when fortunes are made by a single lucky hit and the blind goddess is worshipped accordingly.

The democrats have succeeded in New Jersey, Pennsylvania, Ohio, and in other States and every one speculates on the expected consequences. The sanguine think that peace must come of it ultimately. It may become a party necessity of the democratic party to become a peace party in order to make a definite and intelligible issue before the people. At present their position is without meaning. They are for waging war constitutionally and for the Union. But how one set of States can make war upon another set constitutionally is not easily understood and in what way a Union of consent among States can be made a Union of force without a total change of the government is as hard of comprehension. Not is it easy to conceive how the South is to be conciliated by keeping the bayonet at her throat. John Van Buren is the only man in the North who seems to have any clear or definite scheme of action for the occasion—and armistice; a general convention; the South to be invited to send delegates; if they are sent new guarantees to be offered by the North; if not, the South to be allowed to depart in peace. Whatever the result of his scheme the consequence of an armistice and a convention would be peace. It would not be easy to resume a war once fairly suspended.

NOV. 18TH. Judge King was buried today.[8] He died in his eightieth year, one of our oldest, most esteemed and successful citizens. He came to Charleston fifty seven years ago, a young man in pursuit of fortune with his wits and his learning his only capital. He leaves an ample estate and a well merited reputation for wisdom and justice. He was a lover of books and sacrificed not only to the Severer but the lighter muses. A poem introduced him to public notice. His knowledge was extensive and various. He exhibited in his life a curious illustration of the manner in which one's fortunes are shaped by unexpected events, by what the pious call Providence the thoughtless, Chance. When about two and twenty, Mr. King went from Edinburg to London with the intention of embarking for the East Indies. On reaching London he found the fleet had sailed. It was a period of war, convoy was necessary and was provided periodically only. Some time would elapse before another opportunity offered and he made a voyage to the Mediterranean to employ his leisure. During his voyage he was captured and carried to Spain. From Spain after picking up something of the language he managed to escape and was fortuitously landed at Charleston. A short time after, his poem called the "Wanderer" was published in the city papers, attracted attention and procured him employment. He became a teacher in the Charleston College, was some time after admitted to the bar and in time ranked among the ablest of our lawyers. He was all his life a student and a diligent collector of books. Of his large and valuable library, perhaps the best private library in the South, he bequeathed a large portion to the Charleston College.

Notes

Documentation of the Grayson autobiography is a major task. I have sought a balance between the impossible dream of documenting everything and the reality of limiting myself to items that are clearly relevant to establishing a historical context for Grayson's text. Consequently, I have given priority to identifying items that concern South Carolina, the South, or Washington. On the other hand, when I document I have chosen to provide rather full documentation with the intention of making this a valuable tool for those doing research in nineteenth-century Southern literature. The most valuable resource for scholars has been the notes in *The Letters of William Gilmore Simms*. I found, however, that many of the items I needed to identify were not footnoted in these volumes. I have tried to identify adequately such items. The sources utilizied for my identifications are listed in my bibliography.

Introduction: William J. Grayson, Autobiographer

1. Fred Hobson, *Tell About the South* (Baton Rouge: Louisiana State University Press, 1983) 20, 25.
2. Henry Timrod, "What is Poetry?" *Russell's Magazine* 2 (October 1857): 52-58. Grayson's opening article appeared in 1 (July 1857): 327-37. Timrod clearly still had Grayson and his ilk in mind in his reference to the continuing influence of Lord Kames and his *Elements of Criticism* in his later essay, "Literature in the South," *Russell's Magazine* 5 (August 1859) 385-95.
3. Theodore Rosengarten, *Tombee: Portrait of a Cotton Planter* (New York: McGraw-Hill, 1987) 730.
4. David Duncan Wallace, *South Carolina: A Short History 1520-1948* (Chapel Hill: University of North Carolina Press, 1951) 353. See also J. E. McTeer, *Beaufort Now and Then* (Beaufort, S.C.: Beaufort Book Company, 1971) and Katharine M. Jones, *Port Royal Under Six Flags* (Indianapolis: Bobbs-Merrill, 1960).
5. Rosengarten, *Tombee*, p. 412.
6. Edmund Wilson, *Patriotic Gore: Studies in the Literature of the American Civil War* (New York: Oxford University Press, 1962) 336-41; V. L. Parrington, *Main Currents in American Thought* 2 (New York: Harcourt, Brace and Company, 1927) 101-106. Parrington calls Grayson "no fire eater but a southern moderate—a gentleman of old-fashioned tastes. . . ."
7. Works consulted include: William Sumner Jenkins, *Pro-Slavery Thought in the Old South* (Chapel Hill: University of North Carolina Press, 1935), now dated; the selections in Eric L. McKitrick, *Slavery Defended: the Views of the Old South* (Englewood Cliffs, N.J.: Prentice Hall, 1963); Drew Gilpin Faust, *The Ideology of Slavery* (Baton Rouge: Louisiana State University Press, 1981); Eugene Genovese

made valuable suggestions, and his *The World the Slaveholders Made; Two Essays in Interpretation* (New York: Pantheon Books, 1969) is of great value.

8. George Fitzhugh, *Sociology for the South; or the Failure of Free Society* (Richmond: A. Morris, 1854).

9. On Thornwell there is Charles C. Bishop, "The Pro-slavery Argument Reconsidered: James Henley Thornwell, Millenial Abolitionist," *South Carolina Historical Magazine*, 73: 18-26. Again Eugene Genovese provided helpful directions.

10. *Russell's Magazine* 1 (April 1857): 1-14.

11. Grayson, "What is Poetry?" *Russell's Magazine* 1 (July 1857): 329.

12. *Russell's Magazine* 2 (October 1857): 52.

13. "Literature in the South," *Russell's Magazine* 5 (August 1859): 386-7, 389.

14. Richard J. Calhoun, "Literary Magazines in the Old South," in Louis D. Rubin, Jr., et al., *The History of Southern Literature* (Baton Rouge: Louisiana State University Press, 1985) 157-64.

15. The best studies of intellectual life in the South at this time are Michael O'Brien and David Moltke-Hansen, *Intellectual Life in Antebellum Charleston* (Knoxville: University of Tennessee Press, 1986) and Drew Gilpin Faust, *A Sacred Circle: The Dilemma of the Intellectual in the Old South, 1840-1860* (Baltimore: Johns Hopkins University Press, 1977).

16. Mary C. Simms Oliphant, Alfred Taylor Odell, T.C. Duncan Eaves, *The Letters of William Gilmore Simms* 3 (Columbia: University of South Carolina Press, 1962) 369.

17. For Grayson see *Southern Bivouac* 1 (November 1885): 331-35.

18. Rosengarten, *Tombee*; C. Vann Woodward, *Mary Chesnut's Civil War* (New Haven: Yale University Press, 1981). Mary Chesnut makes one mention of Grayson: "Sandy Brown and Grayson (the poet and friend of Mr. Petigru) are at shovel and tongs." Woodward says simply: "A former U.S. congressman, William John Grayson, combined an ardent defense of slavery with opposition to secession." (p. 393)

19. "The Character of the Gentleman," *Southern Quarterly N.S./Review*, N.S. 7 (January 1853): 53-80.

20. Carl Degler, *The Other South: Southern Dissenters in the Nineteenth Century* (New York: Harper & Row, 1974); John McCardell, *The Idea of a Southern Nation: Southern Nationalists and Southern Nationalism, 1830-1860* (New York: W. W. Norton, 1979).

21. Especially detailed, showing Grayson's interest in biography is his "Hamilton and Burr," in *Russell's Magazine* 2 (February 1858): 385-403. Almost equally important is his review of Simms' *Life of Nathanael Greene, Russell's Magazine* 3 (September 1858): 482-496.

22. Grayson's review, "LaBorde's History of South Carolina College," appeared in *Russell's Magazine* 5 (September 1859): 550-2.

23. Janet Varner Gunn, *Autobiography: Towards a Poetics of Experience* (Philadelphia: University of Pennsylvania Press, 1982) 143.

24. James Olney, *Metaphors of Self; the Meaning of Autobiography* (Princeton: Princeton University Press, 1972) 3.

25. Gunn, p. 23.

26. Gunn, p. 26.

27. Lore Metzger, *One Foot in Eden: Modes of Pastoral in Romantic Poetry* (Chapel Hill: University of North Carolina Press, 1986) xii.

28. William Elliott, *Carolina Sports* (Charleston, S.C.: Burges and James, 1846).

29. Webster appeared in Charleston in 1847. Grayson was a member of the committee. For a description of Webster's visit see C.M. Feuss, *Daniel Webster* II (Boston: Little, Brown) 176-7.

30. Edd Winfield Parks, *Antebellum Southern Literary Critics* (Athens: University of Georgia Press, 1962) 185.

31. Gunn, p. 119.

32. Eugene Genovese, *The Political Economy of Slavery; Studies in the Economy & Society of the Slave South* (New York: Vintage Books, 1967). Fitzhugh's criticism of capitalism is analyzed in *The World the Slaveholders Made; Two Essays in Interpretation* (New York: Pantheon Books, 1969).

33. In addition to his *Intellectual Life in Antebellum Charleston* there is his *A Character of Hugh Legaré* (Knoxville: University of Tennessee Press, 1985). Most recent is his *Rethinking the South* (Baltimore: Johns Hopkins University Press, 1988).

34. *Russell's Magazine* 2 (November 1857): 182.

35. Robert W. Bass, "The Autobiography of William J. Grayson," University of South Carolina dissertation, 1933, p. 330.

CHAPTER ONE

1. Review of Croker's edition of Boswell's *Life of Samuel Johnson* in *Edinburgh Review* (September 1831). In *Essays and Lays of Ancient Rome by Lord Macaulay*. New Edition (London: Longman, Green, and Company, 1897) 170.

2. Jedidiah Morse (1761-1826) was a Connecticut native and Congregational clergyman, who earned the reputation as the "father of American Geography" for his *American Universal Geography*, which went through seven editions early in the nineteenth century.

3. In his edition of the autobiography Samuel G. Stoney reports that according to the *Duellist's Looking Glass*, Grayson's father killed the Frenchman.

4. Mason Locke (Parson) Weems (1759-1823) was the father of modern fictionalized biography. He wandered for thirty-one years up and down the Eastern seaboard from Savannah, Georgia, to New York City, including Beaufort, South Carolina, selling books. His magnum opus in the field of fictionalized biography was his *The Life and Memorable Actions of George Washington*, c. 1800. He also wrote *The Life of Gen. Francis Marion* (1809). Weems settled in Dumfries, Virginia. He died and was initially buried near Beaufort. His remains were later moved to Dumfries.

5. The Reverend Benjamin S. Screven was the minister at the Baptist Church in Beaufort. When Mason Locke (Parson) Weems became ill just as his ship entered Beaufort Harbor, Screven was summoned to give him comfort until his death. The Screvens were long active in the Baptist Church in the area. William Screven established the first Baptist church in Charleston.

6. Ann Rippon is listed in the United States Census of 1800 as a resident of St. Helena Parish, Beaufort County. She is recorded in the census of 1810 erroneously as Ann Rippore. She must have died in 1820, for that census lists her estate as being handled by A. M. Verdier, a well-known Beaufort attorney. In the eighteenth century there were Rippons listed as living on Edisto Island. Grayson locates Ann as living on the side of Parris Island nearest to Edisto Island.

7. A break in the manuscript. The phrase is not completed.

CHAPTER TWO

1. Solomon Saltus was the progenitor of a large family of Saltuses who resided in New York. He engaged in maritime trade between New York and Bermuda.

2. New Utrecht was founded about 1650 by Nicasius De Sille, who built his mansion on his favorite nook of Long Island. He served as a councilor in New Amsterdam and was known as the "lord of the manor" in New Utrecht. By 1738 the hamlet had grown to 282 inhabitants. In the nineteenth century it was one of the four boroughs to be incorporated as Brooklyn, a name derived from the Dutch "Newe Breuschelen."

3. I have been unable to identify Dominie Todd. Although the manuscript reads Uzriel Ogden, Samuel G. Stoney identifies Ogden as Uzal Ogden (1744-1822), who was better known as a controversial clergyman both at Newark, New Jersey, and at the famous Trinity Church in New York City. Ogden was chosen the first bishop of New Jersey in 1798. He was controversial for his laxity in enforcing the doctrines of the Episcopal Church. When suspended by that Church, he joined the Presbytery of New York. Ogden published numerous pamphlets and sermons, the best known of which was *Antidote to Deism: The Deist Unmasked* (1795), refuting Paine's *Age of Reason*.

4. Woodbridge was not the same teacher who became the headmaster of the College of Charleston Academy on January 8, 1800, and not the same teacher who died in the yellow fever epidemic, since he was teaching in New Jersey later than that date. There is another possibility because of this Woodbridge's interest in female education. It is recorded in the *Dictionary of American Biography* that William Woodbridge (1756-1836), the famous first preceptor of Phillips Exeter Academy, came to specialize in the education of females and taught at several unspecified schools after leaving Phillips Exeter.

5. In spite of Grayson's claims of Cotheal's accomplishments, he is not listed in the *Dictionary of American Biography* or the *Cyclopedia of American Biography*.

6. The Kearnys of Newark were a prominent New Jersey family, beginning with the arrival in this country in 1720 of Michael Kearny from Ireland. Stephen Watts Kearny (1794-1848) was the American officer assigned the task of seizing New Mexico and California from the Mexicans. His troubled relations with Stockton and Fremont, who had already engaged the Mexicans in battle, eventually led to winning California. His nephew, General Philip Kearny (1814-62), lost an arm in the Mexican War, and became the first American to win the Cross of the Legion of Honor for service with the French army in Italian wars in 1859. He distinguished himself in the Peninsular Campaign, possibly saving McClellan's forces from a disastrous defeat, and was killed at Chantilly on September 1, 1862. Kearny, New Jersey, was named for him.

CHAPTER THREE

1. Captain David Bythewood of the Schooner *Delancey*. He is listed in the Census of 1810. The baptism of his daughter is recorded in the Register of the Independent (Circular) Congregational Church of Charleston on Wednesday, October 3, 1804.

2. Robert Brown, merchant of Charleston. Possibly this is the Robert Brown, Esq. of Charleston listed in the Census of 1840. There is an account of the marriage of his daughter on April 23, 1839, reported in the *Charleston Observer*.

3. In Greek legend Aeneas was the son of Anchises and Aphrodite. Anchises was struck blind for revealing the name of the child's mother. In Virgil's *Aeneid* he was carried out of Troy on the shoulders of his son and died in Sicily.

4. John Francis De Treville was a captain in the 4th South Carolina in the Revolutionary War. He was wounded at Savannah, Georgia, on October 10, 1779; taken prisoner at Charleston on May 12, 1780; exchanged on June 15, 1781; and served to the close of the war. He was commissioned Brevet Major on September 30, 1783. De Treville died in 1790.

5. Dueling was made illegal in South Carolina only under the Constitution of 1868. An anti-dueling law was passed after Colonel E. B. C. Cash killed Colonel W. M. Shannon on July 5, 1880. The law, passed in 1881, disqualified from public office anyone who had participated in a duel.

6. Jonah Barrington (1760-1834) served as a judge in the court of admiralty in Ireland. He was a member of a Protestant family and attended Trinity College, Dublin. He became a judge in the admiralty in 1798 and served in the House of Commons. He was knighted in May, 1807. He opposed the act of Union and declined an offer to be solicitor general if he would support the act. His extravagant habits led him into debt, and he appropriated money paid into his court to pay off his debts. A commission of inquiry in 1830 deprived him of office. He left England, never to return, dying at Versailles, April 8, 1834. He is known today only for his humorous pictures of Irish society of his day in his *Personal Sketches of His Own Time*, 2 volumes, 1827.

7. Levet died on February 17, 1782, in his seventy-seventh year. Johnson's poem was written before April 18, when it was entered in *Thraliana*. See D. Nichol Smith and E. L. McAdam, eds., *The Poems of Samuel Johnson* (Oxford: Clarendon Press, 1941).

8. The area was known as Hazzard's Neck. Major Hazzard is listed in the 1800 United States Census from Beaufort district. His tombstone in St. Helena's churchyard is inscribed: "To the Memory of Major William Hazzard who died in Beaufort on 19 December 1819, aged 62 years."

9. There is no specific reference in Herbert Aptheker, *American Negro Slave Revolts* (New York: Columbia University Press, 1943) of any plot at this time or place; but there is mention of a unidentified suppression of an insurrection before it took place in South Carolina in 1804. Theodore Rosengarten in *Tombee* also dates this plot as 1804, when Grayson was sixteen. Aptheker does not pretend to catalogue all attempted revolts that never materialized. There was only one major slave insurrection in South Carolina, Cato's rebellion near Stono Creek, in 1739. There was one major conspiracy, suppressed before it became an insurrection. This was the one planned by Denmark Vesey (1767-1822), a freeman in Charleston, who was betrayed by a house servant. Thirty-five slaves were hanged and forty-three were banished.

10. George Jeffreys (1645-1689) was Baron of Wem, and Lord Chancellor of England. His infamy rests primarily, and recent historians believe somewhat unfairly, on his role in the aftermath of the "bloody assizes" of 1685. Jeffreys and four other judges tried rebels in the abortive insurrection of the Duke of Monmouth against the throne of James II. Historians of Grayson's time, including his favorite Lord Macaulay, probably exaggerated the number hanged as 200 or 300. The actual number was probably half that.

11. Samuel Griswold Goodrich (1793-1860) was better known by his penname Peter Parley. He was the publisher of the *Token*, a giftbook annual in which several of

Hawthorne's first tales appeared. His name was a household word for the *Tales of Peter Parley about America;* the first of more than a hundred volumes appeared in 1827. In 1833 he began *Parley's Magazine* for children.

12. Hugh Swinton Legaré (1797-1843) was regarded as the most learned man of his time in Charleston. He was crippled by the effects of his inoculation with smallpox and had to substitute reading for outdoor activities. He studied with Moses Waddel at his famous school at Willington and with Mitchell King at the College of Charleston, before entering the sophomore class at South Carolina College at the age of fourteen. He graduated in 1814 at the head of his class. Legaré went to Europe in 1818 to further his education by studying French in Paris and law in Edinburgh. He returned to South Carolina in 1820 to take charge of the family plantation on John's Island and began to raise sea island cotton. He was coeditor with Stephen Elliott of the *Southern Review* and the chief contributor until it was suspended after eight volumes in 1832. It was popularly known as "Legaré's magazine," and his presence there led to its reputation for learned and scholarly articles and reviews. Legaré was a firm believer in states rights, but he joined the Union party against nullification. He served as attorney general of the state of South Carolina, and as chargé d'affaires in Belgium from 1832-36. He served one term in Congress (1837-39). Legaré was a close friend of President John Tyler, who appointed him Attorney General in 1841 and Secretary of State *ad interim* on the resignation of Webster. He became ill while accompanying Tyler to the unveiling of the Bunker Hill monument and died on June 20, 1843, after an illness of four days.

13. Joseph Clay (1764-1811) was born in Savannah, Georgia. He was a graduate of Princeton (1784), and he served as United States district judge for Georgia and United States judge for the 5th Circuit Court. When legislated out of office, he became a Baptist minister, an effective evangelist, and eventually the pastor of the First Baptist Church in Boston.

14. Robert Gibbes Barnwell (1761-1814) became a very successful rice planter at Laurel Bay, near the Port Royal Broad River in the Beaufort area. As an adolescent he joined his brother's militia company and participated in the skirmish against the British on Johns Island (1779) and later served as a lieutenant at the siege of Charleston (1780). He was captured and imprisoned on the prison schooner *Pack Horse*. He rose to the rank of militia colonel in 1811. His political career included a term as the representative of St. Helena Parish in the 7th General Assembly (1787-88) and as delegate to the state convention to ratify the U.S. Constitution (1788). He served in the United States House of Representatives in the 2nd Congress (1791-93).

15. Benjamin Morgan Palmer (1818-1892) was born in Charleston. He graduated from the University of Georgia and attended Columbia Theological Seminary in South Carolina. He was licensed to preach in the Presbyterian Church in 1842. He served as pastor of the First Presbyterian Church in Savannah from 1841 to 1843 and of a Presbyterian church in Columbia from 1843 to 1855. Palmer edited and founded the *Southern Presbyterian Review.* He was a staunch secessionist and widely influential. He moved to New Orleans in 1856, and he was soon prominent in urging Louisiana to join the Confederate cause. He wrote a life of his famous colleague at Columbia Presbyterian Seminary, James Henley Thornwell.

16. Daniel Baker (1791-1857) was an educator and a Presbyterian clergyman. He was descended from members of a Puritan congregation which settled at Dorchester, Massachusetts, in 1630 but also which spread south, forming a church in 1695, just

above Charleston on the Ashley River. In 1752 their descendants established a parish in Midway, Georgia, where Baker was born and orphaned. He moved to Savannah, Georgia, spent two years at Hampden-Sydney College, and graduated from Princeton in 1815. Baker held Presbyterian pastorates at Harrisonburg, Virginia, Washington, D.C., Savannah, Georgia, and Tuscaloosa, Alabama. In 1840 Baker was sent to the Republic of Texas as evangelistic missionary. He was considered an effective orator for winning conversions, among these William J. Grayson.

17. The Reverend Joseph Roberts Walker came to South Carolina from Pennsylvania to succeed the Reverend John Barnwell Campbell as rector at St. Helena's Parish near Beaufort, where he served as pastor for fifty-five years.

18. Richard Fuller (1804-1876), a South Carolinian, edited the Baptist *Christian Reflector*, published in Baltimore. He engaged in a well publicized debate with Francis Wayland of Brown University concerning slavery, especially on slavery and the scripture. The letters exchanged between the two ministers were published in book form in 1845 under the title *Domestic Slavery Considered as a Scriptural Institution*. He was a Beaufort lawyer until converted during the great revival of 1831. Beaufort legend has it that he invited his lawyer friends to a dinner, at which he announced his giving up law for the ministry. After the war he returned to Beaufort with Secretary of Treasury Chase. Many of his former slaves surrounded him, crying out for joy on his return.

Stephen Elliott, Jr. (1806-1866) was the first bishop of the Protestant Episcopal Church in Georgia. He was an organizer and a leader of the Episcopal Church in Georgia for more than twenty-five years. He was born in Beaufort, South Carolina, the son of the naturalist and later president of South Carolina College, Stephen Elliott. He was another one of the Beaufort intellectuals, graduating from Harvard in 1814. He studied law and practiced in Charleston and in Beaufort from 1827 to 1833 before moving to Georgia.

19. Geographically, Beaufort was exposed to hurricanes. The strongest of the periodical hurricanes to strike there was identified for many years after as "the great hurricane of 1804."

20. The "Barbacue House" stood on the edge of the river beyond where the courthouse now stands in Beaufort. No women were allowed inside the doors; it was a club for men only, to play chess and poker and to drink. In the great storm of 1804, the house was washed away.

21. Findley's poem appeared in the *Charleston Courier* on November 1, 1804. He was apparently fired as an instructor at Beaufort College for being too frank about some of the goings on at the "Barbacue House."

22. Aaron Smith Willington (1781-1862) was born in Wyeland, Massachusetts, and came to Charleston in 1802. With Loring Andrews and W. Cullen Carpenter, he founded a newspaper, the *Charleston Courier*, on January 10, 1803. He became the sole proprietor in 1813, employing the best talent of Charleston as editorial writers, including William Crafts and William Gilmore Simms. Loring Andrews was a native of Massachusetts. There is an announcement of Andrews' death on October 22, 1805, in the *Charleston Courier*.

23. Ambrose Philips (1674-1749) was an English poet whose contemporary reputation rested on Grayson's favorite form of poetry, the pastoral. His pastorals appeared in 1809 in Tonson's *Miscellany*, winning praise from Addison and Steele. He was parodied by John Gay in *The Shepherd's Week* (1744). His quarrel with Alexander Pope,

described by Dr. Johnson as a "perpetual reciprocation of malevolence," resulted from an article in the *Guardian* (1713) hailing Philips, and not Pope, as the successor of Theocritus, Virgil, and Spenser. His enemies derisively referred to him as "Namby Pamby."

24. Colonel Abram Blanding (1776-1839) was born in Massachusetts. He was a student of Dr. Jonathan Maxcy at Rhode Island College (Brown University), who persuaded him to move to South Carolina. He was interested in and active in internal improvements — navigation, roads, canals, railroads, banks. He engineered the waterworks system in Columbia. Blanding was responsible for the planting of trees in the center of the street which bears his name in Columbia. He was also responsible for founding Presbyterian Theological Seminary. He worked with Poinsett in opposition to nullification.

25. It was during the latter part of Charles Pinckney's administration as governor that the old English law of primogeniture was repealed. Edward Rutledge was author of the bill, which passed on February 19, 1791.

26. I take General Foy to be Maximilien Sebastian Foy (1775-1825), a French general of the Napoleonic Wars, who was a leader of liberal opposition in the National Assembly. He was known as much for his misadventures in battles as for his successes.

CHAPTER FOUR

1. Jonathan Maxcy (1768-1820) was a distinguished educator. He was a significant president of Rhode Island College, later Brown University, and of Union College before becoming the first president of South Carolina College in 1804. At South Carolina College he taught belles lettres, criticism, and metaphysics; and he was well remembered by all his students as a teacher and as an orator.

2. Virgil Maxcy (1785-1844), lawyer, legislator, diplomat, was the younger brother of Jonathan Maxcy. He was appointed the first solicitor of the United States Treasury in 1830 and the representative of the United States government in Brussels, Belgium, in 1834. On February 28, 1844, while the guest of President Tyler on the naval frigate *Princeton*, a new gun called the "Peacemaker" exploded, killing him instantly.

3. Milton Maxcy (1782-1817) graduated from Rhode Island College (Brown University) in 1802. He moved with his brother to Beaufort, South Carolina, where he opened a school for boys about 1804. He was admitted to the bar in 1808 and practiced law in Beaufort. He represented St. Helena in the 19th General Assembly. He died in the summer of 1817 of malaria and was buried in St. Helena Churchyard.

4. The author is John Belton O'Neall (1793-1863), who was born near Bush River in Newberry District, South Carolina, of Irish ancestry. He was trained for college at Newberry Academy. He entered the junior class at South Carolina College, graduating in 1812. He joined the militia and rose to the rank of major-general by the time he was thirty-two. He was elected to the state legislature from Newberry District at the age of twenty-three, rising quickly to be speaker of the House. He retired from the legislature in 1827 after supporting a bill that his constitutents thought extravagant. The next year he was elected circuit judge by the legislature and advanced in two years to the South Carolina Court of Appeals. When in 1835 he ruled the test oath devised by nullifiers unconstitutional, through political pressure from the nullifiers his court was abolished. He was reassigned to the Court of Law Appeals, where he served for the remaining portion of his life. In 1859 he became

Chief Justice of South Carolina. O'Neall was a leader in the temperance movement in South Carolina and wrote a column, "The Drunkard's Looking Glass," in the *Temperance Advocate*. He wrote *The Negro Law of South Carolina* (1848) and the *Biographical Sketches of the Bench and Bar of South Carolina*, 2 vols. (1859).

5. George Davis (1787-1810) was born in Maryland. He entered South Carolina College from Laurens District in 1806. After graduation in 1809 he studied law at Laurens, South Carolina. He died within a year in Laurens.

6. Grayson was familiar with South Carolina College as a student, as a state representative concerned with education, and as a trustee. Paul Hamilton Hayne selected him to review Maximilian La Borde's *History of South Carolina College* for *Russell's Magazine* 5 (September 1859): 550-552.

7. James Louis Petigru (1789-1863) was Grayson's classmate and lifelong friend. He graduated first in his class at South Carolina College in 1809 and began the practice of law in Abbeville. He was appointed Attorney General for South Carolina in 1822. He ran unsuccessfully as a Unionist candidate for the S.C. Senate in 1830, but he was elected later to fill a vacancy in the S.C. House of Representatives. Petigru became the acknowledged leader of the anti-nullifiers in South Carolina, chastising his friend Grayson for aligning himself with the nullifiers. He served as United States District Attorney and as South Carolina Code Commissioner. Petigru had many friends and correspondents in the North, and he was one of the best known of the Southern Unionists.

8. Thomas Dupont, Grayson's roommate, was born on July 17, 1789. He entered South Carolina College, as Grayson did, from the Beaufort District. He graduated in 1809, married Agnes Buist, and dropped from sight. No further records exist, even at the University of South Carolina.

9. In spite of Grayson's criticisms of students at South Carolina College, many of his classmates at South Carolina College had distinguished careers. Thomas Galliard was born in St. Stephen's Parish, South Carolina, in 1790. He graduated from South Carolina College in 1809, moved to Monroe County, Alabama, in 1832, where he became a planter. He wrote two books, *The History of the Presbyterian Church*, and *History of the Reformation*. He died in Mobile some time in the 1850s.

James Truman Dent (1790-1869) was born in Maryland, but entered South Carolina College from Georgia, graduating in 1809. He joined the United States Army in 1812, served in the Indian Wars, rising to the rank of major. He died at Tuscaloosa, Alabama.

Robert Blair Campbell (1791-1862) was born at Woodstock, Marlboro District, South Carolina. He rose to the rank of captain in the War of 1812. He had a varied and distinguished government career. He was a one-term member of the United States Congress from 1823-25; United States Consul at Havana, Cuba; member of the Boundary Commission in 1850; United States Consul in London. He resigned at the beginning of the Civil War, lingered in England and died at Eating during the war.

Alexander Bowie (b. 1789) was born at Abbeville, South Carolina. He entered South Carolina College from Abbeville District and graduated in 1809. He served as colonel of the 8th Regiment of the militia in the War of 1812. He was admitted to the bar in Abbeville in 1813. He became an active member of the Abbeville Nullifiers. He moved to Talladega, Alabama, in 1835. He served as president of the Alabama Historical Society. He was Chancellor, Northern Division of Alabama, from 1839 to 1845.

10. The riot resulted from complaints about the food in the Commons, where all students were required to eat. It occurred on March 1, 1827, when students walked

out of the hall in protest. Students engaged in the revolt were reported to the Board of Trustees for expulsion. Twenty-four seniors were expelled, leaving only twelve remaining in the class. No honors were given at the December commencement. The students did get the concession that they could obtain written permission to eat in private boardinghouses.

11. William Murray, Earl of Mansfield (1705-1793), British jurist, served for thirty-four years as Chief Justice of the King's Bench. His most permanent contribution was to commercial law. He had an early reputation for ruling against slavery. His famous ruling in the Somerset case (1772) was only that an escaping slave could not be forcibly removed form England for punishment in the colonies. He did not rule on the legality of slavery itself. Lord Mansfield also made an important ruling for the colonies to the effect that laws passed after the settlement of a colony were not in force there unless the act so indicated, endorsing a position that colonists had long held.

12. The reference is "How sweet an Ovid, MURRAY was our boast! How many Martials were in PULT'NEY lost!" *The Dunciad*, Book IV, 11. 169-70. Murray won a prize at Oxford for a Latin poem on the death of George I.

13. Green's tavern was the chief tavern in the early days of Columbia. On May 15, 1804, a banquet was held there to celebrate the Louisiana Purchase. The builder, Dr. Samuel Green, became postmaster in 1806. He was one of the commissioners of Columbia, and he served several terms as intendant (mayor) of the town.

14. James Gregg (1787-1852) was born in the Marion District, west of the Pee Dee River in South Carolina. He graduated from South Carolina College in 1808, first in a class that included Dr. William Brantly, Chancellor William Harper, and Governor Steven D. Miller. He served as a tutor in South Carolina College until 1813. He married Cornelia Maxcy, the eldest daughter of President Jonathan Maxcy. He was admitted to the bar in Columbia in 1813 and became a solicitor in the Circuit Court of the United States. He practiced law in Columbia, soon becoming the leading lawyer in that town. He served in the House of Representatives from 1822-30.

15. Ainsley Hall, a native of England, built a large store in Columbia and carried on an extensive business in cotton and general merchandise. He married a Miss Hopkins from an aristocratic South Carolina family. The residence adjoining his store was expensively furnished. He supposedly accumulated a fortune of several hundred thousand dollars. Wade Hampton, Sr., bought Hall's house.

16. Colonel Thomas Taylor (1743-1833) was the father of John Taylor, twenty-fourth governor of South Carolina, from 1826 to 1828. He was one of the founders of Columbia. In the Revolutionary Way, he was a colonel in General Sutton's brigade and shared in the victory over Major Wemyss at Fisk Dam on November 8, 1780. He lived long enough to be called "the patriarch of Columbia," dying in 1833 at the age of ninety.

Wade Hampton (1791-1858) was the "middle" Hampton, son of a distinguished father and father of a distinguished son. He left South Carolina College to fight in the War of 1812. On his return he assumed management of "Millwood" plantation near Columbia, where he became famous for breeding blooded horses. Millwood became a social center, to which such men as Dr. Samuel Gridley Howe, Henry Clay, and George Bancroft came for visits. Hampton preferred not to hold public office.

17. Nicholas Herbemont was a professor of French at South Carolina College from 1807-17. He was a French native who married a Columbia native, the widow Smythe, He not only had gardens but pioneered in the wine industry in South Carolina, owning

vineyards near Columbia and producing wines on a small scale. He owned an entire square on the southeast corner of Bull and Lady streets and planted it in flowers, fruit trees, and grape vines, from which "a very fair wine" was made.

18. Samuel G. Stoney identifies "Mr. Joyner" as William Joyner, a relative in his stepfather's family. This was also his stepfather's name.

19. The only reference to Joseph Longworth is in the *Charleston Observer* in an announcement of the death of "Mrs. Ann Beck, relict of Rev. John Beck, at the residence of Joseph Longworth, Esq."

20. Stephen Elliott, Sr. (1771-1830), was another one of the distinguished natives of Beaufort with whom Grayson is concerned in his autobiography. He served for many years in the House and the Senate of South Carolina, and he was the leader in literary activity of Charleston as early as 1812. His vocation was education. He was the first professor of botany at South Carolina College and president from 1814 to 1830. He was the author of the *Sketch of the Botany of South Carolina and Georgia*, 2 volumes, 1821-24. His avocation was literature. Elliott was the founder and coeditor with Hugh Swinton Legaré of the *Southern Review*, the first literary magazine in Charleston to achieve national notice.

21. The *Southern Review* was published in Charleston (1828-32). It was edited by Stephen Elliott, Sr., the distinguished botanist. Its contemporary reputation was largely due to the respect for the learning of the main contributor, Hugh Swinton Legaré. In his mention of Simms, Grayson must have meant the *Southern Quarterly Review*. The *Southern Review* was not one of the several South Carolina magazines under the guidance of William Gilmore Simms.

22. Dr. Henry T. Farmer of Charleston was the nephew of Mrs. Baring, wife of Charles Baring of Pon Pon. He had a large estate on the Combahee River. He is listed as deceased in the account of the wedding of his daughter, Susan Baring, in the *Charleston Observer*, January 9, 1836.

23. The song is still in print. It was written by William Shields (1748-1829), the composer of numerous now forgotten eighteenth-century operas. He apparently wrote the tune for "Auld Lang Syne," and he is also known today for one additional song, his setting of Thomas Moore in "All Those Endearing Young Charms." I was unable to find which opera this song is from or whether it was from one of his operas.

24. The poem, according to Stoney, was "Imagination," published in *The Maniac's Dream and Other Poems* (New York, 1819). The ruins of Sheldon Church in Prince William's Parish are the most beautiful in the area. The church was burned in 1780 when the British passed it on their march from Savannah to Charles Town. It was rebuilt, occupied as a stable by Sherman's troops, and burned again. Charles Fraser sketched it in his *A Charleston Sketchbook*, 1796-1806.

The *Croaker* pieces, a series of humorous and satirical odes, appeared the same year and gave Fitz-Greene Halleck (1790-1867) a reputation that lasted for many years as second only to William Cullen Bryant among American poets.

25. Charles Cotesworth Pinckney (1746-1825) was known as the "old general" to Grayson, but he was much more than a military officer. After matriculating at Oxford, he gained admittance to the Middle Temple and to the English bar as well as to the South Carolina bar. He served as a member of the South Carolina Provincial Assembly and later as a member of both the House of Representatives and the Senate. During the Revolutionary War he was an aide to George Washington at the battles of Germantown and Brandywine. He commanded Fort Moultrie during the attacks on

Charleston. On the fall of Charleston he was taken prisoner by the British and exchanged in 1782. He ended the war as a brigadier general. He was appointed United States Minister to France, but his appointment was unrecognized by the French Directory in reaction to the Jay Treaty. He was one of the three Americans whose negotiations by letters with Talleyrand's ministers precipitated the XYZ affair. Pinckney was appointed by Washington as commander of all forces and posts south of Maryland. He was an unsuccessful Federalist candidate for President in 1800. His brother, Thomas Pinckney (1750-1828), was distinguished as a soldier and diplomat. He also served as the major general in command of the district from North Carolina to Mississippi and as the chief negotiator of the southern boundary between the United States and Spain.

26. William Lowndes (1782-1822) was a congressman from the Charleston District from 1811 to 1822, where he became chairman of the powerful Ways and Means Committee. He died at sea on his way to England. Grayson wrote a biography, which Robert Bass in his South Carolina dissertation (1933) reports was lost in the Charleston fire of 1861. Grayson undoubtedly draws here on the lost biography.

CHAPTER FIVE

1. Beaufort College was chartered by a group of Beaufort citizens in 1795, to be supported by the sale of vacant lots, "escheated and confiscated property in Beaufort Parish." Brantly was first headmaster, a job later held by Grayson's friend Petigru.

William Theophilus Brantly was born in Chatham County, North Carolina in 1787. He entered South Carolina College from the Beaufort District and graduated in 1808. He was ordained to the Baptist ministry in 1809; after which he served in Augusta, Georgia, both as rector of Richmond Academy (1809-1811) and as pastor of the Baptist Church (1821-26) and then as pastor of a Baptist church in Philadelphia (1826-37). He was editor of the *Christian Index* from 1827 to 1833. He was president of the College of Charleston and pastor of the Baptist Church in Charleston (1838-44). He died in Augusta. Among his contemporaries he was famous for his oratory.

2. Richard W. Habersham (1786-1842) was a native of Savannah, a lawyer, who served as United States attorney and Attorney General of Georgia until his death in 1842. He also was a congressman from Georgia.

3. Judge William Law (1793-1874) was described in the *Savannah Newspaper Digest* in his death notice on March 3, 1874, as "our venerated and esteemed fellow citizen."

4. In Greek myth Sisyphus was compelled to roll a stone up a steep hill in Hades. Before it reached the top it rolled down again, and he had to begin all over. Homer does not reveal the reason for the punishment. The myth was revived for the 1950s by the French existentialist, Albert Camus, as a symbol of human defiance of absurdity.

5. Grayson is echoing the Latin motto from Virgil, *Aeneid* II, 49. "*Timeo Danaos et donam ferentes....*" In other words "I fear the Greeks even when they bring gifts."

6. Henry Kollock (1794-1819) was born in New Providence, New Jersey. He was graduated from the College of New Jersey in 1794 and licensed to preach in 1800. He served as pastor of the Presbyterian Church at Princeton and as Professor of Sacred Theology at the College of New Jersey from 1803 to 1806. He then became

pastor of the Presbyterian Church at Savannah, Georgia. He declined the presidency of the University of Georgia in 1810. He journeyed to England in 1817 to do research on a biography of John Calvin, and later died in Savannah.

7. John Tillotson (1630-1694) was an English archbishop famous for his sermons, published in 1682. He was fortunate enough to earn the support of William and Mary, appointing a commission for reconciliation with Dissenters. His sermons were admired by many in Grayson's generation.

8. Samuel Gilman (1791-1858) was born in Massachusetts. He was a Unitarian clergyman and author. In 1819 he assumed the pastorate of the Unitarian Church in Charleston, where he remained the rest of his life. He also preached in the Unitarian Church in Savannah on numerous occasions. He collected the best of his literary works in *Contributions to Descriptive, Critical, Humorous, Biographical, Philosophical, and Poetical Literature* (1856), which included "Ode on the Death of Calhoun," said to have been sung at Calhoun's funeral. The poem best known to his contemporaries was "Fair Harvard."

Anthony Foster was Gilman's predecessor in Charleston, who, while pastor of the Second Independent Church, converted himself and the church to Unitarianism.

9. Reverend Simon Felix Gallagher was a native of Dublin, Ireland, appointed priest of the nascent Catholic Church in Charleston in 1793 by Bishop Carroll. He was renowned for his eloquence. He was elected a professor in the College of Charleston, devoting his salary to the care of the poor. He organized the Hibernian Society in Charleston. He moved to Savannah in 1817 and then to New Orleans, dying about 1830 in Vicksburg, Mississippi.

10. Yellow fever was the great plague for Charleston, Savannah, and Beaufort. This was the 1817 pestilence. Actually, the most severe yellow fever epidemic on record struck Beaufort in the summer of 1800.

CHAPTER SIX

1. Abbe Correa de Serra, Jose Francesco (1750-1823) was the Portuguese botanist and statesman, who was in America from 1812 to 1820. He corresponded with Thomas Jefferson and with members of the American Philosophical Society.

2. Bath still appears on detailed maps as Bath Beach, in the Kings section of Brooklyn, not far from Coney Island.

3. William Smith Shaw (1778-1826) had served as secretary to John Adams during his presidency. He spent many years as librarian at the Boston Athenaeum.

4. James and Mercy Warren were close friends of John and Abigail Adams for many years. Warren was one of Adams's favorite correspondents. Adams said of him: "I write everything to you, who know how to take me." The best coverage of this friendship is in Peter Shaw, *The Character of John Adams* (Chapel Hill: University of North Carolina Press, 1976.

5. In one of the best known coincidences in American history, Thomas Jefferson and John Adams died on the same day, the fiftieth anniversary of the signing of the Declaration of Independence, July 4, 1826. Jefferson expired in his familiar alcove bed at Monticello. Adams's dying words were: "Jefferson still survives." The death of the two founding fathers was viewed as the passing of an epoch.

6. The preacher was William Ellery Channing (1780-1842) and his church was the Federal Street Church in Boston. He both preached and wrote on the importance of

literature for moral regeneration and against slavery in *Remarks on American Literature* (1830), *Abolishing Slavery* (1835), *The Abolitionist* (1836), and *Duty of the Free States* (1842).

7. Daniel E. Huger (1779-1854) was a South Carolina judge and legislator, who resigned his position on the bench to combat radical states rights doctrines when nullification became an issue. Unlike his fellow Unionists Huger became reconciled with John C. Calhoun and later drifted with the majority opinion in South Carolina. He defeated Robert Barnwell Rhett for the United States Senate but resigned in 1845 to open a place for Calhoun to return to the Senate. He became more of a moderate during the States Rights Convention of 1852.

8. At the Virginia Constitutional Convention in 1829 and in debates that followed in 1831 to 1832, pro-slavery and anti-slavery advocates openly clashed over a solution of the slavery question. Western representatives were practically unanimous in opposing slavery; eastern members argued that the slave was the most suitable laborer for the plantation and that to abolish slavery would be to destroy the whole life of their section. Colonization of slaves beyond the Rockies or in Africa was discussed. The sectional differences in Virginia, after the outbreak of the Civil War, were to lead to the secession of the western section and the formation of West Virginia.

9. John James Allen (1797-1871) served one term in the United States House of Representatives from Virginia. He was defeated for reelection in 1834. He returned to Clarksburg, Virginia. He was judge of the Circuit Court from 1836 to 1840 and judge of the Virginia Supreme Court from 1840 to 1867, serving as the presiding judge from 1852 to 1865.

10. The book by Alexis de Tocqueville (1800-59), the author of *Democracy in America*, is *Ancien Régime et la Révolution*.

11. In Sir Walter Scott's *Guy Mannering*, Counsellor Pleydell is an advocate, who is given the comic incongruity of being serious and shrewd in business but fond of fun outside his business hours.

CHAPTER SEVEN

1. Thomas Jefferson, over the violent protests of merchant and shipping interests, as an alternative to war in reaction to British and French blockades and counter blockades and to counter the search and seizure of American ships on the high seas, persuaded Congress to pass the Embargo Act of 1807, which prohibited all American exports to foreign countries. New England was most hurt by the embargo and turned bitterly against Jefferson. To counteract the decline in revenue Jefferson tried to encourage domestic industries. What Jefferson learned from this turmoil was that with such strong opposition with a block of states his embargo was unenforceable by the federal government. Three days before leaving office, he signed a bill for the repeal of his embargo. What was remembered in the South was that opposition from states could make federal laws unenforceable.

2. In response to the Tariff of 1824, called "the tariff of abominations" in South Carolina, John C. Calhoun led his state in issuing an "Exposition and Protest" against the use of the tariff power to protect industry instead of for the intended purpose, in Calhoun's view of the Constitution, of securing revenue. The resolution also asserted the right of "interposition" of a state against unconstitutional action of Congress. It was built on arguments initiated by the Kentucky and Virginia Resolutions.

3. Since the Tariff of 1832 left rates high enough to retain the principle of protectionism, nullifiers in South Carolina elected delegates to a convention that passed the Nullification Ordinance (November, 1832), declaring the tariffs of 1828 and 1832 null and void. The convention prohibited tariff collections in the state and threatened secession if the federal government should use force in the collection of duties.

4. *Paradise Lost* II, 1. 561. "And they found no end, in wandering mazes lost."

5. John Breckinridge of Kentucky obtained from Virginia, largely from the hand of Jefferson, the Kentucky Resolutions as that section's response to the Federalist Alien and Sedition Acts of 1798. Madison authored the similar Virginia Resolutions. The Kentucky Resolutions went further than the Virginia Resolutions in declaring the acts "void and of no force." Both resolutions were later used in nullification arguments in South Carolina.

6. Alexander Pope, *Essay on Man* IV, 11. 367-368. Grayson changes the last two lines of Pope, which read: "Friend, parent, neighbors, first it will embrace, His country next, and next all human race,"

7. John Howard (1726-1790) inherited considerable wealth from his merchant father. He went to Portugal after the earthquake to see what help he could offer. He dedicated himself to prison reform, publishing *The State of Prisons in England and Wales* (1777).

8. Grayson always insisted that nullification was not necessarily secession. Later, when Grayson was under attack for his antisecessionist views by evidence of his earlier support for nullification, he contended that being for nullification was not necessarily being for secession. He did not at that time recognize what his friend Petigru had contended, that nullification could be a prelude for secession.

9. Here are some selective facts on some of the many debaters Grayson mentions, excluding Calhoun, Clay, and Webster.

Robert Young Hayne (1791-1839) was born in the Colleton District. He was elected as to the U.S. Senate in 1824 as a Tariff-for-Revenue Democrat. He served until he resigned in 1832 to become Governor of South Carolina. He was governor from 1832 to 1834, mayor of Charleston 1835 to 1837, and a member of the South Carolina Nullification Convention in 1832. His greatest claim to fame is the notable debate with Daniel Webster in 1830 on the principles of the Constitution.

James Hamilton, Jr. (1786-1857) was U.S. congressman, governor of South Carolina, planter, lawyer, state legislator, land speculator, and diplomatic agent for the Republic of Texas. He was admitted to the bar in Charleston, served in the South Carolina House until his election to the U.S. House of Representatives in December 1822. He was a congressman from 1823 to 1829. He was elected governor in 1830 and actively supported the state's Nullification Convention in November 1832. He was elected to the South Carolina Senate in 1834 and served until 1838. Hamilton acquired property in Texas and lent the new government there large sums of money. He was made commissioner of loans for Texas and diplomatic agent to France, Great Britain, Belgium, and the Netherlands. By 1842 Hamilton was financially overextended because of his loans and speculations and was consequently removed from all Texas offices by Sam Houston. Many of his friends in South Carolina, including James L. Petigru and James Henry Hamilton, lost money for loans consigned and money lent. Hamilton spent his last years pressing the Texas government for settlement of loans and expenses he had incurred on Texas's behalf. His tragedies ended with his drowning at sea when the ship taking him to Texas collided with another in the Gulf of Mexico in 1857.

James Henry Hammond (1807-1864) was congressman, U.S. senator, South Carolina governor, planter, and one of the largest slaveholders in the South. He became a leading spokesman for the South as the Cotton Kingdom prior to the Civil War. He achieved notoriety in the North for his Senate reference to the Negro as the "mud sill" component of Southern labor. Grayson used the term but admitted that it gave grounds for offense. Hammond's diaries, which reveal his intellectual and sexual preoccupations, have been edited by Carol Bleser, *Secret and Sacred: The Diaries of James Henry Hammond, a Southern Slaveholder* (New York: Oxford University Press, 1988).

George McDuffie (1790-1851), U.S. senator, congressman, governor, and state legislator, was born in Columbia. He graduated from South Carolina College in 1813 and soon began the practice of law. He took Calhoun's seat in the U.S. House of Representatives and served there from 1821 to 1834. By the time Grayson arrived, McDuffie was so well known as a debater that people came in from miles away to hear him. He favored nullification, and he was a delegate to the convention in 1834. He served two terms as governor of South Carolina. In 1842 he replaced William C. Preston in the U.S. Senate. Injuries suffered in a duel with William Cumming of Georgia forced his retirement from Congress and affected his health for the rest of his life. He owned a large plantation called "Cherry Hill."

In 1827 Robert J. Turnbull (1775-1833), a wealthy planter and retired lawyer of Charleston, wrote a series of articles in the *Charleston Mercury* advocating resistance to the federal government as the proper course for South Carolina. He argued that the Constitution was "a compact between the States, and there are no parties to it, excepting the people of the different States in their corporate capacities." Political questions were to be settled among the sovereign states, not in the courts. He initiated in South Carolina the attempt to examine the problems between state and federal government in terms of constitutional issues, carrying his views to the very threshold of armed resistance.

10. On the other side, some of the key players were: Daniel E. Huger (1779-1854), lawyer, representative, U.S. senator, already identified.

Richard Yeadon (1802-1870) was born in Charleston. He graduated from South Carolina College and was admitted to the bar in 1824. He supported the Unionist causes in articles in Simms' *City Gazette* and as editor of the *Charleston Daily Courier* from 1832 to 1844. He married a great grandniece of Francis Marion and contributed a long series of articles on the Marion family to Simms' *Southern and Western Magazine*. He was an opponent of secession but supported the Confederacy loyally once war began.

Joel Roberts Poinsett (1779-1851) was a Charleston native who sided with Andrew Jackson in opposition to the nullification measures of South Carolina. He was a member of the South Carolina House of Representatives from 1816 to 1820 and a member of Congress from 1821 to 1825. He served as Minister to Mexico and Secretary of War under President Martin Van Buren. He opposed the Mexican War. The *Poinsettia pulcherina* was named for him since he introduced it to this country from Mexico. He strongly supported the Union.

Richard Irvine Manning (1789-1836) graduated from South Carolina College in 1811, two years after Grayson. During the War of 1812 he served as a militia captain of an artillery company. He served in the state House of Representatives from 1822 until 1824, when he resigned on being elected governor. As governor, he urged reform in the laws concerning slaves. He served in the state Senate from 1830 to 1833 and was the Clarendon delegate at the Nullification Convention (1832 – 3). He voted against the Ordinance and served as vice-president of a Union Party convention that protested the action of the Nullification Convention. He took a seat in the same Congress (1833-35) as Grayson, and he was reelected as a Union Democrat.

11. See previous reference, chapter 4, footnote 16. Wade Hampton's name comes up not from any official political position which gave him a platform to speak from, but from his unofficial position as friend and advisor to many influential politicians. He was so influential in South Carolina politics from his plantation that he was called "the Warwick of South Carolina."

12. Demosthenes (384-332 B.C.) was regarded in Charleston, where oratory was considered an important skill by lawyers and by those with training in the classics, as the greatest of the Greek orators. His speeches on the theme of resistance by Athens to Macedonia were especially admired and taught. He was the exemplary orator for Hugh Swinton Legaré.

CHAPTER EIGHT

1. Dr. Thomas L. Ogier was Grayson's son-in-law. The marriage was announced in the *Charleston Observer* (November 10, 1833). "Married in Beaufort, S.C., on the 31 October, by the Rev. Mr. Walker, Dr. Thomas L. Ogier, of this city, to Miss Marie Willard [Grayson], daughter of the Hon. William J. Grayson."

2. Andrew Jackson rebuffed what he took as Nicholas Biddle's efforts to use the lending power of the Bank to influence politics. When Congress passed the bill in 1832 to recharter the Bank, Jackson vetoed it and in his veto made a ringing populist denunciation of the Bank as a privileged monopoly for the purpose of enriching "the few at the expense of the many." After the election that year Biddle tried to tighten credit in an effort to demonstrate that Jackson's threats against the Bank were alarming the business community. When Biddle lost public support during the credit stringency, Jackson decided to destroy the Bank immediately by ordering all government deposits removed and placed in selected state banks.

3. Lincoln allowed rulings by his generals in cases of treason. His reasoning was that it was better to sacrifice some parts of the Constitution than to lose it all.

4. Edward Everett (1794-1865) was a clergyman, statesman, and, above all, orator. He was briefly professor of Greek at Harvard and editor of the *North American Review*. As a congressman from 1828 to 1835, he was a supporter of John Quincy Adams in opposition to Jackson. He served as Governor of Massachusetts, as Secretary of State, and as U.S. Senator. He is best remembered for his long speech at Gettysburg in contrast to Lincoln's short one.

5. John King Griffin (1789-1841) was a planter from the Clinton and Newberry District of South Carolina. He served in the state House of Representatives (1816-18), and the state Senate (1820-24, 1828-39). He was elected as a States Rights Whig to Congress and served from 1831 to 1841.

John Myers Felder (1782-1851) was born in Orangeburg, South Carolina. He graduated from Yale in the same class (1804) with John C. Calhoun. He was engaged extensively in agriculture and in the lumbering business in that area. He represented his district in the state House of Representatives and in the state Senate. He served two terms in the U.S. House of Representatives, from 1831 to 1835.

John James Allen (1797-1871) served one term in Congress as a representative from Virginia.

John Robertson (1787-1873) was born in Petersburg, Virginia. He was a Whig member of the U.S. House of Representatives (1835-51). Afterwards he was a judge of the Circuit Court. He urged the Southern states not to secede pending a proposed peace convention. Like Grayson he was also an occasional poet. Allen is discussed further elsewhere.

6. John Randolph (1773-1833) was a Virginia planter, a member of Congress, and a defender of states rights. He was a committed critic of most federal projects, including the National Bank, the protective tariff, internal improvements, and anything that interfered with the welfare of a slave society in the South. There was little about the federal government that he did not criticize.

7. The facts are (1) the snubs that Mrs. Eaton, the former Peggy O'Neill of some disrepute and the new wife of Secretary of War John Eaton, received from Mrs. Calhoun and cabinet wives; (2) the Rhea letter which revealed that Calhoun as Secretary of War had favored a censure of Jackson in the cabinet debates of 1818 over Jackson's invasion of Florida. (3) When Calhoun openly espoused the cause of South Carolina in its opposition to a protective tariff, he seemed in Jackson's eyes to be not only not a friend but disloyal to his President. The split was dramatized for those present at the Jefferson Day dinner on April 13, 1830, when at Jackson's toast, "Our Federal Union—it must be preserved." Calhoun countered, "The Union, next to our liberty, most dear." For style, if no longer for substance, I still prefer as an account of Jackson's administration Arthur M. Schlesinger, Jr., *The Age of Jackson* (Boston: Little, Brown and Company, 1950). For massive substance there is the more recent Robert V. Remini, *Andrew Jackson and the Course of American Democracy, 1833-45* (New York: Harper and Row, 1984).

8. Thomas Hartley Crawford (1786-1863) served as a Jackson Democrat from Pennsylvania in the House of Representatives (1829-33). Later he was Commissioner of Indian Affairs and a judge in the District of Columbia Criminal Court (1845-61).

9. Thomas Hart Benton (1782-1858) was born near Hillsborough, North Carolina, but began his career as a colonel of volunteers in the War of 1812 under Andrew Jackson and as a lawyer in the frontier village of St. Louis. As editor of the *St. Louis Enquirer* he insisted that western men have a share "in the destinies of this Republic." He arrived on the Washington scene as senator from Missouri in 1821. During Grayson's time in Congress Benton initiated the legislative battle against the Bank of the United States, fought Clay, Webster, and Whig opposition to sustaining Jackson's veto of recharter (1832) and supported Jackson's removal of government funds from the Bank (1833). Benton sponsored coinage acts to promote "hard money" currency in place of bank note credit and later worked with President Martin Van Buren for a federal "Independent Treasury." Like most Jacksonians, he favored tariff reduction and opposed federal expenditures for local internal improvements. Though pro-Southern and pro-slavery at the time, he rejected Calhoun's doctrine of state nullification of federal law.

Francis Preston Blair, Sr., (1791-1876), journalist and politician, was born in Abingdon, Kentucky. He graduated from Transylvania University in 1811. He entered both journalism and politics at Frankfort and became a strong and loyal supporter of Andrew Jackson. He moved to Washington and established in 1830 a Democratic Party organ, the *Washington Globe*. He quickly became a member of Jackson's unofficial but influential "Kitchen Cabinet." Blair was an ardent Free Soiler, opposing the expansion of slavery into the territories, and a supporter of Martin Van Buren. He was later one of the founders of the Republican Party and an advisor to Lincoln.

10. Martin Van Buren was Jackson's loyal supporter, whose career advanced as Calhoun's relationships with Jackson declined. He was appointed Secretary of State, ambassador to England (rejected by Calhoun's tie breaking vote in the Senate), elected Vice President, and was Jackson's chosen successor for the presidency. Until George Bush's 1988 victory, he was the last Vice President to be elected President.

11. Marquis James, *Andrew Jackson, Portrait of a President* (Indianapolis: Bobbs-Merrill, 1937) 517, states that Andrew Jackson attended the Presbyterian Church of the Rev. John Campbell. Grayson was an Episcopalian.

12. Judge William Smith (1762-1840) was a judge of the South Carolina Circuit Court from 1808 to 1816 and U.S. senator from 1816 to 1823 and from 1826 to 1831. He declined an appointment by President Andrew Jackson to the Supreme Court.

13. Samuel Prioleau (1784-1840) was born in Charleston. His great grandfather came to this country with his Huguenot congregation from France. He attended the University of Pennsylvania, where he studied classics and law. He was admitted to the bar in 1818 and practiced in partnership with Colonel Drayton. He was intendant (mayor) of Charleston and recorder of the city until 1836, when he retired and moved upstate to Pendleton, where he died. He had a fondness for literature and the arts and represented the kind of taste for the classics that Grayson had himself. He lectured on electricity and natural philosophy and contributed regularly to the *Southern Quarterly Review*. He helped establish the "Literary Club," which included Prioleau, William Crafts, Mitchell King, T. S. Grimké, and John Gadsden. He died in Pendleton.

14. William L. Marcy (1786-1857), senator from and later governor of New York, defined the principle of rotation of public office with the aphorism: "To the victors belong the spoils." The statement was made in the Senate in defense of Van Buren against an attach by Henry Clay.

15. William C. Preston (1794-1860) was a South Carolina lawyer, state legislator, and U.S. senator. He was graduated from South Carolina College in 1812 and studied law at the University of Edinburgh. He was admitted to the bar in Virginia and moved to Columbia in 1822. Like Grayson, he was originally a nullifier, serving in the South Carolina House from 1828 to 1833. He was elected to fill the vacancy in the U.S. Senate caused by the resignation of Stephen D. Miller in 1833, the same year Grayson went to Congress. He was reelected for a second term in 1837 but forced to resign his seat because of his support of the Whig Party and Henry Clay. He was succeeded by George McDuffie. He was chosen president of South Carolina College in 1845 and served until he resigned in 1851 because of poor health.

16. Waddy Thompson (1798-1868) was born at Old Pickensville, near the present town of Easley, South Carolina. He graduated from South Carolina College at the age of sixteen. He practiced law, was twice elected to the state legislature, and rose to the rank of brigadier general of the state militia in 1832. He served in the House of Representatives from 1835 to 1841, where he advocated the annexation of Texas. He served as Minister to Mexico from 1842 to 1844 and disapproved of the war with Mexico. He returned to Greenville, where he resumed law practice. Though he and William Gilmore Simms had been on opposite sides in the nullification crisis, he

contributed to Simms's magazine *Magnolia* on Mexican subjects and became a close friend.

17. George Kremer (1775-1854) was a lawyer from Middleton, Pennsylvania, who served in the House of Representatives from 1819 to 1821, and from 1823 to 1829. This was his one moment of fame during his entire tenure. Clay apparently suggested a duel, but he was told that Kremer would issue an apology. Nothing came of an apology or of a duel.

CHAPTER NINE

1. In spite of Grayson's judgment few of those he singles out are regarded as historically important today. John Middleton Clayton (1796-1856) is remembered for his negotiation as Secretary of State under President Zachary Taylor of the Clayton-Bulwer treaty for canal rights in Central America. Theodore Frelinghuysen (1787-1862), who was the vice-presidential candidate on the Whig ticket with Henry Clay in 1844, later became president of City College of New York and Rutgers College in New Jersey. John M. Berrien was the Attorney General aligned with those cabinet members who refused to include the Eatons at their private social functions. Forced to resign his office, he returned to Georgia in 1831 and there bitterly opposed Jacksonian policies. He became a leading supporter in Georgia of South Carolina on nullification. George M. Bibb was a senator from Kentucky who became a Calhoun partisan. William C. Rives of Virginia was appointed by Jackson as Minister to France in 1829. He returned to American in 1832, entered Congress as a Jackson partisan, but, during the nullification controversy, voted against the administration on the Force Bill.

2. Jackson turned the money drawn form the National Bank over to Secretary of the Treasury Roger B. Taney, for deposit in selected state banks, which were christened "pet banks." On March 28, 1834, the Senate, by a vote of 26 to 20, passed a resolution of censure against the President. For a detailed account of the Bank issue I would recommend Remini, *Andrew Jackson*, pp. 142-60.

3. Henry Clay did two things that aroused the ire of Andrew Jackson. In alliance with Calhoun he prevented the confirmation of Martin Van Buren as minister to England. Then he pushed through the Senate resolutions censuring Jackson for removing deposits from the Bank of the United States.

4. Brooke was the confidant who received Clay's doubts about serving in Congress and preference to be a farmer. The strongest of these letters mentioned his dissatisfaction with many of his colleagues in Congress, matching Grayson's views as he looks back on his own experience: "Blackguards, Bankrupts, Scoundrels, Profligacy and Corruption" are the order of the day.

5. Davy Crockett (1786-1836) was a congressman from West Tennessee from 1827 to 1831 and from 1833 to 1835 before going to Texas, where he died at the Alamo on March 6, 1836. He was born near the present Rogersville, Hawkins County, Tennessee, the son of a tavern operator. He achieved some success in the military under Jackson in the Creek Wars of 1813. His backwoods ways were celebrated and recorded in newspapers, almanacs, and an unauthorized biography. The crudeness of the uncouth backwoodsman of the stories was at a variance with his actual personality, which was much more sober and genteel. His autobiography, which he wrote in 1834,

should be read as fiction by an oral storyteller. Crockett's vernacular character persona would be at variance with Grayson's concept of a gentleman.

6. Richard Henry Wilde (1789-1847) was poet as well as congressman. He was a native of Dublin, Ireland, emigrating to the United States in 1797. He moved to Augusta, Georgia, became a member of the bar, Attorney General of Georgia, (1811-13), and a Democrat in the House of Representatives (1815-17, 1823-25, 1827-35). After living in Europe from 1835 to 1840, he returned to live in New Orleans, where he served as a professor of contemporary law at the University of Louisiana, now Tulane University. He was a talented lyricist, best known for his poem, "My Life is Like a Summer Rose."

7. Richard Johnson (1780-1850) was not only the man thought to have killed Tecumseh during the battle of Thames during 1813, but he was also a member of the House of Representatives as a Democrat from Kentucky from 1807 to 1918 and from 1829 to 1837, and Vice President of the United States under Martin Van Buren.

8. Rev. Obadiah Brown, chief clerk of the U.S. Post Office, was the author of a celebrated report on Sunday mails. There was an attempt during the Jackson administration to upgrade the services of the Post Office Department. William T. Barry, who served as postmaster from 1828 to 1835, was the first postmaster to act as a member of the President's cabinet. At this time the Department was embarrassed when Obadiah Brown was accused of conniving with contractors on "straw bids" and of possible corrupting influences on his subordinates. He was forced to resign, but he published an appeal declaring his innocence.

9. As Andrew Jackson was leaving the House of Representatives after the funeral services on January 30, Richard Lawrance, later judged insane, fired two pistols at him, both of which misfired, only the caps exploding. As he fired both shots, Jackson kept coming towards Lawrance, his cane raised. Washingtonians were amazed at the odds of two pistols misfiring successively. The luck of Jackson had prevailed.

10. This was Spencer Perceval (1762-1812), English statesman and prime minister from 1809 until his assassination in 1812. He was educated at Harrow and Trinity College, Cambridge. He was appointed King's counsel in 1796 and entered Parliament that year. He served as attorney general from 1802 to 1806 and as chancellor of exchequer until 1809, when he succeeded the Duke of Portland as prime minister. He was shot dead in the lobby of the House of Commons by John Bellingham who had a grievance against the government. Though judged insane, Bellingham was hanged.

11. See footnote 15, chapter 8. I would add here that Preston was an anti-Jackson Democrat and strongly advocated the annexation of Texas.

12. The Missouri Compromise promised that Missouri be admitted as a slave state and that Maine be admitted as a free state. The territory north of line 36° 30′ should be "forever, free." Missouri adopted a constitution prohibiting free Negroes from entering the state. At Clay's suggestion a resolution passed in Congress requiring that Missouri never enact laws denying citizens of other states their contstitutional rights. Clay, as leader of the Whigs in the Senate, pushed the Tariff of 1842 as a revenue matter needed because of the expiration of the Tariff of 1832. When President Tyler opposed it, the Whig Cabinet resigned.

13. The British humorist Sydney Smith's description of Daniel Webster, quoted exactly, was "Daniel Webster struck me much like a steam engine in trousers."

14. Horace Binney (1780-1875) was the first director of the United States Bank and Whig congressman from Pennsylvania during the 23rd Congress (1833-35).

15. This was an early quarrel in Nashville in 1813, before Benton moved to St. Louis. Jackson was the aggressor, and Benton and his brother Jesse nearly killed him. Benton later fought two duels in St. Louis.

16. Spelled Bouldin. Thomas Tyler Bouldin was a circuit court judge form Virginia and congressman from 1829 to 1833. He died on the floor of the House on February 11, 1834.

17. James Blair (1790-1834) was a planter and sheriff of Lancaster District, South Carolina. He was elected to the House of Representatives in 1821 but resigned in 1822. He was reelected as a Union Democrat in 1829 and served until his death on the floor of Congress on April 1, 1834.

18. Warren R. Davis (1793-1835) graduated from South Carolina College in 1810, the year after Grayson. He served as state solicitor for the Western Circuit in South Carolina. He was a States Rights Democrat, member of the 20th to 23rd Congresses. He died in office on January 29, 1835.

19. Harriet Martineau (1802-36) was an English author who made an extended visit to the United States (1834-39), when she became associated with the new Abolitionist Party. She published an account of American in *Retrospect of Western Travel* (1838), including her impressions of Andrew Jackson.

Octavia Walton Le Vert, who at the height of her fame was called "the belle of the union," was born near Augusta, Georgia. Her father was acting territorial governor of Florida in Pensacola. She was talented; at twelve she could speak French, Italian, and Spanish. She met and charmed Lafayette in his tour of the United States. Later she met and charmed Washington Irving and was frequently his guest at "Sunnymede." Possessing great conversational power, she became a friend of Clay, Calhoun, and Webster. Like Grayson, she reported accurately on their speeches in the Senate. In 1836 she married Dr. Henry Le Vert and lived with him in Mobile. She visited Europe in 1853 on the invitation of the Duke of Rutland. Her memoirs were published under the title, *Souvenirs of Travel*. (1857) She died in Augusta.

CHAPTER TEN

1. In 1788 Jefferson succeeded in getting a law passed in the Virginia legislature prohibiting the importation of slaves. He was opposed to slavery but saw no satisfactory way to abolish it. One of the best recent studies is Jack McLaughlin, *Jefferson and Monticello* (Henry Holt: New York, 1988).

2. In 1839 John Quincy Adams presented in Congress a petition, perhaps forged, from twenty-two slaves. When threatened with censure, he vigorously defended himself. This resolution and the resolution of 1839, providing that a child born in the United States after July 4, 1832, should be free and that the slave trade in the District of Columbia should be abolished after July 4, 1845, were defeated by gag rules. He offended Southern members of Congress in his speech on May 25, 1836, when he first fully enunciated the doctrine of Congress's constitutional powers to emancipate slaves in time of war, a principle Lincoln used thirty years later. Adams was known for his speech-making powers as "old eloquence."

3. The Wilmot Proviso was an issue as a result of the Mexican War controversy. Introduced by David Wilmot of Pennsylvania, an antislavery Democrat, it proposed that any territory acquired from Mexico be forever closed to slavery. It never passed but often appeared as an amendment to relevant bills in Congress. In 1848, urged

by Calhoun, the South Carolina legislature passed a resolution indicating readiness to cooperate with other Southern states in resisting the Wilmot Proviso if it should become law. Mississippi called for a Southern convention, and the South Carolina legislature elected delegates resolved that the passage of the Wilmot Proviso or the abolition of slavery would lead to dissolution. The Nashville Convention (June, 1850) was disappointing to South Carolina, and, on the return to the state, the secessionists sought independent action by South Carolina.

4. Under the influence of "cooperativists" South Carolina waited until the Nashville Convention, which met first from June 3-12, and then again on November 11-18, 1850. The stated purposes of the convention were to promote Southern unity and to form some "mode of resistance" to Northern "aggression" in attempting to exclude slavery from the territory acquired from Mexico in the war. Henry Clay's compromise resolution cost Whig support of any decisive action; only nine of fifteen slave states sent representatives. Moderates controlled the proceedings. The most important of twenty-eight resolutions was one advocating opening of all territories to slavery but actually accepting the extension of the Missouri Compromise line to the Pacific. The meeting adjourned until a second session in November, attended by only fifty-nine delegates, this time denouncing the Compromise of 1850 and upholding the right of a state to secession. This convention failed in its intended purposes, but it sent a warning to moderates in Congress.

5. Whitemarsh B. Seabrook (1792-1855) was thirty-fifth governor of South Carolina (1848-50). He was born in Edisto Island. Although admitted to the bar, he spent most of his time managing the large family plantation, growing sea island cotton on Edisto Island. He was extremely interested in agriculture, serving as president of the State Agricultural Society and doing his own research. He wrote a history of the cotton plant, *Memoir on the Origin, Cultivation, and Uses of Cotton* (1844).

6. Hamilton has been briefly mentioned previously. I would add here that as governor of South Carolina he convened the Nullification Convention in November 1832.

7. Langdon Cheves (1776-1857) served as a congressman (1811-15). He was best known as "Hercules of the U.S. Bank." As president of the United States Bank from 1819 to 1822 he put it into financial order. He was also known for his abilities in architecture, constructing several fine houses in South Carolina.

8. For an account of the impression Cheves made on Mason Locke Weems and of his use of Cheves in his sermons see Archie Vernon Huff, Jr., *Langdon Cheves of South Carolina* (Columbia: University of South Carolina Press, 1976) 87. Huff uses two sources, Grayson and a letter from William Lowndes.

9. Bishop Ellison Capers (1790-1855) was a preacher, deacon, elder, and bishop in the Methodist Church. He worked extensively with the Creek Indians from 1821 to 1844 as the superintendent of missions and, as bishop, with plantation slaves.

10. I might add to what Grayson says that Poinsett was the Unionist activist who asked Jackson to give support to the Unionists in South Carolina.

11. Grayson means Judge John Belton O'Neall (1793-1863), South Carolina Circuit Judge, member of the Court of Appeals, and Chief Justice, who wrote *The Negro Law of South Carolina* (1848) already discussed.

12. The Kansas-Nebraska Act established two new territories and repealed the Missouri Compromise prohibition of slavery north of 36° 30′ leaving the status of slavery to the inhabitants. Receiving the support of the Democratic machine, it was

quickly passed by Congress and signed by President Pierce. Passage of the Act caused many Northern Democrats to desert the party.

13. John Byng (1704-1757), British admiral, was executed in 1757 for failing to do his best to relieve Minorca from attack by the French the previous year. Byng had been sent to save the island, and he had engaged the French fleet; but he decided that his force was insufficient and returned to Gibraltar. A storm of protest was raised in England. He was acquitted of charges of disaffection and cowardice but found technically guilty of neglect of duty in battle, leaving the court with no alternative but to condemn him to death under the newly revised Articles of War.

CHAPTER ELEVEN

1. "I left no calling for this idle trade." Prologue to *Satires to Arbuthnot*, 1. 129.

2. This is a reference to "Chicora" (1856), published with "The Hireling and the Slave." This new poem demonstrated Grayson's interest in Indian lore and what he portrays as pastoral/idyllic life of the primitive Indian.

3. "Country" (1858) presents the advantages of rural life in heroic couplets. His models were Dryden and Pope.

4. "Marion" was published privately by Grayson in Charleston in 1860 after appearing serially in *Russell's* during 1859.

5. In 1806 Samuel Bowles (1762-1850) published an edition of Pope's works with a note attacking the poet's moral character and poetic principles. The controversy, known as the Pope and Bowles controversy, persisted until 1826. Initially, Warton had been attacked by Pope as "the scorn and wonder of our days," in *Moral Essays*, 1, 179.

6. William Cowper (1731-1800) moved to Olney and first gained notice through his collection "Olney Hymns" (published in 1779). His best known work is *The Task*, a poem in six books, published in 1784.

7. Timrod's "What Is Poetry?" was a rejoinder to Grayson in *Russell's Magazine* 2 (October 1857).

8. Bowles described the dispute over Pope's poetical methods as the "invariable Principles of poetry." Byron's best defense of Pope was in his "An Answer to Some Observations of Thomas Campbell, Esq." in his "Specimens of British Poets," in *Literary Journal* 5: 526-36. Grayson undoubtedly saw a similarity between his defense of Pope against the rise of Romanticism in Charleston and Byron's defense of Pope in England.

9. "Every language of a learned nation necessarily divides itself into diction scholastick and popular, grave and familiar, elegant and gross; and from a nice distinction of these different parts, arises a great part of beauty of style." Johnson's *Lives of the Poets*, edited by Matthew Arnold (New York: Russell and Russell, 1881) 183.

10. Horace cautions the poet against making his images resemble a sick man's dreams. Horace, *De Arte Poetica*, 7. "*Velut aegri somnia.*"

11. The quote is from Shelley's *A Defense of Poetry*. "Poetry is the record of the best and happiest memories of the happiest and best minds."

12. John Selden (1584-1654), an eminent lawyer and judge, wrote *The Nativity of Christ*, published in 1661.

13. Benjamin Franklin Butler (1818-1893) was a Massachusetts lawyer, state representative, and senator. As a major general in the Union army, he captured the

forts guarding Hatteras inlet. Later a military ruler of New Orleans, he issued order No. 28 (December, 1862), which threatened to regard any female molesting his troops "as a woman of the town plying her avocation." This order and his execution of a civilian for taking down the American flag received considerable publicity in Charleston as the consequences of federal occupation of a Southern city.

14. Savage's great biographer was, of course, Samuel Johnson, whose *Life of Richard Savage* was printed anonymously in 1744.

15. *Marmion, A Tale of Flodden Field*, a poem in six cantos by Sir Walter Scott, published in 1808.

CHAPTER TWELVE

1. The Convention of the People of South Carolina convened first in the First Baptist Church at Columbia on December 17, 1860. David F. Jamison of Barnwell was elected president, and the convention was then adjourned to meet in the Charleston the next day. An ordinance of secesssion was passed on December 20.

The Montgomery Convention assembled at Montgomery, Alabama, on February 4, 1861, to organize the Confederate States of America. Six states of the Lower South answered the first role call. Texas delegates arrived March 2. After Howell Cobb of Georgia was elected the presiding officer, the convention worked in secret session. It drafted a provisional constitution on the model of the Constitution of the United States, with additional provisions for states rights. Jefferson Davis was elected president and Alexander Stephens, who had been a Unionist, vice-president.

2. The passage referred to is from *An Account of the European Settlements in America* (New York: Arno Press, 1972) 261-62.

3. "We know of no great revolution which might not have been prevented by compromise early and graciously made." This quote comes from "Hallam's Constitutional History," available in *Historical Essays Contributed to the Edinburgh Review* (London: Oxford University Press, 1913) 83.

4. This was supposed to have been made in a dispatch in 1815. The exact quotation is "Nothing except a battle lost can be half so melancholy as a battle won." Supposedly he also made this remark to a lady with a passion to see a great victory. Wellington added: "Madam there's nothing so dreadful as a great victory excepting a great defeat."

5. Fort Sumter was fired on April 12, 1861. The signal shot for all batteries to begin firing was fired at 4:30 A.M. The guns at Fort Sumter remained silent till about 7:00 A.M. when the fire was returned by eighty-five officers and men with some help from forty-three workmen. The surrender, on Saturday, April 13, came after thirty-four hours of bombardment. More than 4000 shells were fired. What pleased Grayson was that no one was killed.

6. On October 29, 1861, Du Pont left Hampton Roads for Port Royal with seventeen wooden cruisers and a force of about 12,000 under Thomas W. Sherman. After a bombardment on November 7, the Federals acquired a base for operations in the area by taking possession of Forts Beauregard and Walker.

7. In the 1740s South Carolina developed her second great staple crop, indigo. This crop was tried even earlier, but, after 1695, greater profits from rice displaced it in favor. Eliza Lucas married Charles Pinckney, and was the mother of Charles Cotesworth and Thomas Pinckney. She planted the first indigo seed in St. Andrew's parish,

helping to revive interest in its cultivation. Bounties were granted in 1748 to boost planting. The removal of the bounty after the Revolution destroyed the industry. Some remnants of the industry remained after the Revolution in the Orangeburg area but were eventually supplanted by the development of coal tar dyes.

8. Jefferson Davis (1808-1889) was reportedly surprised when he was elected president of the Confederacy, expecting a military command instead. His military experience in the Mexican War led him to believe that he could serve not only as president but also as his own Secretary of War. He had strongly held opinions about the talents of his generals—for example, high respect for General Braxton Bragg, who was dangerously aggressive, and little for General Joseph E. Johnston, who fought defensive battles. Jefferson Davis was easily a target for blame for what went wrong in the war because he always sought to promote the interests of the entire South over those of bickering individual states. He also tended to believe that all his actions were both correct and ethical.

9. There are many things that could be said about these British leaders. I can only select from what might be most relevant to Grayson's reference. William Pitt (1759-1806), English statesman and prime minister, attempted to pass a slave abolition bill. In spite of his parliamentary talents, he failed.

Robert Stewart Castlereagh (1769-1822) was responsible for British policy in the peace settlements at the close of the Napoleonic Wars. In response to the threat from Napoleon he advocated a union of Ireland and Britain.

George Canning (1770-1827)—foreign secretary, associate of Pitt, prime minister—was a fine speaker, with a remarkable ability to put country above personal interest. Both Castlereagh and Canning were engaged in various negotiations with the United States during the Monroe presidency.

10. Lord John Russell (1792-1878) was twice the prime minister of England and the great champion of parliamentary reform and of various liberal measures. His powerful intellect more than compensated for his frail physical appearance. Lord Henry John Temple Palmerston (1784-1865) was one of Britain's ablest and most powerful foreign secretaries and prime ministers. He was not only highly efficient but also open minded, good-humored, and tactful in dealing with colleagues of widely differing opinions. These traits would have attracted Grayson, but he cannot forget the British neglect of the South. On the outbreak of the Civil War, Palmerston acknowledged the duty of the British government to remain neutral.

11. The exact date was November 7. The occupation of the forts there established a base for subsequent operations against Charleston and Savannah.

12. The great Charleston fire occurred on December 11-12, 1861. It originated near the Cooper River and swept across the peninsula to Council Street on the Ashley River. Both halls used by the Secession Convention were destroyed. Property losses were enormous.

13. These were homes on Tradd Street and were two of the finest old homes destroyed by the Charleston fire. Both women were known for their entertaining. Harriott Pinckney (1776-1866) was known for her treatise on states rights.

14. In an effort to close off Charleston harbor federal forces sank two stone fleets in December, 1861, and in January, 1862. In June, 1862, Union troops landed on James Island and attacked Fort Lamar at Secessionville on June 16. The attack was repulsed and the troops withdrew. Rear Admiral S. F. Du Pont attempted to take Charleston with nine ironclads on April 7, 1863. The vessels were driven off by the harbor forts.

There was a combined naval and land assault against Morris Island, and a siege of Fort Wagner was begun the next day. Morris Island was evacuated by the Confederates on September 7. Charleston was not abandoned by Confederate forces until February 17, 1865.

CHAPTER THIRTEEN

1. Thomas Wigg (d. 1759) was a South Carolina Royal Assembly representative from St. Helena Parish. Having moved there from Beaufort, he became a prominent planter on Port Royal. He served as Surveyor and Comptroller of Her Majesty's Customs at Charleston. One daughter married a Grayson; another married a Hazzard.

2. George Butler, eldest brother of United States Senator Pickens Butler (1786-1821), was a lawyer and Edgefield district attorney. He graduated third in (his) Grayson's class (1809) at South Carolina College. Judge O'Neall (*Bench and Bar of South Carolina* II, 476) remarks: "If he had been spared to live long, he would have been a distinguished lawyer and an eminent man."

3. Benjamin Rush (1745-1831) was born near Philadelphia and educated at the College of New Jersey (Princeton). He studied medicine in Edinburgh. In 1774 he published "An Address to the Inhabitants of the British Settlements in America," opposing slavery. He wrote much on medicine and on moral philosophy in *Essays, Literary, Moral & Philosophical* (Philadelphia, 1798). When the College of Philadelphia merged with the University of Pennsylavania he became for many years a famous professor at the university. Although he believed that yellow fever was caused by unsanitary conditions, he also contended that many diseases had a common trouble spot in pressure and spasms in the veins, which could be relieved by blood depletion.

4. The correspondent was James Louis Petigru, who died in Charleston on March 9, 1863. Stoney explains the fragmentary structure of this chapter as the result of Grayson's turning his attention to the memoir of his friend. It is true that some of the material in this chapter was reworked for his memoir of Petigru and some material may have been removed from this chapter for the life. Nevertheless, Grayson's associational organization, as he roams through old letters and vivid memories, is rather effective.

5. One of the best descriptions of Moses Waddel's academy at Willington, South Carolina, is in Grayson's *James Louis Petigru* (34-35). "The Willington school was a sort of Eton or Rugby of American manufacture, and the doctor at its head the Carolina Dr. Arnold. He had great talents for organization and government. His method appealed largely to the honor and moral sense of his pupils. They were not confined with their books unnecessarily in a narrow schoolroom. The forest was their place of study....Monitors regulated the classes and subdivisions of classes, and preserved the order and discipline of the institution with the smallest possible reference to its head. It was a kind of rural republic, with a perpetual dictator."

6. A brief break in the manuscript.

7. Stoney identifies this quotation as coming from Petigru's description of Elizabeth Savage Heyward, daughter of Thomas Heyward, signer of the Declaration of Independence. Her salty language amazed the young Petigru.

8. This is a classmate of Grayson and Petigru, previously discussed. Thomas Creech (1659-1700) was a teacher at Oxford and headmaster of Sherbourne School, known for his translations of Lucretius and of Horace. His *Odes, Satyrs, and Epistles of*

Horace (1684) was dedicated to Dryden and survived through editions in 1688, 1715, 1720, 1737. His translations gave little credit to the poetry. In his own translation of Horace, Pope reproduced Creech's rendering of the opening of Book I, epistle vi, adding the satirical couplet: "Plain truth, Dear Murray, needs no flowers of speech, So take it in the very words of Creech." Creech committed suicide, apparently because of unrequited love.

9. Frank Hampton (1829-1863) was a son of General Hampton, younger brother to Wade Hampton III. He was a man of astonishing physical prowess. He was a regular at Planter's Hotel, where Mrs. Calder was hostess. He lived at Woodlands plantaton and at Cashiers, North Carolina. See *James Louis Petigru*, 57-58.

10. Joseph Allston (1733-1784) of All Saints, Waccamaw, was governor during the war of 1812. William H. Bull went from college to be a tutor in the family of Joseph Allston, who was governor of South Carolina from 1812-1814. In 1801 he married Theodosia Burr and they lived at "The Oaks." Their one son, Aaron Burr Allston, died on June 13, 1812. On December 30, 1812, Theodosia Burr Allston departed to sail from Georgetown to New York on the schooner *Patriot*. The ship sank in a severe gale off Cape Hatteras.

11. The facade of the old Planter's Hotel is preserved as the facade for the Dock Street Theatre. Tait is described by Grayson in his life of Petrigu as "a man of many adventures." He served in the Revolutionary War with a commission of captain in Robert's Artillery. "At the close of the war, or when the excitement of revolution grew strong in France, he hurried across the Atlantic to offer his sword to the new republic. His experience in France was not entirely happy, but he rose to the rank of General. He was totally rejected on his return to America. He was among the inventors of perpetual motion. He went to Philadelphia to perfect his machine, and was heard of no more. He died, perhaps, in the poor house." Grayson discusses this in detail in *James Louis Petigru*, 55-56.

12. The longest break in the manuscript, three to four pages, occurs here. The missing material in the career of the Petigru may have been included in Grayson's memoir of James L. Petigru.

13. Stephen Decatur Miller (1787-1838) was senator and twenty-fifth Governor of South Carolina. He was the father of Mary Chesnut. He was born near Lancaster County, South Carolina. He opposed Calhoun's doctrine of nullification. He served as governor from 1828 to 1830. He was elected U.S. senator in 1830, resigning his seat in 1832 because of ill health. He was a member of the Nullification Convention of 1832 and of the special session to rescind the nullification resolution in 1833. He moved to Mississippi in 1835 and died there in 1838.

14. Grayson apparently intended this as his epitaph for Petigru and he uses it as such in his memoir. He has apparently adapted Goldsmith's passage from "The Deserted Village" (Austin Dobson, *The Poetical Works of Oliver Goldsmith*. London: Oxford University Press, 1949, p. 26), ll. 93-96.

> And, as a hare, whom hounds and horns pursue,
> Pants to the place from whence at first she flew,
> I still had hopes, my long vexations pass'd,
> Here to return—and die at home at last.

The other quoted passages are from ll. 187-93; 167-71.

APPENDIX

1. Robert Smalls was a slave on the South Carolina steamer *Planter*, used to remove guns from Cole's Island. He commandeered the ship and with several other slaves sailed past Fort Sumter to join the federal fleet. He took with him five guns in addition to the two on the ship and reported that Cole's Island had been abandoned. Smalls served the rest of the war in the federal navy and he was prominent in Reconstruction politics in South Carolina.

2. Josiah Tattnall (1791-1871) took command of the naval defenses of Georgia and South Carolina. He relieved the wounded Buchanan in command of the ironclad *Virginia*. He destroyed his ship to prevent her capture. Censured for this action, Tattnall demanded a court-martial, which acquitted him on July 5, 1862.

3. John Clifford Pemberton (1814-1881) was a native of Philadelphia, a West Point graduate, a veteran of the Seminole War and the Mexican War, who resigned his position as superintendent of the military academy at West Point to join the Confederate army. He was eventually to surrender to Grant at Vicksburg. He was always under some suspicion in the South because of his Northern birth. There was a dispute between Generals Pemberton and Ripley, another Northerner, who joined the Confederate army. Pemberton wanted to abandon the outlying forts and defend Charleston proper. Ripley disagreed and won the argument. Pemberton later tried the same tactics in Vicksburg, which he surrendered to General Grant after a long siege.

4. Over the objections of his division commanders General H. W. Benham, with about 9,000 troops, began an assault on the Confederate positions around Secessionville on James Island on June 16, 1862. The assault was repulsed by 500 men under Colonel T. G. Lamar. Benham was relieved of his command. He was then arrested for having disobeyed. He suffered the final humiliation of having his appointment as a brigadier general revoked.

5. This is an epitaph, included in the manuscript, but not previously published. Charles C. Lee died at Hanover Courthouse after the battle known as Malvern Hill. There is an account of his promise and heroic death in Douglas Southall Freeman, *Lee's Lieutenants* II (New York: C. Scribner's Sons, 1946) 606. "Two colonels of particular promise had been lost in the closing battles. Gaston Meares of Third North Carolina and C. C. Lee, a young West Pointer, who commanded the Thirty-Seventh North Carolina. Both these men almost certainly would have risen to the rank of general officers."

6. In South Carolina the Secession Convention continued its life as the government for the time it was to take to ratify a Confederate constitution. After the collapse at Port Royal, it was reassembled to save the state. It took over the powers of a regular government by creating an executive council composed of Governor Pickens and four others. Using the excuse of an emergency, it suspended parts of the Constitution and made the Council responsible only to itself. These actions aroused a storm of protest. Grayson's account and analysis is more detailed than those in the standard histories.

7. Pierre Gustave Toutant Beauregard (1818-1893) actually commanded the attack on Fort Sumter and was popular in Charleston as the "Hero of Sumter." He turned over his command in the West to Bragg in June, 1862, to go on sick leave. Jefferson Davis relieved him on the charge of leaving his post without authority. When he was

restored to command, he was sent to Charleston in charge of the defenses of the Carolina and Georgia coasts.

8. Mitchell King (1783-1862) was a long-time lawyer and city recorder in Charleston. He was born in Scotland. He was a voracious reader and an imitator of the style of Addison and Steele in the *Spectator* papers. He arrived in Charleston November, 1805. He opened a school and wrote verses under the name "Wanderer" for the *Courier*. In 1806 he joined the faculty of the College of Charleston. He also undertook studies in law. He became professor of chemistry and natural philosophy at South Carolina College in 1811. He was admitted to the bar in 1810. His interests in literature paralleled Grayson's, and his political commitments were close to those of Grayson's friend Petigru. He was known in Charleston as Judge King.

Selective Bibliography

PRIMARY SOURCES

Manuscripts:

Manuscript Room, South Caroliniana Library, University of South Carolina: The Autobiography of William J. Grayson; The War Diary of William J. Grayson.

Published Works of William J. Grayson:

An Oration, Delivered in the College Chapel, Before the Clariosophic Society Incorporate, and the Inhabitants of Columbia on the 3rd December, 1827. Charleston, S.C.: Miller, 1828.

Letter to His Excellency Whitemarsh B. Seabrook, Governor of the State of South Carolina. On the Dissolution of the Union. Charleston, S.C.: Miller, 1850.

The Union, Past and Future: How It Works and How to Save It. Charleston, S.C.: Miller, 1850.

The Letters of Curtius. Charleston, S.C.: Miller, 1851.

The Hireling and the Slave. Charleston, S.C.: Russell, 1854.

The Hireling and the Slave, Chicora, and other Poems. Charleston, S.C.: McCarter, 1856.

The Country. Charleston, S.C.: Russell and Jones, 1858.

Marion. Charleston, S.C.: Privately printed, 1860.

Remarks on Mr. Motley's Letter in the London Times on the War in America. Anonymous. Charleston, S.C.: Evans & Cogswell, 1861.

James Louis Petigru. A Biographical Sketch. New York: Harper, 1866.

Bass, Robert Duncan. "The Autobiography of William J. Grayson," Ph.D. dissertation, University of South Carolina, 1933. This was the most complete edition. There is a copy in the South Caroliniana Library. I was unable to locate the other copy in the

Cooper Library at the University of South Carolina. Bass provides a good introduction to Grayson's life. Instead of documenting the text he records all of Grayson's corrections and most of the variant readings.

Major periodical publications:

Stoney, Samuel G., ed. "The Autobiography of William John Grayson." *South Carolina Historical and Genealogical Magazine* 48-51 (July 1947-April 1950). Stoney omits chapter 11 and several other passages. The text is only lightly documented.

Puryear, Elmer L., ed. "The Confederate Diary of William John Grayson." *South Carolina Historical and Genealogical Magazine* 63 (1962): 137-49, 214-26. The edition is incomplete and only lightly documented.

Significant periodical publications by William J. Grayson:

"What Is Poetry?" *Russell's Magazine* 1 (July 1857): 327-337.

"LaBorde's *History of South Carolina College,*" *Russell's Magazine* 5 (September 1859): 550-552. A more extensive review appears in *Russell's Magazine* 6 (December 1859): 254-267.

"The Character of the Gentleman," *Southern Quarterly Review* N. S. 7 (January 1853): 53-80.

"The *Edinburgh Review* Reviewed," *Russell's Magazine* 1 (April 1857): 1-14.

"A Philadelphia Lawyer's View of the Constitution," *Russell's Magazine* 1 (April 1857): 74-80.

"The Evangelical Christians of the United States of America." *Russell's Magazine* I (August 1857): 385-395.

"The Duel," *Russell's Magazine* 1 (August 1857): 439-454.

"The Life and Times of Aaron Burr and History of Republic of United States of America, as traced in Writings of Alexander Hamilton," *Russell's Magazine* 2 (February 1858): 385-403.

"Trescott's *Diplomatic History,*" *Russell's Magazine* 2 (February 1859): 425-430.

"Marion: A Poem," *Russell's Magazine* 4 (December 1858): 212-228; (January 1859): 313-321; (February 1859): 406-414; (April 1859): 8-14.

"The Dual Form of Labor," *Russell's Magazine* 6 (December 1859): 254-67.

SECONDARY MATERIALS:

The sources for much of the research material used to document the autobiography of William J. Grayson were found in the Library of Congress, the South Carolina Historical Society, the Georgia Historical Society, the South Caroliniana Library of the University of South Carolina, the Charleston Library Society, the South Carolina Department of Archives and History, and in special collections at Clemson University. The most valuable single reference has been the published volumes of the *South Carolina Historical and Genealogical Magazine*. Standard reference books and many historical monographs on nineteenth-century South Carolina have been of value. I have tried to list the items that have been the most useful for my approach to the autobiography and for documentation.

Alderman, Edwin Anderson; Smith, Charles Alphonso; Metcalf, John Calvin, eds. *Library of Southern Literature*. 15 vols. Atlanta: Martin and Hoyt Company, 1907-1929. *Biographies*, vol. 15.

American Council of Learned Societies. Johnson, Allen; and Dumas Malone, eds. *Dictionary of American Biography*. 20 vols. New York: Charles Scribner's Sons, 1928-58.

Aptheker, Herbert. *American Negro Slave Revolts*. New York: Columbia University Press, 1943.

Bailey, N. Louise; Morgan, Mary L.; and Taylor, Carolyn R., eds. *Biographical Directory of the South Carolina Senate, 1776-1985*. 3 vols. Columbia: University of South Carolina Press, 1986.

Bain, Robert; Flora, Joseph M.; and Rubin, Louis D. Jr., eds. *Southern Writers: A Biographical Dictionary*. Baton Rouge: Louisiana State University Press, 1979.

Barnwell, John. *Love of Order: South Carolina's First Secession Crisis*. Chapel Hill: University of North Carolina Press, 1982.

Biographical Directory of the American Congress, 1774-1971. Washington, D.C.: U.S. Government Printing Office, 1971.

Biographical Directory of the South Carolina House of Representatives, 1791-1815. N. Louise Bailey, ed. Vol. 4. Columbia: University of South Carolina Press, 1984.

Bleser, Carol, ed. *The Hammonds of Redcliffe*. New York: Oxford University Press, 1981.

———. *Secret and Sacred: The Diaries of James Henry Hammond, A Southern Slaveholder*. New York: Oxford University Press, 1988.

Boatner, Mark M., III. *The Civil War Dictionary*. New York: David McKay, 1959.

Burton, E. Milby. *The Siege of Charleston, 1861-1865*. Columbia: University of South Carolina Press, 1970. This is the work useful for those who want background for Grayson's war diary.

Calhoun, Richard J. "Southern Literary Magazines, III: The Ante-Bellum Literary Twilight, *Russell's Magazine*." *Southern Literary Journal* 3 (Fall 1970): 89-110.

————. "William J. Grayson," in Rathbun, John W.; and Monica Grecu. *American Literary Critics and Scholars, 1850-1880. Dictionary of Literary Biography*. Detroit: Gale Research, 1988.

Cardozo, Jacob N. *Reminiscences of Charleston*. Charleston, S.C.: Joseph Walker, 1866.

Carson, James Petigru. *Life, Letters and Speeches of James Louis Petigru*. Washington, D.C.: W. H. Lowdermilk and Company, 1927.

Cote, Richard N.; and Patricia H. Williams, eds. *Dictionary of South Carolina Biography*. Easley, S.C.: Southern Historical Press, 1985. This is useful but incomplete.

Davidson, Chalmers Gaston. *The Last Foray: The South Carolina Planters of 1860, A Sociological Study*. Columbia: University of South Carolina Press, 1971.

Degler, Carl N. *The Other South: Southern Dissenters in the Nineteenth Century*. New York: Harper and Row, 1974.

Duyckinck, Evert A.; and George L. Duycinck, eds. *Cyclopedia of American Literature*. 2 vols. New York: Scribner's, 1855-56.

Easterby, J. H. *A History of the College of Charleston*. Charleston, S.C.: Scribner Press, 1935.

Eaton, Clement. *A History of the Old South*, 2nd ed. New York: Macmillan Co., 1966.

Elliott, William. *Carolina Sports by Land and Water*. Charleston, S.C.: A. Morris. 1846. This is an antebellum classic, still underrated, and undoubtedly influential on Grayson's own descriptions. I am indebted to my colleague Ben Skardon, whose master's thesis under Edd Parks at the University of Georgia is still one of the best introductions to Elliott.

Ellis, Ralph E. *The Union at Risk: Jacksonian Democracy, States' Rights, and the Nullification Crisis*. New York and Oxford: Oxford University Press, 1987.

Faust, Drew Gilpin. *A Sacred Circle: The Dilemma of the Intellectual in the Old South, 1840-1860*. Baltimore: The Johns Hopkins University Press, 1977. This is an important study. I value it for the section on George Frederick Holmes. The stress is on Romanticism with some sacrifice of conservative, more neoclassical views.

————, ed. *The Ideology of Slavery: Proslavery Thought in the Antebellum South, 1830-1860*. Baton Rouge: Louisiana State University Press, 1981. These selections give the best overview from primary sources of proslavery thought in the South. Grayson is omitted from the text and from the bibliography.

Freehling, William W. *Prelude to Civil War: The Nullification Controversy in South Carolina, 1816-1836*. New York: Harper and Row, 1965.

Genovese, Eugene D. *The Political Economy of Slavery: Studies in the Economy and Society of the Slave South*. New York: Pantheon Books, 1969.

————. *Roll Jordan, Roll: The World the Slaves Made*. New York: Pantheon Books, 1974.

Gillespie, Neal C. *The Collapse of Orthodoxy: The Intellectual Ordeal of George Frederick Holmes*. Charlottesville: University Press of Virginia, 1972.

Hayne, Paul Hamilton. "Ante-Bellum Charleston," *Southern Bivouac* I (November 1885): 327-36.

Hecht, Marie B. *John Quincy Adams: A Personal History of an Independent Man*. New York: The Macmillan Company, 1972. The section on Adams in Congress at the time Grayson was there was the most helpful for an understanding of events that occurred there.

Hollis, Daniel W. *University of South Carolina*. vol. 1. Columbia: University of South Carolina Press, 1951.

Hubbell, Jay B. *The South in American Literature 1608-1900*. Durham, N.C.: Duke University Press, 1954. In this standard history there is the best account of Grayson. Hubbell fails to see the literary importance of the autobiography.

Huff, Archie Vernon, Jr. *Langdon Cheves of South Carolina*. Columbia: University of South Carolina Press, 1976.

Jenkins, William Sumner. *Pro-Slavery Thought in the Old South*. Chapel Hill: University of North Carolina Press, 1935.

Jones, Katherine M. *Port Royal Under Six Flags*. Indianapolis and New York: Bobbs-Merrill, 1960.

Kibler, Lillian A. *Benjamin F. Perry: South Carolina Unionist*. Durham, N.C.: Duke University Press, 1946.

Hennig, Helen Kohn, ed. *Columbia, Capital City of South Carolina, 1786-1936*. Columbia, S.C.: R. L. Bryan, 1936.

La Borde, Maximilian. *History of the South Carolina College From Its Incorporation, December 19, 1801, to December 19, 1865.* 2nd ed. Charleston, S.C.: Walker, Evans and Cogswell, 1874.

Latner, Richard B. *The Presidency of Andrew Jackson: White House Politics 1829-1837.* Athens: University of Georgia Press, 1979. This study provides the best thumbnail sketches of the personalities involved.

McTeer, J. E. *Beaufort Now and Then.* Beaufort, S.C.: Beaufort Book Co., 1971.

Metzger, Lore. *One Foot in Eden: Modes of Pastoral in Romantic Poetry.* Chapel Hill: University of North Carolina Press, 1986.

O'Brien, Michael. *A Character of Hugh Legaré.* Knoxville: University of Tennessee Press, 1985.

———— and David Moltke-Hansen, eds. *Intellectual Life in Antebellum Charleston.* Knoxville: University of Tennessee Press, 1986. This valuable series of essays escaped my attention when it came out. It is the best reevaluation of intellectual life in antebellum Charleston. I am glad to see that the Classical/Neoclassical tradition in Charleston is stressed as well as the Romantic.

————. *Rethinking the South.* Baltimore: Johns Hopkins University Press, 1988. This study arrived too late for me to use it, but I recognize it as the kind of study that should make possible a better understanding of Grayson by providing a more accurate historical context for understanding Southern writers and intellectuals.

National Encyclopedia of American Biography. Clifton, N.Y.: J. T. White, 1892———. 15 vol. Supplements, 1926———.

Oliphant, Mary C.; Alfred Taylor Odell; and T. C. Duncan Eaves, eds. *The Letters of William Gilmore Simms.* 6 vols. Columbia: University of South Carolina Press, 1952-56.

Olney, James. *Metaphors of Self; The Meaning of Autobiography.* Princeton, N.J.: Princeton University Press, 1972.

O'Neall, John Belton. *Biographical Sketches of the Bench and Bar of South Carolina.* 2 vols. Charleston, S.C.: Courtenary and Company, 1859; reprinted Spartanburg, S.C.: The Reprint Co., 1975.

Parks, Edd Winfield, *Antebellum Southern Literary Critics.* Athens: University of Georgia Press, 1962. Parks does not consider the chapter on poetry in the autobiography.

Parrington, V. L. *Main Currents in American Thought: An Interpretation of American Literature from the Beginnings to 1920.* 3 vols. New York: Harcourt, Brace and Company, 1927-30.

Perry, Benjamin F. *Reminiscences of Public Men.* Philadelphia: J. D. Avil and Co., 1883. Perry and Hayne are the best contemporary witnesses to the character of Grayson as Southern gentleman.

Remini, Robert V. *Andrew Jackson and the Course of American Democracy, 1833-1845.* III. New York: Harper & Row, 1984. This source is the most recent and most factual account of the events in the Jackson administration of concern to Grayson in his autobiography.

Rippy, J. Fred. *Joel R. Poinsett, Versatile American.* Durham, N.C.: Duke University Press, 1930.

Rogers, George C., Jr. *Charleston in the Age of the Pinckneys.* Norman: University of Oklahoma Press, 1969.

Roller, David C.; and Robert W. Twyman, eds. *The Encyclopedia of Southern History.* Baton Rouge: Louisiana State University Press, 1979. The entry on Grayson is the one other contemporary source that seems to understand the basic fairness of the man.

Rosengarten, Theodore. *Tombee: Portrait of a Cotton Planter: With the Plantation Journal of Thomas B. Chaplin (1822-1890).* New York: Morrow, 1986. Rosengarten shows the most sensitive understanding of the importance of Grayson's autobiography, making clear that this is a different work from *The Hireling and the Slave.*

Rubin, Louis D., Jr., et al. *The History of Southern Literature.* Baton Rouge: Louisiana State University Press, 1985. There is cursory mention of Grayson, only brief mention of his contributions to periodical criticism and of his poem *The Hireling and the Slave.* There is no recognition of the autobiography.

Schlesinger, Arthur M., Jr. *The Age of Jackson.* Boston: Little, Brown and Company, 1945.

Schultz, Harold S. *Nationalism and Sectionalism in South Carolina 1852-1860.* Durham, N.C.: Duke University Press, 1950.

Sloan, Nell S. *Tales of Beaufort.* Beaufort, S.C.: Beaufort Book Shop, 1963.

Snowden, Yates, ed. *History of South Carolina.* 5 vols. Chicago, New York: Lewis Publishing Co., 1920.

Sydnor, Charles. *The Development of Southern Sectionalism, 1819-1848.* Baton Rouge: Louisiana State University Press, 1948.

Taylor, George Rogers, ed. *Jackson vs. Biddle's Bank: The Struggle over the Second Bank of the United States.* 2nd ed. Lexington, Mass.: D. C. Heath, 1972.

Wauchope, George Armstrong. *The Writers of South Carolina.* Columbia, S.C.: The State Company, 1910.

Wallace, David Duncan. *South Carolina: A Short History, 1520-1948.* Chapel Hill: University of North Carolina Press, 1951.

————. *History of South Carolina.* Volume IV: *Biographical.* New York: American Historical Society, 1934.

Wilson, Edmund. *Patriotic Gore: Studies in the Literature of the American Civil War.* New York: Oxford University Press, 1962. It was Wilson's finding merit in the poetry that led me to a realization of the value of Grayson's prose.

Wiltse, Charles M. *John C. Calhoun.* 3 vols. Indianapolis: Bobbs-Merrill, 1944-51.

Woodward, C. Vann, ed. *Mary Chesnut's Civil War.* New York and London: Yale University Press, 1981.

Index